M000111184

HUMAN RIGHTS AND
THE CARE OF THE SELF

HUMAN RIGHTS AND THE CARE OF THE SELF

ALEXANDRE LEFEBVRE

DUKE UNIVERSITY PRESS DURHAM AND LONDON 2018

©2018 DUKE UNIVERSITY PRESS

All rights reserved. Printed in the United States of America on
acid-free paper ∞. Designed by Courtney Leigh Baker and typeset
in Whitman by Graphic Composition, Inc., Bogart, Georgia

Library of Congress Cataloging-in-Publication Data
Names: Lefebvre, Alexandre, [date–] author.
Title: Human rights and the care of the self / Alexandre Lefebvre.
Description: Durham : Duke University Press, 2018. | Includes
bibliographical references and index.
Identifiers: LCCN 2017045249 (print) | LCCN 2017051070 (ebook)
ISBN 9780822371694 (ebook)
ISBN 9780822371229 (hardcover : alk. paper)
ISBN 9780822371311 (pbk. : alk. paper)
Subjects: LCSH: Humanistic ethics. | Human rights—Philosophy. |
Humanism—Social aspects. | Self-realization—Moral and ethical
aspects. | Self-actualization (Psychology)
Classification: LCC BJ1360 (ebook) | LCC BJ1360 .L44 2018 (print) |
DDC 172/.1—dc23
LC record available at https://lccn.loc.gov/2017045249

Chapter 1 was previously published as "The End of a Line: Care of the
Self in Modern Political Thought," *Genealogy* 1, no. 2 (2016): 1–14, and is
republished with permission.

Chapter 2 was previously published as "Mary Wollstonecraft, Human Rights,
and the Care of the Self," *Humanity: An International Journal of Human
Rights, Humanitarianism, and Development* 7, no. 2 (2016): 179–200, and is
republished with permission.

Chapter 5 was previously published as "Human Rights and the Leap of Love,"
Journal of French and Francophone Philosophy 24, no. 2 (2016): 68–87, and is
republished with permission.

COVER ART: Eleanor Roosevelt carrying her suitcase at LaGuardia
Airport, New York City, 1960. Photo by Lawrence W. Jordan.
Franklin D. Roosevelt Presidential Library and Museum.

IF I AM INTERESTED IN HOW THE SUBJECT
CONSTITUTES ITSELF IN AN ACTIVE FASHION THROUGH
PRACTICES OF THE SELF, THESE PRACTICES ARE
NEVERTHELESS NOT SOMETHING INVENTED
BY THE INDIVIDUAL HIMSELF. THEY ARE MODELS
THAT HE FINDS IN HIS CULTURE AND ARE PROPOSED,
SUGGESTED, IMPOSED UPON HIM BY HIS CULTURE,
HIS SOCIETY, AND HIS SOCIAL GROUP.

—MICHEL FOUCAULT, "THE ETHICS OF THE CONCERN
FOR SELF AS A PRACTICE OF FREEDOM," 1984

Contents

Acknowledgments

Many colleagues and friends have provided invaluable assistance and constructive criticism at various stages of this project. From the University of Sydney, I thank Charlotte Epstein, Duncan Ivison, Jane Park, John Keane, Kiri Flutter, Joy Twemlow, Megan Quinn, Marco Duranti, Moira Gatens, and Simon Tormey. I am also indebted to what I hope will one day be known as the UNSW Foucault school: Ben Golder, Paul Patton, and Miguel Vatter. Keith Ansell-Pearson, Jane Bennett, Leonard Lawlor, Ella Myers, and Felisa Tibbitts provided advice and encouragement at crucial points. Courtney Berger was her usual wonderful editorial self, and I am lucky to have her patient and excellent direction. I am especially grateful for three wonderful colleagues, Danielle Celermajer, Samuel Moyn, and an anonymous reviewer for Duke University Press, all of whom helped me more than I could have hoped for, and for my wife, Melanie White, and her tender loving care. This book is dedicated to Melanie, to our beautiful daughter Beatrice, and to my parents Georges and Joanne.

I thank the following journals and their publishers for permission to reprint modified versions of three articles in this book. Chapter 1 was previously published as "The End of a Line: Care of the Self in Modern Political Thought," *Genealogy* 1, no.2 (2016): 1–14; chapter 2 was previously published as "Mary Wollstonecraft, Human Rights, and the Care of the Self," *Humanity: An International Journal of Human Rights, Humanitarianism, and Development* 78, no. 2 (2016): 179–200; and chapter 5 was previously published as "Human Rights and the Leap of Love," *Journal of French and Francophone Philosophy* 24, no. 2 (2016): 68–87. I also thank the Franklin D. Roosevelt Presidential Library and Museum for allowing me to use the photograph of Eleanor Roosevelt on the front cover of my book. I first encountered it in Allida Black's book on Roosevelt, *Casting Her Own Shadow*, where it is accompanied by a caption: "ER [Eleanor Roosevelt] traveled simply and without fanfare. Often this amazed those who found themselves in her company—as it did Lawrence Jordan Jr., who in the fall of 1960 photographed a solitary, seventy-six-year-old ER deep in thought and carrying her own luggage." It is difficult to say why some pictures mark you, but this one has stayed with me as the image of a life well lived.

Introduction

On August 13, 1948, Eleanor Roosevelt gave a major speech on human rights at the Sorbonne in Paris. Twenty-five hundred people packed into the great auditorium to hear her, and she, the most seasoned of public speakers, confessed to feeling "nervous and apprehensive."[1] Her fears were for naught and the address was a success. The chair of the United Nations Commission on Human Rights and former first lady persuaded her audience of the supreme importance of personal freedom for human rights. She amused them with improvised stories of Soviet stubbornness on the Human Rights Commission. And she introduced a phrase that would come to shape present-day human rights policy. Speaking of the need to see such basic rights as freedom of speech and freedom of assembly as more than abstract ideals, she proposed that they are tools with which to craft "a way of life."[2]

Human rights as "a way of life" is an interesting phrase, but what does it mean? Roosevelt did not define or elaborate it in her speech, but it often comes up in her later speeches and writings. Indeed, the idea of human rights as a way of life is at the heart of her best-known remark on human rights: "Where, after all, do universal human rights begin? In small places, close to home—so close and so small that they cannot be seen on any maps of the world. Yet they are the world of the individual person; the neighborhood he lives in; the school or college he attends; the factory, farm or office where he works. Such are the places where every man, woman and child seeks equal justice, equal opportunity, equal dignity without discrimination. Unless these rights have meaning there, they have little meaning anywhere."[3] The message here is that to be effective human rights must become integrated into the day-to-day of ordinary people. If human rights are not nestled into the small places of life, they run the risk of seeming remote to most people. They would have the air of abstract (not to mention pious) principles. And they would seem to concern only great and far-off institutions. We could say, then, that the viability of the human rights project depends on whether it can guide us in everyday life. That is one reason why Roosevelt advocated for human rights in terms of a way of life.

But there is another reason as well. It is less explicit in her work, perhaps, but no less present or deeply felt. To appreciate it we must remember that in addition to her many roles as human rights campaigner, diplomat, journalist, and social critic, Roosevelt also wore another hat: advice columnist. For decades she wrote a monthly column, "If You Ask Me," for the *Ladies' Home Journal*, advising readers on any number of topics, from politics to art to housekeeping. And late in life she wrote a short and much-loved book, *You Live by Learning: Eleven Keys for a More Fulfilling Life*, in which she tries to answer the thousands of letters received over the years asking her, in essence, "What have you learned from life that might help solve this or that difficulty?"[4]

This vocation as an advice-giver shines through in Roosevelt's reflections on human rights and gives a crucial insight as to why it is so very necessary for human rights to become a way of life. It is not only for the health and viability of the human rights project. Nor is it even for the cause of justice or the improvement of the wider world. It is for the sake of the individual. Her view, her advice, is that a person who lives according to the ideals of human rights—that is, who uses the norms of human rights to shape their own personal outlook and lifestyle—will be better and potentially happier than someone who does not. A person guided by these principles will have a real chance, in her words, to infuse their life with a "spirit of adventure," a fearlessness in living that is intrinsically rewarding.[5]

Roosevelt is important to the story I want to tell, but she is only one figure in it. Many others also view human rights in a therapeutic light. Some are deep in the past of the human rights tradition, such as Mary Wollstonecraft and Alexis de Tocqueville. Others are contemporaries of Roosevelt, such as Henri Bergson and Charles Malik. Today, this perspective can be observed in parts of the human rights education movement. Naturally, none of these people see the relation between human rights and personal transformation in the same way. They respond to problems and pressures of their own place and time; they propose different values and virtues for human rights to help cultivate; and they recommend a mix of practices and techniques to achieve their goals. But underlying all of them is a view that the ideals, norms, and practices of human rights are a means to bring out the best in oneself for the sake of one's self.

Care of the self is the main concept of this book. As we will see, it is a complex idea and comes from the later work of the French philosopher and historian Michel Foucault. The use I make of it, however, is simple to state. I contend that several well-known figures in the human rights tradition advance human rights as a means for individuals to concern themselves with, work upon, and improve themselves. To use an expression that might sound glib at first, they see human rights as a tool for "self-help," one that provides strategies for people to become more resilient, happier, fulfilled, present, loving, exuberant, and even joyful.

This thesis is counterintuitive. Very much so: it rubs against the grain of two fundamental assumptions in human rights law, theory, and activism.

The first assumption concerns the goal of human rights. It is to *protect* people whose rights are at risk of violation, and not to transform those people nor the ones who advocate human rights. Whatever else human rights may be, there is overwhelming agreement between scholars and practitioners, advocates and critics, that the purpose of human rights is to protect all people everywhere from severe political, legal, and social abuse. When, for example, we think of the institutional world of human rights—with its covenants and conventions, international courts, and small army of monitoring agencies—we naturally assume that its mission is to protect people and safeguard their dignity, autonomy, security, or whatever fundamental feature of human life may be in jeopardy. From this perspective, personal transformation seems like a distraction from more serious business.

Things are even less promising when we turn to the second assumption. It concerns, for lack of a better word, the object of human rights: *other* people. Today human rights have become the standard-bearer of global justice. For people from rich and privileged places, and especially from North Atlantic countries where human rights have so powerfully channeled and shaped a moral and political imagination, the cause of human rights is embraced as a way to help other, less fortunate people. Thus, to suggest, as I do, that human rights are as much about caring for one's own self as for other people may seem indulgent or just plain immoral. It appears to funnel a leading institution for global justice into yet another kind of self-help for the already privileged.

There is no general way to allay these suspicions. Each of the main authors I treat in this book envisages a different relationship between personal transformation and protection, and between care for the self and care for other people. They also work from (and intervene in) different and historically specific understandings of what human rights are and do. Although they share a certain core and minimal definition of human rights—as moral and/or legal entitlements belonging to every person—we will see that the specific human rights concepts, laws, practices, and cultures vary from author to author.

Caveats aside, I wish to put forward two hypotheses. On the one hand, all of the authors I have singled out believe that protection and personal transformation, and care for the self and care for others, are complementary and mutually reinforcing. They never face the tragic dilemma of having to choose one set of goals at the expense of the other. On the other hand, and this is crucial, they also maintain that personal transformation and care of the self is not only irreducible to the protection and care of others; it is primary and pursued for its own sake. That is to say, each author considers, in the first instance, how human rights can enhance the well-being, happiness, and power of individuals in and for themselves, and how human rights entail, but only as an offshoot, protection and care for other people. Although there is no conflict between these self-oriented and other-oriented goals, there is a definite and unexpected priority.

This book contributes to the field of human rights and to the study of the care of the self. With respect to human rights, my goal is to demonstrate that a past and present feature of human rights discourse and practice is to inspire individuals to a new way of life and to care for themselves. To be clear, most human rights authors and documents do not conceive of human rights in this way. It is definitely a minority position! Nor do I undertake a comprehensive survey of the care of the self in human rights. Additional authors, movements, and events are pointed out for future study. This book is simply an attempt to mark a facet of human rights that lies hidden in plain sight. I want to show how, time and again at pivotal moments in the history of the tradition, human rights have been claimed as a relevant, valuable, and even necessary answer to personal cares and troubles. Just as significantly, I also want to show how human rights come to be anchored in the nitty-gritty of everyday life as a technique to care for the self.

My second contribution pertains to the care of the self. As we will see, Foucault developed this concept through a series of studies on ancient philosophy. Yet, for various reasons, he was skeptical that it could extend to modern political thought, and in particular, to modern political philosophies based on rights. He even warned against looking for the care of the self in the place I presume to find it! Needless to say, I need to explain why there is room to see his misgivings as hasty. But my goal is not to argue with Foucault. It is to suggest that human rights renew the care of the self for our present moment. Care of the self does not simply not die out in modern and contemporary political thought. By turning to the field of human rights, we see it thrive as one form of response to social and political problems that wreak spiritual and personal distress.

Method: The Author Study

This book is made up of nine chapters. Three are general in nature and develop themes found throughout the book: chapter 1 introduces the concept of the care of the self, chapter 3 anticipates objections to viewing human rights in terms of care of the self, and chapter 6 addresses the relationship between care of the self and social and political criticism and resistance. The majority of the book, however, consists of chapters dedicated to particular authors who, I argue, link human rights to care of the self: Wollstonecraft (chapter 2), Tocqueville (chapter 4), Bergson (chapter 5), Roosevelt (chapter 7), Malik (chapter 8), and contemporary human rights educators (chapter 9). To round off this introduction, I would like to explain, first, why I have composed this book primarily as a series of author studies, and second, why I have chosen to discuss these particular authors.

If the reader will indulge me a moment, I can best address the first question—why author studies?—by explaining how I arrived at the idea for this book. A few years ago, I published a short work on the French philosopher Henri Bergson titled *Human Rights as a Way of Life*. I wrote it because I felt Bergson had a very strange, but also strangely attractive, notion of human rights. I will revisit it at length in chapter 5, but for now a one-line summary will do. Bergson thinks that the purpose of human rights is to introduce all human beings to a way of living in the world—he calls it love—untouched by hatred. At the time, I thought this was a genuinely unique position. Bergson talked about human rights in terms of love rather than law, of emotions rather than practical reason, and most of all, he emphasized the role human rights play in ameliorating the self rather than helping other people. The way he sees it, you should live your life according to human rights not for the sake of other people, but simply because being in love is a better and more joyful way to be. And this, I thought, was an original take on human rights. "To my knowledge," I averred, "[Bergson] provides the first and only account of human rights as a medium to improve upon, relate to, and care for ourselves."[6]

I was mistaken. Soon after finishing that book I began to realize that Bergson was not as singular as I had made him out to be. No one else saw human rights in terms of his notion of love, that much is true. But stepping back from the precise contours of that notion, I have come to believe that several celebrated authors in the history of human rights are also fundamentally concerned with the care of the self. This is the reason the book you are reading is written the way it is, that is, as a series of author studies. Rather than focus on any one author in depth, I have chosen to survey a number of them, as if to say to my reader:

"Look, care of the self can be found here, and here, and here!" My author studies, in other words, are meant to build up a theme through repetition. Now I've tried my best to make these chapters as accessible as possible, both in the sense of not presupposing prior knowledge of any author, and also, I hope, of being able to interest a general reader with wider discussions of human rights, political thought, and ethics. But over and above any value my interpretations of this or that author may have, the result I'm seeking is to be had by holding them all up together in order to produce a cumulative effect. By showing how often care of the self recurs in the history of human rights, my goal is to identify it as a persistent phenomenon, one that deserves further scholarly attention in and of itself, and that could also be tapped as a resource for contemporary practice.

The next question—why *these* authors?—is trickier to answer. That is because the two reasons we might most naturally expect are ruled out. First of all, in the coming pages it will become abundantly clear that no two authors envisage care of the self in the same way. There is no one way to care for the self using human rights, and the reader will not be able to flip to the end of this book to find a model or formula that would state, *this* is how you do it. What we will encounter instead are many different proposals about *how* to care for the self with human rights, and perhaps more importantly, many different explanations as to *why* we might want to do so. Thus, although I claim that care of the self is a persistent phenomenon in human rights, it is undoubtedly a plural one as well. The authors I discuss in this book are not connected by a shared sense of what care of the self in human rights means, is, or does.

But neither, if I can express it this way, are they bound together in disagreement. To put it simply, the authors I have selected do not engage or even acknowledge one another. Setting aside the close and warm relationship between Roosevelt and Malik, in all my reading I have turned up only a handful of passing references made by one author of another, each of which is dismissive to boot. Thus, the plurality I mentioned a moment ago is not arrived at through vigorous engagement and disagreement, as if one author (say, Tocqueville) recognized that a predecessor (say, Wollstonecraft) proposed to use human rights to care for the self in *this* way but that he recommends to instead use them in *that* way. Not at all: the realization that human rights can be used to care for the self takes on the status of a fresh insight for each author, one arrived at from the perspective of their own historical moment, through a distinct intellectual tradition, and to address a specific practical problem.

What does connect these authors? The glue is none other than the concept of the care of the self. As we will see in chapter 1, it is possible to extract from

Foucault's later writings and interviews quite specific criteria as to what counts as the "care of the self" in the traditions he is working through. I have used these criteria to select authors. My procedure is straightforward: if an author writing on human rights meets the criteria for the care of the self fully and robustly, then he or she is in. That is why, for example, I discuss Wollstonecraft rather than Thomas Paine, Malik rather than René Cassin, and human rights education rather than international human rights law. In a manner of speaking, this might be called cherry-picking: I have made my case for care of the self in human rights by selectively choosing the best exemplars in the tradition. This is how I have attempted to constitute a new object of inquiry in human rights. As I said a moment ago, this handful of authors is by no means a definitive list, and readers may well discover additional candidates. That would be excellent: the more the merrier! At the risk of repeating myself, my aim in this book is simply to establish the continued presence of care of the self in human rights and to propose that the value of human rights lies partly in the role they can play in enabling practices of personal transformation and self-improvement.

[1]

THE CARE OF THE SELF

In this first chapter I present Michel Foucault's concept of "care of the self." Straightaway, though, I should say that this is not a book on Foucault. I discuss him to the extent that his later work on ethics and care of the self allows me to spotlight an aspect of human rights.

What do I mean? A much-discussed topic in recent human rights scholarship is the role human rights play in shaping subjectivity and our sense of self. In fields as diverse as political theory, history, art and literary criticism, philosophy, sociology, and anthropology, several works examine how human rights are central not only to the protection but also to the formation of individuals. I would venture to say that there is an excellent book on how human rights impact nearly every human capacity or faculty, whether that is our political imagination, our aesthetic sensibility, our felt awareness of the suffering of others, our self-conception as agents, or even our notion of what it means to be a person.[1]

These studies are crucial to my argument, but none exactly capture the phenomenon I am trying to identify: how human rights are used as a tool for self-transformation and self-improvement for the sake of oneself. That is why I draw on Foucault. His definition of care of the self encapsulates features that are surprising to find in the human rights tradition. As I said in the introduction, we do not expect to find a preoccupation with personal transformation at the heart of the human rights imagination. And it is certainly counterintuitive to discover a priority given to caring for oneself in an idea and institution devoted to global justice and concern for the other. Yet read with a certain Foucauldian eye, these themes of self-care are discoverable time and again at key junctures in the history of human rights. So much so, in fact, that by tracking these multiple iterations it is possible to identify a persistence of the care of the self, mutable and porous though it may be, that human rights have never been without.

But the value of using Foucault's notion of the care of the self to study human rights is not only historical. It is a resource for us here and now. To begin with, it helps to make key human rights authors speak to us anew. The main ones I discuss—Wollstonecraft, Tocqueville, Bergson, Roosevelt, and Malik—struggle against problems that are still very much with us. Chivalry, in Wollstonecraft's sense, is far from dead; neither is the individualism, xenophobia, conformity, and materialism that Tocqueville, Bergson, Roosevelt, and Malik respectively address. That all of them reach for human rights as a therapeutic aid may lead us to recognize attitudes and practices that can be adapted for our own use.

More generally, and these specific authors aside, there is another advantage to viewing human rights in terms of care for oneself: it gives human rights education and advocacy an additional anchor. Today, as we will see later, Roosevelt's slogan for human rights has truly caught on: over the past twenty years or so, policy documents, educational initiatives, and international law have routinely advocated for human rights to become "a way of life." But a shortcoming of much of this discourse is that it is virtually silent as to what can motivate people to do so. *Why*, to adopt a language of moral individualism that I believe human rights need to engage, perhaps even mimic, in order to be widely heard—*why* is it personally advantageous to adopt human rights as a way of life? Why should *I* do it? How will it help *me*? These are hard questions, especially in light of the diverse audiences of human rights education. But if human rights can be aligned with care of the self, one line of answer could be opened up.

I am getting ahead of myself. Before we turn to any particular human rights author, before we assess his or her ongoing relevance, and before we examine how care for the self can complement care for others in contemporary practice, we need to first ask what care of the self is.

Morality: Code, Conduct, and Ethics

"Care of the self" (*le souci de soi-même*, in French) is the defining concept of Foucault's later period (1981–84). It is the cornerstone of the work he produced in the last four years of his life, which includes two books, the delivery of five lecture series (published posthumously), and roughly a dozen essays and interviews.[2] One way to introduce it is to say that, for Foucault, care of the self is a morality; that is to say, it is a particular kind of morality that emerges at a specific time and place. That time and place is Western antiquity: ancient Greece, Rome, and early Christianity. But given that Foucault has a rather idiosyncratic understanding of what morality is and does, this is not a particularly helpful starting point. We should begin, instead, by taking a step back and looking at his conception of morality in general.

A handy overview is found in the Introduction to *The History of Sexuality*, volume 2: *The Use of Pleasure* (1984). This piece is a gateway to Foucault's later period and serves as an introduction to this book and to its companion volume, *The History of Sexuality*, volume 3: *The Care of the Self* (1984).[3] In it he states his reasons for undertaking a two-volume study of ancient Greco-Roman culture and, in particular, a study of its sexual practices. In brief, the classical world emphasizes a valuable dimension of morality that today has faded from sight (which he calls "ethics"). To reach this claim, however, he begins by setting out a broad schema of what he takes morality to be in and of itself and, from there, marks out the place and importance that care of the self occupies within it.

Let's start as Foucault does: with the big picture. Morality, he says, has three components. He calls them "moral code," "moral conduct," and "ethics." Each particular historical morality has its own distinct codes, conduct, and ethics. Nevertheless, Foucault insists that morality, any morality, is always an amalgam of these three components.

"Moral code" and "moral conduct" work as a pair and are straightforward to understand. By *moral code* Foucault means "a set of values and rules of action that are recommended to individuals through the intermediary of various prescriptive agencies."[4] *Moral conduct* refers to the actual behavior of individuals, and considers whether or not it conforms to the code.[5] A moral code, then, consists of the prescribed rules and principles of a morality, and moral conduct denotes whether or not the code is followed in practice.

There are any number of moral codes and instances of moral conduct to cite as examples. Perhaps not surprisingly, the field of human rights abounds with them. It is even tempting to think that these two categories exhaust it. On the one hand, the world of human rights is replete with moral and legal codes, such as the Universal Declaration of Human Rights and the panoply of conventions designed to enact and supplement it.[6] So too, on the other hand, is the international human rights apparatus (both governmental and nongovernmental) dedicated to ensuring that these codes are honored and that the conduct of nation-states lives up to what they affirm on paper.[7] The notions of moral code and moral conduct thus seem apt to cover the basic goals of the human rights project. The question, though, is whether or not they capture all of its aims.

To get a handle on this, we need to return to Foucault and his third component of morality: ethics. This is the one he is keen to discuss. Distinct from codes and conduct, *ethics* refers to the relationship that the self establishes with itself in relation to the precepts that make up the code. Ethics, he writes, is a process "in which the individual delimits that part of himself that will form the object of his moral practice, defines his position relative to the precept he will follow, and decides on a certain mode of being that will serve as his moral goal. And this requires him to act upon himself, to undertake to know himself, to monitor, test, improve, and transform himself."[8] It is clear that when Foucault uses the term *ethics* he does not mean something interchangeable with *morality*, as we often do in ordinary language. Neither does he refer to what that word designates in Anglo-American philosophy, namely the metaphysical and epistemological examination of ethical concepts (metaethics) or the investigation of the criteria for evaluating actions (normative ethics). For Foucault, rather, ethics designates the relation the self establishes with itself through a moral code, and, more specifically, the work the individual undertakes on him- or herself in order to become a subject of that code.

An example helps. Take the precept that enjoins sexual fidelity between marital partners.[9] One way to look at it is in terms of code and conduct. We could trace it back to a particular prescription (say, by a moral or religious authority). We could also look at the degree to which marital fidelity is actually honored in a given society. Yet to consider this precept only from the perspective of code and conduct misses something essential about how morality functions, namely how individuals take up the code to constitute themselves as moral subjects in the first place. A person might, for example, use the prescription to identify that part of himself that needs attention and work, in this case to get one's desire or attention under control. An individual could also take up the precept to identify the kind of person he wishes to become—for example, a dependable and serious partner. (Contrariwise, it is perfectly possible to stake an ethic by breaking moral rules. Think, to continue the example, of someone who refuses to be bound by what he sees as the puritanical rules of his milieu.)

In sum, for Foucault, morality is more than a set of rules or exhortations for individuals to follow. Moreover, and this is crucial, morality does not work simply to regulate relations between people. A core aspect of morality is also to establish the relation we have to ourselves, what Foucault calls "*le rapport à soi*," or more specifically, "the kind of relationship you ought to have with yourself."[10] *Ethics* is the name he gives to this process of self-constitution.

Care of the Self

Where does "care of the self" fit in this trio of code, conduct, and ethics? To use Foucault's language, it belongs to a historical period in Western culture that gave strong priority to ethics. He coins the phrase "care of the self" to demarcate a long tradition in the history of morality that begins in ancient Greece, migrates to Rome and flourishes, and persists into early Christianity and beyond. What makes this period special for Foucault is that it centers on the exhortation for individuals to be concerned with themselves, to attend to themselves, and to work upon themselves.

To introduce care of the self, it is helpful to start with the original French phrase it translates: *le souci de soi-même*. Notably, Foucault's final book is titled *Le souci de soi* (1984), but the phrase makes its thematic appearance in his work a few years earlier, in his 1981–82 lectures at the Collège de France.

> To start with I would like to take up a notion about which I think I said a few words last year.[11] This is the notion of "care of oneself" ["*souci de soi-même*"]. With this term I've tried my best to translate a very complex, rich, and frequently employed Greek notion which had a long life throughout Greek culture: the notion of *epimeleia heautou*, translated into Latin with, of course, all the flattening of meaning which has so often been denounced or, at any rate, pointed out, as *cura sui*. *Epimeleia heautou* is care of oneself [*souci de soi-même*], attending to oneself, being concerned about oneself, etc.[12]

Foucault makes this remark at the beginning of his lecture course in order to indicate his topic for the year. He also signals the tangle of languages and traditions that he will be working through. In this short paragraph, one idea is translated into three languages: "*epimeleia heautou*" (ancient Greek), "*cura sui*" (Latin), and "*souci de soi-même*" (French). English speakers can add a fourth to this list: "care of the self."

The core meaning of this phrase is the same in all languages. It designates attention to oneself and work on oneself. At the same time, however, there is some slippage in that the Greek and French phrases convey something that the Latin and English do not. *Epimeleia* and *souci* signify a sense of worry and preoccupation, such that in the phrases *epimeleia heautou* and *souci de soi-même* the self is a source of anxiety as well as an object of concern.[13] *Le souci de soi-même* is an attitude of concerned attention for oneself as well as a practice of working on oneself.

Ethics and *care of the self* are not synonymous. Although each and every historical morality has an ethical component (insofar as all morality must concern itself with the relation the self establishes with itself in relation to a code), Foucault is clear that only one moral tradition centered on the exhortation to care for the self: ancient Greek and Roman (and, to a degree, early Christian) culture. "What we have there," he observes, "is an entire ethics that pivoted on the care of the self and that gave ancient ethics its particular form. I am not saying that ethics *is* the care of the self, but that, in antiquity, ethics as the conscious practice of freedom has revolved around this fundamental imperative: Take care of yourself [*soucie-toi de toi-même*]."[14] The imperative to care for the self is thus a modality of ethics. It is a particular way in which the relation to oneself is envisaged and actualized within a tradition.

Much of Foucault's lectures and writings on the care of the self are taken up with descriptions of the practices and exercises of the ancient schools of philosophy: Platonic, Cynic, Epicurean, and Stoic. In a sense, this focus is perfectly understandable. These schools are treasure troves of practices and discourses to cultivate the self. And so, over four years Foucault fills volume after volume—seven in total, if we count the lecture series—describing in loving detail the various exercises to care for the self in antiquity.[15] Some exercises are physical and corporeal, such as dietary regimens.[16] Others are spiritual in nature. For example, in his 1981–82 lecture course *The Hermeneutics of the Subject,* Foucault covers the following exercises: nightly examination of conscience to prepare restful sleep (*HOS* 345, 364, 480–84), the drilling into memory of key precepts so as to have them ready for action (*HOS* 360–62, 367), daily meditation to withdraw from the world and remain undisturbed by what is taking place (*HOS* 47–48, 537–38), regular trials of endurance to help resist temptations (*HOS* 421–32), arts to cultivate listening so as to better receive instruction (*HOS* 338–52), and daily reflection on one's own death in order to better appreciate what you have and to bear what is to be expected (*HOS* 417–18, 477–88).

This is only a handful of the techniques Foucault discusses. There are many more. But the question is, why are they so important to him? It is worth asking because Foucault is not interested in recovering or resurrecting any particular exercise. He never enjoins us, for example, to meditate or to abstain from certain pleasures.[17] And it is crystal clear that he doesn't urge a return to a Greco-Roman lifestyle. Even if this were an attractive option—and for Foucault, it certainly is not[18]—it simply wouldn't be possible. As he says, "you can't find the solution of a problem in the solution of another problem raised at another moment by other people."[19] But if this is his opinion, the question remains: Why spend so much time and energy on describing exercises that are arguably only of historical interest?

His answer is direct. The ancient tradition is much more than a fascinating cultural phenomenon. It is an "event in thought" (*HOS* 9). It is, he elaborates, "an important phenomenon not just in the history of representations, notions, or theories, but in the history of subjectivity itself or, if you like, in the history of practices of subjectivity" (*HOS* 11). In detailing the spiritual exercises of the ancient tradition, Foucault is trying to extract something striking and more general: a conception of ethics and morality—and so too of subjectivity—which is not only singular and impressive but also, he adds, "still significant for our modern mode of being subjects" (*HOS* 9).[20]

How and why Foucault thinks this ancient tradition remains significant will be relevant for us later on. At this point, I simply want to identify its main features. This is somewhat difficult as Foucault never explicitly lists, one by one, the defining criteria of the care of the self. Yet three themes recur in his later writings. They concern the purpose, object, and mode of the care of the self. Taken together, they make the care of the self—that is, the morality (and especially the ethics) of the ancients—a genuine event in the history of subjectivity.

1. *The purpose of the care of the self is to transform the self.* To use two of Foucault's favorite expressions, care of the self is a "poetics" and a "cultivation" of the self. Within this tradition, the self is not seen as a fixed substance or pre-given essence. It is a material to be crafted in light of an end or telos. As Foucault states, the purpose of the practice of care of the self is to "change, purify, transform, and transfigure oneself" (*HOS* 11). Ancient ethics does more than modify conduct. Its true goal is to revolutionize our ethos and way of being in the world, right down to our desires, perceptions, ideals, pursuits, and self-understanding.

2. *The object of the care of the self is the self.* Foucault is emphatic that for the ancients, the self—or more precisely, one's own self—is the definitive object of the care of the self. "Under no circumstances," he warns, "can this activity, this practice of the care of the self, be seen as purely and simply preliminary and introductory to the care of others. It is an activity focused solely on the self and whose outcome, realization, and satisfaction, in the strong sense of the word, is found only in the self. . . . One takes care of the self for oneself, and this care finds its own reward in the care of the self. In the care of the self one is one's own object and end" (*HOS* 177). The stridency of these remarks should not be misunderstood. Foucault is not saying that care of the self is by nature individualistic or egoistic, as if it must take place at the expense of other people or by ignoring them. He claims, rather, that in ancient morality the care of the self is a self-sufficient moral end. It is not preparatory labor for care of others.

3. *The mode of the care of the self is voluntary.* Foucault is equally emphatic

that care of the self is not prescribed by law or rule. To the contrary, it presupposes the freedom and choice of the individual undertaking it. "Whatever the effects of austerity, renunciation, prohibition, and pernickety prescriptiveness [the care of the self] may induce, it is not and basically never was the effect of obedience to the law" (*HOS* 317). To speak plainly, I do not try to lead a certain lifestyle or practice certain exercises because I have been commanded by someone else. I do so because I want to transform and improve myself. Caring for oneself is, Foucault insists, "a choice about existence made by the individual. People decide for themselves whether or not to care for themselves."[21] It may sound odd to hear Foucault speak in such voluntarist tones, but he is firm that care of the self is "without relation to the juridical per se."[22] Self-initiated subjectification is the nonprescriptive core of this moral system.

To summarize, for Foucault, the care of the self (*le souci de soi-même*) is a particular dispensation of ethics (that is, the relation we have to ourselves in relation to a moral code) that lies at the heart of Greco-Roman morality. It is special and valuable—an "event in thought," no less—thanks to its unique combination of purpose (to transform the self), object (the self in and of itself), and mode (free and voluntary). When I thus propose to discover care of the self in the human rights tradition, all three criteria must be present. It must prioritize the need for personal cultivation and a poetics of the self. It must regard the self and caring for the self as a self-sufficient moral end. And it must remain nonprescriptive and allow individuals to voluntarily take on human rights codes and practices to cultivate the self. That is the task set for this book.

Two Interview Comments

Equipped with a working definition, it might seem as though we are ready to go off in search of the care of the self in human rights.

Not quite yet. Before starting down this path I need to address an obstacle Foucault puts before us. He believes that care of the self is unlikely to be found in modern or contemporary political thought. Worse, he could be interpreted as saying that the venerable tradition of the care of the self—which begins in ancient philosophy and orients Western culture for more than a thousand years—is interrupted, perhaps even killed off, by the obsession in modern political thought with law, rights, norms, and a juridical conception of the subject. To put the issue starkly, the very place where I seek to discover a concern with care of the self (namely, modern theories of law, rights, and human rights) may in fact be responsible for its demise.

This objection is significant. Accepting it would be fatal to my two goals in this book. Obviously, it would block off investigation of the care of the self in human rights. It would also deny the possibility that human rights renew the care of the self for modern and contemporary audiences. In the second half of this chapter, then, I walk a fine line. I present Foucault's view that the ascendancy of law and rights in modern political thought drives out care of the self. But I also prepare an alternative narrative for the rest of my book to fill in, one in which human rights appeal to generations of scholars, activists, and policymakers as the right kind of tool to care for the self in light of problems that plague their own time and place.

Now, I do not mean to suggest that Foucault was "anti-rights" or "anti-human rights," whatever that might mean. From the late 1970s until his death in 1984—a period that overlaps almost exactly with his later work on ethics and care of the self[23]—he appealed often and forcefully to the language of rights and human rights in relation to a number of social and political causes. To cite a handful of examples, he called on human rights to protect prison inmates,[24] to shame the Socialist Party of France for failing to protest the deportation of a prominent lawyer for asylum seekers,[25] to criticize the Iranian prime minister Mehdi Bazargan,[26] to defend suicide and euthanasia,[27] to promote gay rights,[28] and to defend refugees and demand humanitarian aid.[29] Still, for all his appeals to rights and human rights, Foucault's later work is laced with observations that show him to be skeptical, to put it mildly, that modern political thought (and its rights-based approach) fosters or is even amenable to an ethic of care for oneself.

Two sets of interview comments by Foucault are revealing. They come from different contexts: one is tactical and political, the other is scholarly and historical. Yet they converge on a doubt that, broadly speaking, either rights-based politics or rights-based political thought can be pressed into the service of ethics and care of the self.

The first is an interview Foucault gave in 1982 for *Christopher Street*, a prominent New York gay magazine. This was during the time that Foucault was deep in his work on ethics. What is remarkable about this interview is that Foucault seems to almost subconsciously run through the components that make up morality (i.e., code, conduct, and ethics, which I discussed in the previous section) to formulate a response to a question about rights:

> [Question:] Today we no longer speak of sexual liberation in vague terms; we speak of women's rights, homosexual rights, gay rights, but we don't know exactly what is meant by "rights" and "gay." . . .
>   [Foucault:] I think we should consider the battle for gay rights as an episode that cannot be the final stage. For two reasons: first because a

right, in its real effects, is much more linked to attitudes and patterns of behavior than to legal formulations. There can be discrimination against homosexuals even if such discrimination is prohibited by law.

... That in the name of respect for individual rights someone is allowed to do as he wants, great! But if what we want to do is to create a new way of life [*mode de vie*], then the question of individual rights is not pertinent.[30]

Without a doubt, Foucault supports the cause of gay rights. A legal code protecting the rights of homosexuals may well be a first step, but it is an indispensable one. But upon endorsing this moral and legal code, he immediately shifts gears to consider such rights from the perspective of conduct and ethics. In the first paragraph of his answer he insists on the importance of conduct: it is one thing for homosexuals to have rights on paper, but what really matters are attitudes on the ground and whether or not the code is respected. For us, however, it is the second paragraph of his answer that really matters. Foucault goes out of his way to deny that rights (and by implication, human rights) are a site for ethical subjectivation: individual rights, he states, are not pertinent to the creation of a way of life and the manner in which we relate to ourselves. If I can be permitted to extrapolate from this quotation, it is as if Foucault is pro-rights on the one hand, pro-care of the self on the other hand, yet never shall the two meet. Each line should be pursued on its own—one political and tactical, the other ethical and existential—even if they have no business coming together.

Let's look to the second interview. It also takes place in 1982, just as Foucault was wrapping up his research on ancient ethics—what, in a lecture, he calls his years-long Greco-Latin "trip."[31] The interviewers ask about his post-trip plans, so to speak: specifically, if he intends to seek out care of the self in contemporary politics and political thought. On its face, this suggestion seems perfectly plausible. Much of Foucault's past work had been on modern political topics (such as discipline, governmentality, and biopolitics). It is only natural to wonder how ancient philosophy and care of the self might relate to it. Foucault is intrigued by the possibility yet guarded in his response.

[Question:] Could the problematic of the care of the self be at the heart of a new way of thinking about politics, of a form of politics different from what we know today?

[Foucault:] I admit that I have not gone very far in this direction, and I would very much like to come back to more contemporary questions to try to see what can be made of all this in the context of the current political problematic. But I have the impression that in the political thought of the nineteenth century—and perhaps one should go back even farther, to Rousseau and Hobbes—the political subject was conceived of essentially as a subject of law [*sujet de droit*], whether natural or positive. On the one hand, it seems to me that contemporary political thought allows very little room for the question of the ethical subject. I don't like to reply to questions I haven't studied. However, I would very much like to come back to the questions I examined through ancient culture.[32]

Why is Foucault reluctant to take on board the suggestion that ethics and the care of the self might have a role to play in modern and contemporary political thinking? True to his word not to reply to questions he hasn't studied, he never explains his reasons. Still, he provides a clue. Modern political thought, he says, conceives of the subject as a "subject of law." And this, he continues, has the effect of allowing "very little room for the question of the ethical subject."

In the following section I try to understand what Foucault meant by this. Our first task will be to see what exactly the "subject of law" is. In the interview he takes the term for granted and doesn't comment further, even though it serves to characterize the political thought of several hundred years. With a definition of the subject of law in place, we will be able to, first, flesh out his view that modern political thought marginalizes ethics, and second, assess whether or not his opinion is conclusive.

The Juridical Age

Le sujet de droit is a commonly used term in French. It denotes a legal person, that is, a bearer of legal rights and duties.[33] But while this captures part of Foucault's meaning, his usage has a wider scope. This can be gleaned from another spoken remark, this time in a roundtable discussion at Berkeley in 1980, conducted in English. Foucault describes the birthplace of the subject of law, a historical period of Western societies that he names "the juridical age." Read in this context, it becomes clear that the *subject of law* refers to much more than a bearer of legal rights and duties. It designates an entire conception (an episteme, if you like) of politics, government, and subjectivity.

I think that Western societies have known an age of, how could you say, a juridical age, a juridical period, which started from the twelfth or thirteenth century and lasted till the beginning of the nineteenth century with great political constitutions, the great civil and penal codes of the nineteenth century, and that those juridical structures are now going down and disappearing. Anyway, from the thirteenth century to the beginning of the nineteenth century, the hope, the dream of all Western societies has been that it could be possible to govern people through laws, through courts, through juridical institutions. And the idea of writing constitutions with human rights and so on, the project of writing codes, which would be either universal for humanity, or at least universal inside the nation, was the dream of a juridical way of government. The coincidence between the art of governing and juridical structures has been I think one of the great trends of this long period—from the thirteenth to the nineteenth century.[34]

As is to be expected from a roundtable discussion, Foucault paints with broad strokes. Yet it is a version of a narrative that he sets out on other occasions as well.[35] He claims that Western societies existed in a juridical age for roughly six hundred years. Its key feature—indeed, what makes the age "juridical"—is the coincidence between "the art of governing" and "juridical institutions." Or, put more plainly, the juridical age was guided by a belief (and aspiration) that it is possible to govern primarily by means of law and juridical institutions.

This definition of the juridical age may seem straightforward. Yet perhaps there is more to it than meets the eye. The reason is that it is ambiguous as to *what*, exactly, is being governed by law and juridical institutions. What is the "subject," as it were, of the juridical age? "People," Foucault says at the roundtable. But the word *people* can refer to different things.

One possibility is that Foucault refers to the notion of *a* people (*un peuple*, in French), such that in a juridical age the members of a particular country or community are governed primarily by laws and juridical institutions. No doubt, this is part of his meaning. In the roundtable discussion, he singles out standard devices of government by law—such as constitutions, human rights, and tribunals—as hallmarks of the juridical age. Here we have a first definition of the subject of law. It is the government of a people by means of law and juridical institutions.[36]

But there is another way to read this passage. We must keep in mind that a main topic of Foucault's later period is how people "govern" themselves—that is to say how *an individual person* conducts, controls, and guides him or herself. For example, in his 1980–81 lecture course, Foucault proposes to examine the problematic of government (and governmentality) "from a different angle," namely, "as the government of the self by oneself in its articulations with relations with others."[37] Continuing this line of investigation, he devotes his entire 1982–83 course to the same topic, titling his lectures *The Government of the Self and Others*. In short, the problem of how individuals govern themselves—"the government of the self" and its aims, techniques, and relation to the government of others—is a mainstay of Foucault's later period.

With this in mind, a second definition of the subject of law comes to light. It is the government of the self by means of law and juridical institutions. We thus have two definitions of the subject of law. Loosely speaking, the first subject of law, that is, the government of *a* people by law, is "political" in nature. It designates a particular technique of power—one in which the art of governing a people coincides with juridical structures—and is distinct from other techniques to govern a people that Foucault delineates elsewhere in his work, such as those of disciplinary power and biopower.[38] The second subject of law, that is, the government of *the self* by law, is different. It is "moral." It refers to a particular phase in the history of morality in which the art of governing the self is undertaken (executed, as it were) by means of a legal code.

To appreciate the implications of this twofold definition of the subject of law (as political *and* moral), a passage from the Introduction to *The Use of Pleasure* is indispensable. In it, Foucault outlines an epochal shift away from a morality based on ethics to one based on code.

> If it is true, in fact, that every "morality," in the broad sense, comprises the two elements I have just mentioned: codes of conduct and forms of subjectivation [i.e., ethics]; if it is true that they can never be entirely dissociated, though they may develop in relative independence from one another—*then we should not be surprised to find that in certain moralities the main emphasis is placed on the code*, on its systematicity, its richness, its capacity to adjust to every possible case and to embrace every area of conduct. With moralities of this type, the important thing is to focus on the instances of authority that enforce the code, that require it to be learned and observed, that penalize infractions; *in these conditions, subjectivation occurs basically in a quasi-juridical form*, where the moral subject refers himself to a law, or set of laws, to which he must submit at the risk of committing offenses that may make him liable to punishment. It would be quite incorrect to reduce Christian morality—one probably should say, "Christian moralities"—to such a model; and yet it may not be wrong to think that the organization of the penitential system at the beginning of the thirteenth century, and its development up to the eve of the Reformation, brought about a very strong "juridification"—more precisely, a very strong "codification"—of the moral experience.[39]

As I explained in the first half of the chapter, Foucault's thesis in the Introduction to *The Use of Pleasure* is that every morality is made up of three components: code, conduct, and ethics. But in this passage Foucault adds a crucial observation: different historical moralities may well privilege a certain component, often at the expense of one or the other two. This is especially true, he believes, of moralities that emerge in the modern age. Modern moralities emphasize code and conduct almost to the complete neglect of ethics, such that the government of the self is envisaged as obedience to law. To use Foucault's terms, in this period morality and moral experience undergo a "strong juridification" or "codification." That is why modern code-based morality is a key element of the juridical age: it reconfigures the government of the self in the image of law and prescription.

Ancient (ethics-oriented) and modern (code-oriented) moralities differ in kind for Foucault. The morality of classical philosophers is based on a choice—"a personal choice," he stresses time and again[40]—to care for the self in order to lead a good, beautiful life. "What I tried to show," he says reflecting on his later work, "is that nobody is obliged in classical ethics to behave in such a way as to be truthful to their wives, to not touch boys, and so on. But if they want to have a beautiful existence, if they want to have a good reputation, if they want to be able to rule others, they have to do this."[41]

Modern (so-called "juridical") morality has a different attitude. Prescriptive in nature, it conceives of morality as compliance with a code. As Foucault states in the above passage, "In these conditions, the moral subject refers himself to a law, or set of laws, to which he must submit at the risk of committing offenses that may make him liable to punishment."[42] From this perspective, morality is no longer a question of how the subject actively constitutes itself in relation to a code, as it was for the ancients. It becomes a matter of how the self is constituted by and through the prescriptions of a code. As Foucault states elsewhere, "we pass from a morality that was essentially the search for a personal ethics to a morality as obedience to a system of rules."[43]

In his interview comment I cited earlier, Foucault names Hobbes and Rousseau as representatives of this shift in morality. But clearly he is pointing to something much bigger: namely, the congruence between categorical societies—that is, societies bound together by codes—and a vision of morality as founded on rules, on dos and don'ts. Indeed, the two major branches of modern-day philosophical ethics, Utilitarianism and Kantianism, both envision morality in terms of a criterion or procedure for what agents ought to do.[44] They are part and parcel of the juridical age. As Foucault says elsewhere, we "inherit a secular tradition that sees in external laws the basis for morality. . . . We seek the rules for acceptable behavior in relations with others."[45]

This is the "subject of law." It is shorthand for the model of political *and* moral government by law that emerges in the modern or juridical age. And, given this duality, we could say that for Foucault the juridical age is a decisive period not only in the history of law and politics but also, and perhaps primarily, in the history of subjectivity. For if he feels justified in declaring that a morality based on care of the self is an "event in thought" and "an extremely important phenomenon in the history of subjectivity," it seems only fitting to accord the same status to the juridical age. It undertakes a no less decisive transformation of morality and what Foucault calls *assujetissement* (translated in English as "subjection" or "subjectivation"). By placing the subject of law at the heart of morality—that is, by undertaking the government of the self and subjection by means of law—the juridical age relegates the component of morality that the ancients had privileged: ethics. In truth, Foucault's verdict is more severe. The juridical age does not simply underemphasize ethics; it subsumes it altogether under the category of the code. For when the constitution of the subject is accomplished through the prescriptions of a code, the juridical age effectively jettisons ethics as a unique dimension of morality and moral experience. Ethics loses its place and standing as a distinctive component of morality.

At last we revisit Foucault's interview comment I cited earlier: "It seems to me that contemporary political thought allows very little room for the question of the ethical subject." We now can speculate as to why: modern and contemporary political thought downgrades the role and importance of ethics (and thus too, of care of the self) because it fixates on the subject of law.

In light of his comments on the juridical age, there are two (complementary) ways to interpret this comment. The modest option is that, according to Foucault, there is little room *within* modern political thought for the problem of ethics to emerge. We are unlikely to find much reflection on ethics in this tradition because its canonical authors construct their theories on the idea that the political government of others, and the moral government of the self, coincide with law and juridical institutions.[46] By drawing attention to the centrality of the subject of law in modern political thought, Foucault's comment can be understood as an explanation for why it leaves so little room for ethics, and also as a caution against looking for care of the self there.

But perhaps Foucault is saying something more far-reaching. Maybe his claim is not just that ethics is absent within modern political thought, but, more strongly, that modern political thought is part of a broader movement—call it the juridical age—that marginalizes ethics and the care of the self as such, that is, as core elements of morality. In this respect, modern political thought would be one flank in a more general campaign, also being carried out in such fields as philosophy and religion, to remake morality and the moral imagination in the image of a code. Read this way, the purpose of his interview comment is not merely to identify the absence of ethics in modern political thought. His indictment runs deeper. Modern political thought (together with its avatar, the subject of law) would be a key player in a wider, even epochal movement to marginalize ethics and drive care of the self from the world.

[2]

THE JURIDICAL SUBJECT AS ETHICAL SUBJECT: WOLLSTONECRAFT ON THE RIGHTS OF MAN

Given what I said in the previous chapter, it is uncertain whether or not Foucault would have admitted that care of the self can be found within the human rights tradition. After all, this tradition has its roots in an episteme (i.e., modern political thought, and more generally, the juridical age) that he believes eclipses the morality his later work explores (i.e., care of the self). On top of that, readers familiar with Foucault will recognize two strands from his earlier writings that seem hostile to the very idea of human rights: namely, his critique of foundationalist conceptions of subjectivity (chiefly humanism), and his critique of theories of sovereignty guided by a rights-based understanding of power and government.[1]

Nevertheless, I am confident that two features of my project would have found his favor. Or, better put, there are two qualities in each of my human rights authors that Foucault himself admires. They are diagnosticians. And they are ethicists.

By diagnosticians I mean they seek to identify those dangers specific to their own milieu that harm people to the depths of their souls. That is to say, these human rights thinkers and actors do not react to evils and dangers that have plagued humankind since the beginning of time. They address modern—that is, historically modern—dangers and ills. For example, when Wollstonecraft criticizes patriarchy, she does not decry a timeless and placeless domination of women by men. She uncovers a specific form of it: late medieval and early modern chivalry. Tocqueville, for his part, says that democrats suffer feelings of isolation and restlessness. This is not because they are selfish, a condition that every age has known; it is because they are individualistic, a misfortune unique to democracy. The same goes for Roosevelt, Malik, and certain present-day human rights educators: they cast human rights as a therapy to target harms and pressures that are endemic, and often specific, to their own time and place. That is why, to use Foucault's term, they can be called "diagnostician[s] of today."[2]

They are also ethicists, in Foucault's special sense. As we will see in the coming pages, there is no single way to care for the self using human rights. What we have, instead, is an untotalizable plurality: human rights keep on being used, in different ways and for different reasons, to mend the self for the sake of the self. Yet, at the same time, there is an underlying coherence. Behind all of the different conceptions of the care of the self in human rights lies a single imperative: "Transform yourself! Become other than who you currently are!" Each author I discuss, in other words, claims human rights as a tool to help people unbecome what they have become and to unlearn what they have learned.

This resonates with Foucault. As we have heard him say, care of the self seeks to "change, purify, transform, and transfigure," all of which involve gaining a critical distance from oneself.[3] More than that, these goals are personal aspirations for him. They are the essence of what it means to be a philosopher, not only in antiquity, but also in our own day and age. As he states in *The Use of Pleasure*, "What is philosophy today—philosophical activity, I mean—if it is not the critical work that thought brings to bear on itself? In what does it consist, if not in the endeavor to know how and to what extent it might be possible to think differently, instead of legitimating what is already known?"[4] And in a rare personal aside, Foucault speaks of an urgent need—his own and one he tries to elicit in his readers—to "refuse who we are," "to think otherwise," and "to get free of oneself."[5] In this vein he uses a French word for which English has no equivalent: *égarement*.[6] Roughly translated as "straying afield of oneself," it is the action of getting distance from what is represented as the morality, reason, and common sense of one's time.[7]

No single word better describes the uses that human rights are put to in order to care for the self. The authors and actors in my book all envisage an égarement in which individuals gain distance and relief from the pressures and common sense of their time. The difference from Foucault, and the possibility he never entertained, is that they use human rights and the juridical subject of human rights to do so.

The First Great Human Rights Debate

This chapter is on Mary Wollstonecraft. Writing as she does in the wake of the French Revolution, she is the first author to have viewed human rights as a means to care for the self. But that is not the only reason why she is the starting point of my book. It is also because her account of how human rights can remake and care for the self is the most powerful, moving, and least academic I know of. The problem she seeks to redress is painful and real: the desperation of women who live according to the values and virtues of her time. And her solution is a clear case of how the juridical subject of human rights is put to "ethical" (in Foucault's sense) use. For Wollstonecraft, the great potential of the so-called "rights of man"—which are for her truly universal, *human* rights[8]—is to inspire individuals to a new way of life. She hopes that these rights can help women to personally, practically, and affectively escape their attachment to a culture that devastates any chance they may have to live happy, full lives.

Vindication of the Rights of Woman is Wollstonecraft's systematic dissection of the state of her culture, and her most forceful statement as to how human rights can serve as a release from it. Before turning to it, I must say a word about its context: the "pamphlet war" of late eighteenth-century Britain. Pamphlet war is the name given to the flurry of publications in Britain commenting on the Revolution of 1789 in France. Over the following decade approximately four hundred "pamphlets" (which often were full-blown books) were published in Britain debating the events and meaning of the French Revolution. As one historian writes, "This meant that there were over four hundred voices all fiercely contesting what exactly had happened in France, why it had happened, what it meant for Britain and where events were now headed."[9]

Most of these contributions were minor and faded quickly into obscurity. Others became classics of political thought. Three of the most famous are Edmund Burke's *Reflections on the Revolution in France* (1790), Thomas Paine's *The Rights of Man* (part 1 published in 1791, part 2 published in 1792), and Wollstonecraft's *A Vindication of the Rights of Men* (1791) and *A Vindication of the Rights of Woman* (1792). As we can tell from the titles, the debate between these authors swirls around the issue of universal rights, and more specifically, the meaning of "The Rights of Man and Citizen," declared and passed by France's National Constituent Assembly in 1789. Roughly speaking, Burke sees such rights as a vehicle for the worst destructive tendencies of the Revolution, whereas Paine and Wollstonecraft believe they enshrine the value and importance of the individual human being. But stating the opposition bluntly in this way covers up what I take to be the crucial difference between the Burke–Paine debate on the one hand, and the Burke–Wollstonecraft debate on the other. The first centers on the power of the newly minted doctrine of the rights of man to destroy (Burke) or remake (Paine) the social and political order. The second has a different focus and set of stakes. It concerns the potential for the rights of man either to distort (Burke) or regenerate (Wollstonecraft) the self.[10]

This is not the place to recount Burke's critique of human rights. Yet one observation bears mentioning. I began this book by claiming that it is unusual to think of human rights in terms of care for oneself. That said, the opposite claim is made loudly and often. A great many critics have proposed that, far from perfecting a talent for living well, human rights foster the art of living badly! Marx and his successors, for example, claim that human rights instill and reinforce an impoverished ethos of moral and political individualism.[11] Other authors, as diverse as Jeremy Bentham and Milan Kundera, find a mutual attraction between human rights discourse and a supercilious, sneering way of life.[12] And today a range of critics link human rights to a certain kind of bloodlessness and narrow universalism, both political and spiritual, which is really only acquiescence to our state of affairs.[13]

I address these objections later in the book. But the grandfather of this kind of attack on human rights is Burke. His critique not only comes chronologically first but also takes precedence in terms of scope, emotion, and sheer magnificence. Written during the early days of the French Revolution, *Reflections on the Revolution in France* is arguably the first great work on human rights. Hostile though it may be, *Reflections* is nevertheless pertinent to a discussion of the care of the self. Burke's view is that the rights of man declared in the French Revolution threaten to devastate the system of manners and customs that had previously nurtured the self's relation to itself. It is as if a life guided by these rights is the surest way to fall prey to the rising pressures of equalization and abstraction that he associates with modernity, to undermine any ability to care for oneself (not to mention care for others), and ultimately, to become prideful, vicious, sanctimonious creatures.[14]

I have elsewhere discussed Burke's attack on the rights of man from the perspective of self-formation.[15] Here I only suggest that Burke and Wollstonecraft are perhaps not so far removed from one another as one might assume. Their conclusions are miles apart, certainly. He believes that human rights ruin the relation we have to ourselves; she sees them as a powerful tool to re-create the self. Nevertheless, they debate on a shared terrain. Both conceive of human rights in terms of law *and* as a comprehensive way of life. Their dispute, in other words, proceeds from a mutual appreciation that the "rights of man" are more than a bundle of legal entitlements or constitutional guidelines; they are also

an ethical device or standpoint that can be used, for better or worse, to cultivate the relationship that we have to ourselves. From this perspective, then, a
dispute over the care of the self lies at the heart of the first great human rights
debate.

The Unhappiness of Women

In discussing Wollstonecraft it is best to begin with the concrete problem. As
I suggested a moment ago, she is a diagnostician. She analyzes the character
of women (and also of men) as shaped by a particular dispensation of culture.
She identifies, in other words, what is specific to her time and place, and in
particular, its specific ills. Her guiding question is never, "What is the essential
nature or character of woman?" Nothing could be further from her premise
that gender differences are socially and historically constructed. Her approach
is instead to ask, "What is the character of women as constituted by the present
modification of society?"[16]

This is an enormous question. It takes the whole of *Rights of Woman*—along
with other works, most notably her novella *Maria, or the Wrongs of Woman*[17]—
for Wollstonecraft to give her answer. For it is with only a touch of hyperbole
that she states, "it would be an endless task to trace the variety of meannesses,
cares, and sorrows, into which women are plunged by the prevailing opinion"
(*VRW* 137). But to gain a first impression we can avail ourselves of Sylvana Tomaselli's vivid depiction of the kind of woman Wollstonecraft both loathed and
pitied.

> [She is] a married woman who divides her time between her mirror and
> fashionable society, consults astrologers and succumbs to every fad, is too
> afraid to tarnish her reputation by taking a lover, yet is flirtatious, and
> unfaithful in thought, if not deed, who having sent her infants to wet-
> nurses, takes little interest in them on their return home, who worries
> that her daughters might outshine her when they come of age, cannot
> concentrate long enough to improve herself by reading, affects physical
> frailty, pretends to be ill whenever it suits her, lacks all reserve before her
> husband, children and servants, and fears not God, but dreads the loss of
> her looks more than anything else on earth.[18]

This is the type of woman Wollstonecraft thinks her time and place produces,
and similar characterizations are rife in *Rights of Woman*.[19] Clearly, such a person is contemptible for Wollstonecraft. But why? Yes, she will neglect her duties. She will also very likely be mean and uncaring to those ostensibly closest to

her. But that's not the worst of it. The real problem, Tomaselli rightly concludes, is that she will be condemned to "an empty, and in all probability, embittered existence."[20] In every line of this description a different unhappiness rears its ugly head: whether it is the fleetingness of beauty and the ability to please, being at the mercy of opinions and fads, having desires that cannot be satisfied for fear of stigma, or seeing one's own children as annoyances and even eventually as rivals. Such a person will be alarmingly brittle. She will be gripped by "emotions which rather embitter than sweeten the cup of life" (VRW 101). And she will be ensnared in a system of values and so-called "virtues" that, in the end, lead only to resignation, bitterness, or rage.

What role do human rights play in this bleak diagnosis? I argue that Wollstonecraft advances a conception of human rights with two facets. One is juridical and political, the other educational and ethical. These two facets of human rights are complementary and reinforcing. More than that, they combat oppression in different ways and are both needed if women are to escape their predicament.

In her juridical theory, Wollstonecraft insists on the need for women to enjoy the same basic legal, civil, and political status as men. She aims to advance rights that will end male conjugal and political power and to create the conditions for women to function as free, independent, and enfranchised agents. Yet as significant as this argument is, I address it only briefly. In part, my reason is that it is excellently developed in commentaries on Wollstonecraft.[21] But my sense is that it is also the less original facet of her theory of human rights.

That distinction is reserved for her educational theory of human rights. My main argument in this chapter is that, for Wollstonecraft, the key human rights advanced in the French Revolution—universal rights to equality, liberty, and what she calls "friendship"—are indispensable to redress the oppressive relation women have to *themselves*. As distinct from the juridical dimension of her theory, Wollstonecraft does not here call on human rights to secure the conditions for the education of women (for example, rights to equal access to education). Her point is more basic. She proposes human rights as the very content and medium of instruction, that is, as educational in and of themselves. She implores women to view themselves *in the image of* human rights, for example, *as* self-determining agents free of spurious needs and passions, and *as* human rather than female beings. If women strive to do that—if, differently put, they use human rights to modify their self-understanding, needs, and desires—then they will have taken the first crucial step in constituting themselves in such a way as to gain distance from a culture that saddens and enfeebles them.

I can translate this into Foucault's idiom. Wollstonecraft treats human rights from the perspective of ethics, understood as the relationship an individual establishes to him- or herself (*le rapport à soi*) in relation to a code. Her aim is to encourage women to become the subject announced in the great political declaration of her time: a free and equal being. Here I should like to recall that favorite word of Foucault's to describe the work of ethics: égarement, defined as the action of gaining distance and perspective from what is represented as the morality, reason, and common sense of one's time. In *Rights of Woman* Wollstonecraft's deepest wish is to spark an égarement, a desubjectification such that women could unbecome what their milieu of chivalry has led them to become. Her book—and indeed her life, which I touch upon later—testifies to a sense of being inside and outside of a world, of trying to resist it, to reform it, and, just as importantly, to live as well as one can within it. Human rights are her tool to do all these things at once.

The Juridical Theory of Human Rights

In this section I briefly sketch Wollstonecraft's legal and political—what, following Foucault, I call her "juridical"—theory of human rights. At the outset, though, it is important to observe that it is an open question in Wollstonecraft scholarship as to whether or not she has a theory of rights at all. Several leading interpreters claim she doesn't.

Barbara Taylor's *Mary Wollstonecraft and the Feminist Imagination* (2003) is a good example. While Taylor acknowledges that Wollstonecraft's writings abound with references to rights, she finds that most are "cursory" and "pragmatic": "Natural-rights was for her not a primary intellectual commitment but one of a quiverful of intellectual weapons to be kept sharp and handy for contestation."[22] As Taylor sees it, after the opening pages of *Rights of Woman*, Wollstonecraft "appears almost to lose interest in the question of rights," and that her main concern "is less with the institutions that oppress women than with the experience of *being* female, with the emotional violence and intellectual debilitation on which feminine subjectivity is founded."[23] Taylor is not alone. Janet Todd, Virginia Sapiro, and Sandrine Bergès all remark that Wollstonecraft's major work is curiously mistitled. It is a work on education dressed up as a political treatise.[24] These authors do not claim that "rights talk" is unimportant for Wollstonecraft. They acknowledge that her discussion of natural and political rights is part of a broader argument about the democratization of the public and private spheres. Nevertheless, they conclude that rights are a secondary topic for Wollstonecraft, one quickly displaced by her focus on education and perhaps reserved for a future treatise.[25]

This view is not unanimous. Other commentators affirm that Wollstonecraft has a theory of right, and a robust one at that. Daniel O'Neill sees her as engaged in a project to extend the "rights of man" to women and to undercut the civil and domestic rights of patriarchy. He suggests that Wollstonecraft sketches a defense of both "first" (civil and political) and "second" (social and economic rights) generation human rights for women.[26] Lena Halldenius goes further. She claims that a theory of rights is primary to *Rights of Woman*. To do so she distinguishes between two kinds of liberty that Wollstonecraft seeks to preserve. The first is social and political liberty: the freedom of individuals from dependence on an arbitrary will. The second is moral liberty: the freedom of individuals to form and trust their own judgment. Her conclusion is that, on Wollstonecraft's account, "moral liberty needs social [and political] liberty."[27] In order for individuals to have a duty to improve their minds and cultivate virtue, moral and legal rights must be in place for them to do so.

Halldenius's argument is amply grounded in *Rights of Woman*. Wollstonecraft often observes how unjust laws thwart any chance for women to overcome narrowness of mind and pursue true virtues. "The very constitution of civil governments," she writes, "has put almost insuperable obstacles in the way to prevent the cultivation of the female understanding" (*VRW* 129). Wollstonecraft also makes the positive point: only with equal legal rights will women have the opportunity to collectively and individually flourish. Granted, she never systematizes this idea. Nowhere does she catalogue the rights necessary to break down hierarchies of various sorts. Yet she calls for equal civil and political rights in so many domains—in civil society (*VRW* 239), politics (*VRW* 237), education (*VRW* 67–70, 129), and domestic life (*VRW* 162, 235)—and with such insistence as to make her intention clear. Following Halldenius, then, I agree that a juridical theory of rights is central to *Rights of Woman*.

Here, then, are two opposed camps. A majority of Wollstonecraft scholars deem rights a topic of secondary importance in *Rights of Woman*. A minority emphasize it is fundamental. Yet they share a key assumption. They presume that rights and education are distinct. The majority state that Wollstonecraft's interest in rights takes a backseat to her preoccupation with education. The minority claim that for Wollstonecraft rights provide a space or framework for education to take place. All of them, in other words, present Wollstonecraft's interest in rights as though it were an exclusively juridical (or legal, or constitutional, or political) topic. Granted, these commentators acknowledge that rights and education are interrelated. None of them would take issue with Bergès's observation that "Women have a right to be educated, but also, in order to enjoy any other rights, they need to be educated."[28] Yet no one claims that Wollstonecraft treats human rights *in terms of* education, such that human rights and education can be one and the same thing, or more exactly, that human rights can be educational in and of themselves. That is my position.

The Wollstonecraft Paradox

How does that work? What does it even mean to say that human rights are educational in and of themselves?

Allow me to approach these questions with an insight by Joseph Slaughter in *Human Rights, Inc.* (2007). As I explain later, this is a work very near to, and yet very far from, my own conception of human rights as care for oneself. But at its core is a rich and valuable idea I have relied on. To use Slaughter's language, there is a "tautology" (and also a "teleology") at the heart of human rights discourse in that it aims to produce subjects (i.e., real, empirical, living and breathing human beings) in the image of the juridical subject it presupposes that human beings already are. As he puts it, the human rights project is essentially tied to "the project of becoming a person," and in particular "[to] the development of a human person and personality capable of occupying the place of the 'human' in international human rights law."[29]

The tautology that Slaughter identifies is at play in the authors I treat in this book. Wollstonecraft, Tocqueville, Bergson, Roosevelt, and Malik (as well as others I mention passingly) may well disagree as to who or what the universal subject of human rights is. But, if we can bracket their differences for the moment, Slaughter's tautology is apt to describe their efforts. They all conceive of the universal subject of human rights as a figure to designate, on the one hand, what we are declared by law to already be (i.e., a dignified, self-determining, equal human being) and, on the other hand, what we should aspire to personally become (i.e., a dignified, self-determining, equal human being). To borrow Slaughter's elegant formulation, they presuppose "that the person *is* a person in order to effect the person *as* a person."[30]

Slaughter doesn't mention Wollstonecraft in *Human Rights, Inc.*, as she is well outside the historical period he studies (the mid-twentieth-century drafting of the Universal Declaration of Human Rights). Yet she offers a striking example of his thesis on the tautological nature of human rights. For proof I quote a passage from *Rights of Woman* in which Wollstonecraft expresses the paradoxical notion that our inherent natural or human rights must be "procured": "Pleasure is the business of woman's life, according to the present modification of society, and while it continues to be, little can be expected from such weak beings. Inheriting, in a lineal descent from the first fair defect in nature, the sovereignty of beauty, they have, to maintain their power, *resigned the natural rights, which the exercise of reason might have procured for them,* and chosen rather to be short-lived queens than labor to obtain the sober pleasures that arise from equality" (*vrw* 129–30, emphasis added). Following Slaughter's penchant for identifying "paradoxes" of human rights, I name the idea expressed in this passage the Wollstonecraft Paradox: our natural rights—which she also refers to as our "inherent" rights (*vrw* 272, 294)—must be procured. Through care and effort we must become, in our hearts and minds, in our flesh and blood, the juridical subject we are said already to be.[31]

This paradox has two components. First, Wollstonecraft says it is possible for people to resign their natural rights. Second, she says it is possible for people to procure their natural rights (even if, as in the case of women in the eighteenth century, this possibility is systematically thwarted). And at the end of the passage she adds a clause that is crucial for us. In speaking of the "sober pleasures" that arise from equality, she links the procurement of natural rights to personal improvement and fulfilment. This is the kernel from which I develop her conception of human rights in terms of care of the self.

Paradox 1: To Resign Our Human Rights

Start with the first component of the paradox. The notion of "resigning" natural rights is standard fare in early modern political theory. To name but one prominent example, John Locke uses it in *Second Treatise of Government* (1689) to describe the founding moment of the commonwealth, wherein individuals hand over ("resign") their power to legislate and to adjudicate disputes to a common legitimate authority.[32] Wollstonecraft too draws on this idea in *Vindication of the Rights of Men*, published a year prior to *Rights of Woman*. "The birthright of man," she says, "is such a degree of liberty, civil and religious, as is compatible with the liberty of every other individual with whom he is united in a social compact, and the continued existence of that compact."[33] This formulation has all the features we might expect of a definition of natural rights. It stipulates equality and grants civil and religious freedom, but on condition that individuals resign a portion of their natural right to a common authority.

Her use of the word *resign* in *Rights of Woman* differs markedly from those standard usages. It is biting and critical. In the passage I quoted in the previous section, Wollstonecraft is not referring to the fact that everyone, or at least all citizens, resign a portion of their rights in a legitimate polity. She is talking about how women—specifically, women who put stock in a certain kind of feminine beauty and the power that comes with it—willingly resign their natural rights in the context of a particular dispensation of culture.

Part of Wollstonecraft's meaning is that women in her milieu do not care about, or even care for, equal rights. Educated as helpmates and playmates for men, as creatures of sensuality and passion, universal rights appear to middle-class and rich "educated" women either as irrelevant to their way of life or else as a threat to it. As she scathingly puts it, such women are taught to "despise the freedom which they have not sufficient virtue to struggle to attain" (*vRW* 126). This, then, is one sense in which Wollstonecraft speaks of women "resigning" their rights. Regarded as "foreign to their sex," the cause of equal rights is consigned to disinterest or regarded with hostility.[34]

But there is a second, more devastating component to Wollstonecraft's criticism. It stems from her conviction that women forfeit their humanity by resigning their natural rights. As hard as it is for us to hear, the message is not that women are perceived as inferior by men. Thanks to their education they really are so. In *Rights of Woman*, Wollstonecraft repeatedly states her belief that, with few exceptions, women of her day are less than human: "brutalized," in her deadly literalism (*vRW* 185). She writes of women as "insulated" and "stripped of the virtues of humanity" (*vRW* 107). She laments that, in them, "the characteristics of humanity can scarcely be discerned" (*vRW* 125). She calls women "brutes" and "animals" (*vRW* 87, 105). Even her depiction of women as "pale-faced creatures who are flying from themselves" trades on the inhuman (*vRW* 237, 124). In short, Wollstonecraft attacks the typical education of an eighteenth-century woman—based as it is on a desultory instruction in lady-like subjects geared to securing a favorable marriage[35]—as denaturing. Raising females "as women [rather] than [as] human creatures" distorts and diminishes their humanity (*vRW* 74).

Two criticisms are thus bound up in Wollstonecraft's complaint that women resign their natural rights. The first concerns the "rights" part of natural rights. Women, she believes, are largely indifferent or hostile to the cause of equal civil, political, and domestic entitlements. The second criticism is different. It concerns the "nature" (or the "human") part of their natural rights. Women, she argues, have been made into beings in whom the humanity that underpins natural rights can scarcely be recognized. In this respect, the phrase *resigned the[ir] natural rights* is another way of describing what I earlier called Wollstonecraft's diagnosis of the unhappiness of women. It captures the disempowerment and disfigurement of women—political, social, domestic, but also affective, cognitive, and existential—from within a culture of chivalry.

"Chivalry" is the name Burke gives to the beloved world he thinks the French Revolution has doomed.[36] It is an order based on a hierarchy of the sexes in which men and women are unequal parts of an organic whole. But whereas for Burke the end of chivalry is nigh, Wollstonecraft reads the situation very differently. She emphasizes just how far down its roots go, how entrenched chivalry is in the everyday attitude of its men and women alike. Her goal is thus nothing short of trying to bring about the break that Burke fears has already happened. She wants to pry the mores of her milieu loose from the grip of chivalry.

Suffice it to say, this is a monumental task. Such reform must be comprehensive, even total. In perhaps the most famous sentence of *Rights of Woman*, Wollstonecraft announces her program: "It is time to effect a revolution in female manners—time to restore to them their lost dignity—and make them, as a part of the human species, labor by reforming themselves to reform the world" (*VRW* 117). To do this, however, she must confront a major obstacle. Bluntly put, men and women are fond of chivalry. They are attached to it. They have formed their self-understanding in its image. How then to proceed? What tactics can Wollstonecraft use to displace one ethos (i.e., chivalry) in favor of another based on human rights and its ethic of liberty, equality, and friendship between the sexes?

There is no single answer. Some of Wollstonecraft's strategies are stick-like: negative and critical. Others are carrot-like: positive and constructive. The stick is easy to explain. She needs to show women how the life they currently lead is awful on any number of registers. Here Wollstonecraft launches several kinds of criticism. She attacks women from a perfectionist point of view for failing to live up to their potential (*VRW* 76, 136). She puts forward a deontological argument and claims that chivalry leaves women indisposed to fulfill their duties to God, spouse, friends, and children (*VRW* 143–47, 235–36). Most importantly, she will deploy a hedonistic critique to reproach chivalry on its own terms: it is a terrible bargain in terms of the pursuit of pleasure. At best, beauty and the power to please and amuse men will procure a few years of "regal sway" (*VRW* 104). To drive home her view, she cites a "lively writer" who asks, "what business have women turned of forty to do in the world?" (*VRW* 78). Now, we might expect Wollstonecraft to coax her reader to exclaim, "Oh! What a horrible thing to say!" But not at all. On the basis of the values of chivalry, she agrees entirely (*VRW* 147). The statement has a clarifying Swiftian tone. And that's just the point: a culture that spits out women at the age of forty is a perfect *reductio* proof of its own insanity as a culture of pleasure.

Through these lines of attack, Wollstonecraft seeks to demolish her reader's attachment to chivalry from nearly every known moral and psychological position: perfectionist, religious, deontological, consequentialist, and hedonistic. She needs to impress on them the sheer madness—the irrationality, unhappiness, indignity, and desperation—of having willingly resigned their natural rights. This is the stick.

But Wollstonecraft also has a carrot up her sleeve. It is human rights. She will show her reader that a life oriented according to liberty, equality, and friendship is preferable in every way to chivalry. It will be better for our loved ones, in our ability and desire to care for them. It will be better for our community in that we can realize our potential. But most of all it will be better for ourselves. It holds out the prospect of a fuller life to which chivalry cannot compare.

Paradox 2: To Procure Our Human Rights

If for Wollstonecraft human rights hold out the prospect of personal fulfillment, is it fair to say that she offers a modern version of the care of the self? Is it even appropriate to align her with this kind of morality? A Wollstonecraftian might object on one issue in particular: Foucault's insistence that caring for oneself is a self-sufficient moral end and not preparatory work to care for others. Wollstonecraft does, after all, emphasize duties to care for others (mainly in the context of marriage, motherhood, and the family).[37] She also develops a rich ethic of care toward nonhuman animals (vrw 268–69).[38] It might then seem that the discourse of "care of the self" doesn't fit with Wollstonecraft's multidimensional account of the relationship between duties, rights, care of self, and care of others.

Yet in several places Wollstonecraft is explicit that a woman's first duty is to herself as a rational being: "Connected with man as daughters, wives, and mothers, their moral character may be estimated by their manner of fulfilling those simple duties; but the end, the grand end of their exertions should be to unfold their own faculties and acquire the dignity of conscious virtue" (vrw 95). And again, "Speaking of women at large, their first duty is to themselves as rational creatures, and the next, in point of importance, as citizens, is that, which includes so many, of a mother" (vrw 235). And so, while it is true that if women fail to attend to themselves they will not properly do their duties— for example, without cultivating her understanding, a mother will be either tyrannical or indulgent toward her children (vrw 140, 145, 272)—the accent of *Rights of Woman* falls on this defining feature of the care of the self: women must unfold their faculties and cultivate their reason primarily for their own sake. Their dignity depends on it.

Here again is the problem: Women have lost their dignity not because they have lapsed from the standards set by their society, but because they have fully imbibed them. Chivalric society may call beauty, sensuality, chastity, and bashfulness the key virtues of women. But we know perfectly well what Wollstonecraft thinks: there are virtues and then there are "virtues," values and then "values." Some lead to perfection and the potential for happiness, others to imperfection and unhappiness. The problem is how to tell them apart. What standard can tell the good virtues from the bad?

Human rights are the answer. The promise of human rights, as I interpret Wollstonecraft, is to provide women (and less pressingly, men too) with a standard to select which particular values and virtues to cultivate, and which kinds of experiences, desires, and goals to pursue. Her hope is that by viewing themselves in the light of human rights—that is, *as* the juridical subject of human rights—women will have a reliable guide to cultivate the right kinds of values and virtues that will break the hold chivalry has on them. If they do that—if, that is, they adopt the juridical subject of human rights to orient future work on themselves—they will, in Wollstonecraft's fine phrase, procure their natural rights. They will become in their person the juridical subject they are already said to be: free, equal, sociable, dignified human beings.

This idea of procuring one's own inherent human rights is complex. For the sake of clarity, allow me to break it down as a four-step process.

Step one, which is really no step at all, is the depressing situation we have heard Wollstonecraft describe: women as having lost ("resigned") their dignity and humanity through the bad education of chivalry. Raised into enfeebling virtues and passions, they are made, and then make themselves, constitutively unfree and unequal.

Step two is where human rights come in. Wollstonecraft urges individuals (and again, women in particular) to adopt human rights as a perspective on themselves, that is, to view themselves as the universal, free, and equal juridical subject of the Declaration of the Rights of Man. Obviously, doing so doesn't magically make it come true. A lifetime of enculturation into chivalry isn't suddenly erased because a person starts reflecting on him- or herself as free and equal. What such reflection does, however, is provide an all-important foothold, an anchor point to guide work on the self. As an attitude or perspective, human rights furnish a standard to ask of any virtue—really, of any value, desire, or pursuit—"Will this help me to become free? Will this help me to become equal?" If the answer is yes, then it is a humanizing option; if not, then not. The juridical subject of human rights, in other words, shifts the reflexive relation people have to themselves and thereby serves as the basis for individuals to develop qualities of character to conduct themselves differently.

Step three is the momentous one: it involves actually doing the work of cultivating the self. Here, of course, the possibilities are open-ended. A point I am keen to argue in later chapters is that human rights are not—or rather, are certainly not necessarily—homogenizing. They are not doomed to produce cookie-cutter subjects. In the particular case of Wollstonecraft and the Rights of Man, for example, there are any number of ways to work on the self so as to become free, equal, and dignified. Someone could choose to develop courage, or forbearance, or open-mindedness, or reliability, or perspicacity, or whatever combination of these and other virtues holds out a prospect to become freer and more equal.

Step four is what Slaughter calls the tautology of human rights, wherein the individual becomes, in his or her own person, what the juridical theory of human rights posits them to already be. Or, in terms of what I earlier named the Wollstonecraft Paradox, step four is achieved when individuals succeed in procuring their natural rights by becoming a free and equal subject in their person.

I admit that, laid out as a series of steps, this process seems abstract. To give it flesh I will conclude by looking at how Wollstonecraft adapts three key universal rights of the French Revolution—equality, liberty, and what she calls friendship—to care for the self in conditions of chivalry.

Equality as Care of the Self

The main controversy that travels throughout Wollstonecraft's writings— whether fictional, educational, political, and even epistolary—is the sexual division of virtues.[39] We have seen her rail against the commonplace wisdom of her time that males and females should cultivate different virtues. For Wollstonecraft, this has had disastrous effects on both sexes. But women clearly get the worst of it. Within chivalry they are taught to cherish virtues that are actively enfeebling, such as frailty, delicacy, sensuality, and the like (VRW 115– 19). Moreover, they tend to receive only the degraded version of virtues said to define them, such as untutored bashfulness rather than acquired modesty, or the forbearance of weakness and dependence (VRW 104–5, 209–11). That is why the sexual division of virtue renders women constitutively unequal. Women become "stripped of virtues that should clothe humanity" (VRW 107).

The solution to this problem is clear: boys and girls, as well as men and women, must be taught that there is only one road to happiness and perfection, or more accurately, one bundle of virtues to strive for (VRW 79, 87, 117). What is remarkable, however, is that Wollstonecraft presents this solution in the language of human rights: "Surely there can be but one rule of right, if morality has an eternal foundation, and whoever sacrifices virtue, strictly so called, to present convenience, or whose *duty* it is to act in such a manner, lives only for the passing day, and cannot be an accountable creature" (*VRW* 106). Here, Wollstonecraft adopts a core principle of the French Revolution that is bound to ring in the ears of her audience. The principle is this: a single set of universal rights must displace the feudal world of unequal entitlements and duties. This revolution has occurred in the legal and political world. It is now time to reform the moral and quotidian one. But for this to happen, more is required than substituting one legal order for another. Deep personal transformation must take place. All human beings must recognize that there is but a single road to excellence, worthiness, and happiness. Or, to put the point directly, every individual must recognize him- or herself as a human being, rather than primarily as a man or women. Only then will the revolution of equality be achieved at the level of manners.

Equality is thus as much an ethical and attitudinal term for Wollstonecraft as it is a legal one. The universal subject declared by the French Revolution— the human in "human rights"—is not merely someone who holds the same legal rights and duties as everyone else. It is also someone who regards him- or herself *as an* equal, *as a* human being. This is what Wollstonecraft wishes for women. As she says, "I wish to show that elegance is inferior to virtue, that the first object of laudable ambition is to obtain a character as a human being, regardless of the distinction of sex; and that secondary views should be brought to this simple touchstone" (*VRW* 76–77). This is the power of equality: it serves as a perspective, an "ethic" in Foucault's sense, for women to relate to themselves as human beings in the first instance. It is, moreover, a standpoint to care for the self by selecting and cultivating virtues that are genuinely humanizing. It is thus to demonstrate the appeal of equality that Wollstonecraft will dedicate much of *Rights of Woman* to showing how attractive it is to be human, how preferable being human is to being either a man or woman in a world of sexualized virtues and chivalric manners.

In short, the equal and universal subject of human rights plays two roles in *Rights of Woman*. It is a legal concept to designate a universal set of rights and duties. It is also an educational concept to lead individuals to regard themselves as human and take the first step toward caring for themselves. It is thus in two different but related senses that we should read Wollstonecraft's rebuke of Germaine de Staël: "It is not empire,—but equality that [women] should contend for" (*VRW* 186). Certainly, Wollstonecraft argues that women should lay claim to legal and political equality. But it is just as imperative for women to labor to achieve equality as a way of life, that is, as a way of viewing and working upon themselves. For Wollstonecraft, this is the only way to overcome lingering attachments to the sexualized virtues of chivalry and false promises of happiness and pleasure.

Liberty as Care of the Self

The terms *tyrant* and *slave*, and *tyranny* and *slavery*, are among the most prominent in *Rights of Woman*. Wollstonecraft sees tyranny between the sexes everywhere she looks. Men tyrannize over women in political, civil, and domestic spheres (*VRW* 67–71, *passim*). The reverse is true as well: women play to the weakness of men and obtain illicit sway over them (*VRW* 78, 87, 104, 129). But Wollstonecraft is not concerned only with tyrant–slave relations *between* sexes. In her attack on the tyranny of the sexes, she revives one of the great themes of classical moral and political philosophy (think Book IX of Plato's *Republic*): the tyrant is first and foremost a slave and the unhappiest of beings. More than anyone, he or she is at the mercy of appetite, passion, opinion, and circumstance.

Wollstonecraft deploys this theme to powerful effect in *Rights of Woman*. Consider this surprising line: "When, therefore, I call women slaves, I mean in a political and civil sense; for, indirectly, they obtain too much power, and are debased by their exertions to obtain illicit sway" (*VRW* 262). The slave here is not powerless in the ordinary sense. Just the opposite: she has obtained too much power by illegitimate means. She is a tyrant. The key point, however, is that she is debased and degraded. She has spent a lifetime cultivating virtues that may appeal to (certain sorts of) men, but that leave her defenseless and miserable. Such a tyrant is exposed to every kind of unhappiness: she is a slave to impermanent sensory pleasure (*VRW* 137, 270), intemperate passion (*VRW* 172, 212), and opinion and propriety (*VRW* 184, 234, 243). In the language of the ancients, she is as far away from the ideals of *ataraxy* (absence of inner turmoil) and *autarky* (self-sufficiency in which one needs nothing but the self) as possible. Specifically, Wollstonecraft laments that because women are encouraged to pursue this kind of power over men—in the present dispensation of politics and culture they can have no other—they turn away from virtues that could buffer the vicissitudes of passion, sensibility, and circumstance. In becoming tyrants, then, women are made uniquely vulnerable to the world and to themselves.

When Wollstonecraft thus calls for the "independence" of women, she again speaks in a double register. She clearly means to advance the cause of political, civil, and domestic freedom for women. But it bears emphasizing that in the first paragraph of *Rights of Woman*, Wollstonecraft treats independence as an ethic or disposition: "Independence I have long considered as the grand blessing of life, the basis of every virtue—and independence I will ever secure by contracting my wants, though I were to live on a barren heath" (*VRW* 67). This is the kind of independence under threat by the current education of women and the view that girls must be raised to be charming mates (*VRW* 97, 98, 101). In advocating independence—or as she puts it elsewhere, "sovereignty" over oneself (*VRW* 137) and "self-government" (*VRW* 144)—Wollstonecraft designates a relationship to oneself as much as a relationship to others.

This ethics-centered conception of liberty is explicit in her critique of Rousseau. In her words: "'Educate women like men,' says Rousseau, 'and the more they resemble our sex the less power will they have over us.' This is the very point I aim at. I do not wish them to have power over men; but over themselves" (*VRW* 138).[40] Power, in this sense, is Wollstonecraft's name for a measure of control over one's own needs and desires. Truly, this kind of self-control is neither "inherent," nor does it come easily or naturally. It takes a lifetime of hard work to procure. (As Jonathan Lear remarks in a different context, "To become human does not come that easily.")[41] But the first step is to see oneself in the light of human rights, namely as a free and independent agent. Only then will women be able to care for themselves and procure virtues that will make them free in a meaningful and practical sense. Only then will women cease to be slaves to men, to themselves, and to circumstance. And only then can women aspire to become the best and happiest kind of person known to Wollstonecraft: a friend.

Friendship as Care of the Self

In *Rights of Woman*, Wollstonecraft explicitly names "friendship" a natural right (*VRW* 143). It designates a personal and intimate relationship that can grow between free and equal beings. More exactly, it refers to a relationship that can grow between individuals who strive for virtues that make them "respectable," in the sense of being worthy of respect (*VRW* 124).

The roots of Wollstonecraft's identification of "friendship" as a natural right are difficult to pinpoint. But along with its Aristotelian resonance, it seems safe to suggest that she is in part trading on its connection with the more commonly used revolutionary idea of "fraternity." One effect of speaking of friendship rather than fraternity, of course, is to shed androcentrism. But whichever term she uses (i.e., friendship or fraternity), Wollstonecraft still has to contend with the fact that neither fits seamlessly into the standard grammar or discourse of rights talk.

This takes a word of explanation. Today, the revolutionary phrase *liberté, egalité, fraternité*" is cited as if it were one indivisible package: with any one of these terms comes the other two. But as Mona Ozouf has shown, this was not always the case. First of all, its emergence as a tightly knit slogan can be traced to the efforts of Ernest Renan in the late nineteenth century.[42] And even when *fraternity* was evoked by the revolutionaries themselves in connection with *liberty* and *equality*, it was acknowledged as the odd term out, "the poor relation."[43] Of the three, it is the least established in Enlightenment thought. Moreover, unlike liberty and equality, which can be easily coded into the language of rights, fraternity seems of another order—"of duties rather than rights, of bonds rather than statutes, of harmony rather than contract, of community rather than individual. It is more carnal than intellectual, more religious than juridical, more spontaneous than contemplative."[44]

Yet it is precisely this anomalous status of fraternity as a natural right that appeals to Wollstonecraft. Indeed, she does something inventive with it. Rather than try to wrench the notion of fraternity and friendship into the juridicized orbit of liberty and equality, she does the opposite. She presents liberty and equality as attitudinal or dispositional qualities that liken them to friendliness and fraternity. In so doing she is able to treat all three terms (i.e., liberty, equality, and friendship) as if they were of a kind: natural rights with the power to impart a state of the soul.

Wollstonecraft most often discusses friendship within the context of marriage.[45] She refers to it as the "most holy band of society" (*vrw* 99). Her claim is that friendship, not love, should be the basis and goal of marriage (*vrw* 186, 205). This does not mean that marriage should be unaffectionate or sexless. It means that marriage ought not to be based on a chivalric kind of love in which women strive to be pleasing and men to be seductive. Not surprisingly, Wollstonecraft is exceedingly critical of this sort of love.[46] Inevitably, it leads to contempt, the very opposite of the mutual respect of dignity upheld by human rights. Consider her remarks on the impermanence of chivalric love:

> Half the sex, in its present infantine state, would pine for a Lovelace; a man so witty, so graceful, and so valiant: and can they *deserve* blame for acting according to principles so constantly inculcated? They want a lover and protector; and behold him kneeling before them—bravely prostrate to beauty! The virtues of a husband are thus thrown by love into the background, and gay hopes, or lively emotions, banish reflection till

the day of reckoning come; and come it surely will, to turn the sprightly lover into a surly suspicious tyrant, who contemptuously insults the very weakness he fostered. (*VRW* 205)

Chivalric love is an awful trap, particularly for women. Raised in the expectation of love, and trained in the arts to elicit it, they soon find it has a built-in expiration date. "Love," Wollstonecraft observes, "from its very nature must be transitory" (*VRW* 99). It may burn brightly at first, yet soon it will be succeeded by one of two things. Either it ends in shared indifference and disappointment, or else it can bloom into friendship. But it is not as if these alternatives present themselves as live options to choose between. It is not as if Lovelace or his would-be lover can simply decide one fine day to be friends. Their entire education and constitution prevent it. Neither has been prepared for friendship—either to be a friend or to want one. Their fate is mutual contempt.

Friendship is the highest reward for having cared for the self. It is a natural right, yes, but one with preconditions: it flourishes only between beings who have worked on and cared for themselves. As Wollstonecraft states in *Rights of Men*, "true happiness [arises] from the friendship and intimacy which can only be enjoyed by equals."[47] Or, as she puts it in *Rights of Woman*, friendship is possible only between those with hearts "made to beat time to humanity, rather than to throb with love" (*VRW* 209). This is why men and women must procure equality and independence, so as to "merit" the regard of their spouse (*VRW* 99). As ever, though, they should do so not primarily for the sake of their spouse but for themselves. Only if they care for themselves through human rights will they enjoy the sweet side of life and know what it is like to be "beloved by one who can understand him [or her]" (*VRW* 171).

Human Rights as a Style of Existence

My goal in this chapter was to present a clear case for how human rights can operate in terms of care of the self. In so doing I also wanted to begin to push back against Foucault's view that the juridical subject—and its conception of government of the self by law—is inhospitable terrain for ethics and the care of the self. In the previous chapter I cited from several works to convey his skepticism. To conclude this chapter, I quote from an interview in which he seems to open the door, at least a crack. In it he revisits the question of whether care of the self—or, as he calls it here, an "aesthetics of existence"—persists into modernity. "A history of the techniques of the self and the aesthetics of existence in the modern world needs to be done. A moment ago I mentioned the 'artistic' life, which had such a great importance in the nineteenth century. But we could also envisage the [French] Revolution not simply as a political project but as a style, a mode of existence with its own aesthetic, its own asceticism, and its particular form of relation to oneself and to others."[48] It is a pity Foucault never read Wollstonecraft. Her life is a case study of a "revolutionary" mode of existence (and one that became famous, which is to say infamous, immediately after her death). As Virginia Woolf attests, along with many subsequent biographers, Wollstonecraft's life "was an experiment from the start."[49] She did her best to live up to the ideals of her work. She became an independent author at a time when few women dared. She sought friendship in love. And, most importantly for us, her writings envisage the Revolution just as Foucault suggests: as a political event *and* as a style of existence. Putting it this way is not to diminish her achievement. To say she advances a "style" of living conveys the depth of her project: to instill the ideals of the revolution and its declaration of natural rights as a comprehensive way of life.[50]

To be honest, I'm not sure if what Foucault calls for is feasible within the field of human rights: "a history of the techniques of the self and the aesthetics of existence." My trouble is with the word *history*, which implies some measure of continuity, narrative coherence, and myriad relays between past and present events. I have not been able to uncover that in studying care of the self in human rights.[51] First of all, as I said in the Introduction, the authors I have singled out never mention one another, so it is difficult (if not artificial) to establish intellectual filiations.[52] They also differ with respect to how they define human rights: as recent historical scholarship has made abundantly clear, it cannot be assumed that a late eighteenth-century notion of human rights maps onto present-day institutions and discourses.[53] Last, because they reach for human rights in response to particular problems, the practices and models they recommend are not interchangeable. Their problems and solutions are strongly contextual: what works to overturn chivalry (Wollstonecraft) will not address individualism (Tocqueville), which in turn will not cure conformity (Roosevelt), and so forth. They are specific fixes for specific issues.

But perhaps such plurality is not a weakness. It is certainly not from the perspective of ethics: the more multifaceted, supple, singular solutions offered by human rights to care for the self the better! But also I mean that perhaps it is not a methodological liability either. That there is little continuity in this domain, and that there is no unified set of techniques or guidelines that one author or tradition consciously borrows from another makes the recurrence of the care of the self in human rights all the more remarkable. Precisely because it is never raised to the level of an explicit theme, it has the quality of appearing as a fresh insight arrived at by authors working from particular historical moments, distinct intellectual traditions, and specific practical problems. What connects them is a repeated intuition that human rights provide indispensable resources to care for the self. Thus, if a history cannot be written, something like a gallery can be presented: a series of tableaux, one next to the other, which, in repeating a theme, gives form and life to it. My chapter on Wollstonecraft has been the first picture at this exhibition.

[3]

CRITIQUE OF HUMAN RIGHTS AND CARE OF THE SELF

At the end of the previous chapter I described this book as a portrait gallery of the care of the self in human rights. The tour will resume with the following chapter on Alexis de Tocqueville. Before that, however, I would like to take a brief detour in order to outline the contemporary critique of human rights and the care of the self. No one has yet criticized them together, that is, from the perspective of how they work together and mutually reinforce one another in the way I am trying to set out. Even so, it is striking that contemporary criticisms of the care of the self on the one hand, and of human rights on the other, dovetail to a remarkable degree. In critical theory and progressivist circles, they are indicted for similar shortcomings.

I speak from experience. When I present this research at conferences and workshops I am often met with perceptive critics who raise versions of the same objection: that the discourse of human rights *and* the discourse of the care of the self are problematic for similar, and in my case compounding, reasons. Both can be said to be depoliticizing and lead individuals to care about themselves (*their* own rights, *their* own well-being) rather than collective concerns. Both can thus also be said to undermine the ethos required for a flourishing democratic politics. Both—and this is when the bite of the criticism really sinks in— can be said to sit all too cozily with neoliberalism and its own depoliticizing tendencies. Last, as the final nail in the coffin, both can be said to be spiritually impoverishing because they enshrine individualism as a way of life. From this point of view, the combination of human rights and care of the self is a noxious cocktail. It mixes a diminished critical sensibility with distaste for political life and tops it off with an existentially stultified way of being in the world.

This is an impressive set of criticisms. In this chapter I sketch the dovetailing critiques that political theorists have made of the care of the self and of human rights. I do so because these critics mark out something real and important. Disengagement and individualism, both political and ethical, are directions human rights and the care of the self can take. But they are not necessary ones, or so I will argue alongside my selection of human rights authors. My aim, then, in outlining potential pitfalls of human rights and the care of the self is to set the stage for an ongoing theme of my book. Namely, illustrious figures in the tradition recommend human rights to ward off precisely these pitfalls—along with the powerful forces that support them—in our own person and for our own sake.

Critique of the Care of the Self

A survey of the criticisms of the care of the self and human rights made by political theorists is too big a task to attempt here. For the sake of manageability, I focus on two powerful critics: Ella Myers on the care of the self and Wendy Brown on human rights.

Most discussion of the care of the self in political theory—both for and against—takes place in the context of what has come to be known as the "ethical turn."[1] As with any branch of political theory, the ethical turn has many expositors. It includes preeminent authors in the field such as William Connolly, Jane Bennett, Simon Critchley, Judith Butler, and Martha Nussbaum. What unites them is a desire to identify what kind of ethos is most conducive to a flourishing democratic politics. They seek, in other words, to elaborate the right kind of sensibility to draw citizens into democratic activity and to foster the virtues and emotions necessary for democratic life, such as open-mindedness, respect, commitment, tenacity, and love. Naturally, many proposals are made about how to do this. Some are inspired by Foucault's later work on the techniques of the self, which is pressed into the service of generating a pluralistic ethos.[2] Others take Emmanuel Levinas and his ethic of charity and generosity as their point of departure.[3] Appeals are also made to Auguste Comte, J. S. Mill, and Rabindranath Tagore and their respective notions of a "religion of humanity."[4] Yet, as diverse as these efforts are, they share a point of view. They see ethics as coming to the rescue of democratic politics.

For the sake of clarity, I can draw a bright contrast (too bright, no doubt) between my own approach to human rights and the current discussions dominating the ethical turn. The ethical turn in political theory investigates the following question: How can ethics support democracy? From this perspective, ethics has instrumental value as an indispensable treatment for an ailing democratic politics. Granted, the various ethics advanced by these theorists may be praised as admirable in their own right. Yet the attention of this scholarship is directed at how ethics can support a democratic politics.[5] My approach addresses the reverse question: How can human rights support the care of the self? From this point of view, human rights and human rights culture are an instrument—a "technique," to use Foucault's language—in the service of ethics, and not the other way around. Although I too treat the relation between democratic politics and ethics, the priority I give to caring for oneself as an end in itself is distinct from the main concern of the ethical turn in political theory.

Let's look at the critics of the ethical turn. There are two kinds: external and internal. External critics argue that the ethical turn as a whole is an intellectual and practical dead end. For them, a focus on ethics and ethos in contemporary democratic theory distracts from the real and messy work of collective political life. It is dismissed as the kind of political retreat that the dominant social, economic, and political powers of today demand and promote.[6]

These are not the critics I wish to engage. Because they oppose the ethical turn as a whole, they are not attuned to shortcomings of care of the self in particular. Internal critics, by contrast, are those political theorists who affirm the importance of the ethical turn, yet criticize care of the self as the wrong direction for it.[7]

Ella Myers offers the strongest, most robust version of this argument. In *Worldly Ethics* (2013) she begins her assessment of the ethical turn on a sympathetic note, agreeing that it is crucial to cultivate the right kind of ethics in order to sustain a flourishing democracy. The trouble, she says, is that the two leading positions of the ethical turn do just the opposite. Care of the self (inspired by Foucault) and care for the Other (inspired by Levinas) are "ill-equipped to nourish associative democratic politics. The dyadic relations that are labelled ethical in both of these cases narrow attention to the figures of self and Other and obscure the worldly contexts that are the actual sites and objects of democratic action."[8]

It is worthwhile to cite at length the dedicated criticism she makes of the care of the self in democratic political theory:

> The care for the self is a flawed basis for elaborating a democratic ethics. Although the notion that purposeful work on the self can contribute to collective citizen action is no doubt appealing, an ethics capable of animating associative democratic activity . . . cannot take the self's relationship to itself as its starting point. The therapeutic ethics that emerges from Foucault's and Connolly's work tends to treat democratic activity as a consequence or extension of self-care, a view that overlooks the unique orientation toward shared conditions that associative democracy requires. Unless the self's reflexive relationship to itself is driven from the start by concern for a worldly problem, there is no reason to believe that self-intervention will lead in an activist, democratic direction. Any reflexive relationship that might enhance democratic subjectivity depends upon collective political mobilizations that both inspire and continually guide work on the self. A viable democratic ethos should focus less on inciting and enriching individual care for oneself than on activating collaborative concern for social conditions. Only in tandem with such world-centered practices of care can arts of the self acquire democratic significance.[9]

Myers asks a simple but pointed question: Does care of the self lead to greater concern for a democratic polity? Her answer is no: on its own, we shouldn't expect care of the self to do so. On the one hand, it is perfectly possible for certain kinds of self-care to be incompatible with democracy. She worries, for example, that consumerist aspects of Connolly's therapeutic ethics "runs the risk of being captured by prevailing habits and beliefs that can render arts of the self nondemocratic, even antidemocratic."[10] On the other hand, as we see in this passage, Myers claims that if techniques of the self do help to sustain democracy it is because they are always already animated by a concern for a shared democratic world. To use her terms, the ethic (i.e., the reflexive relation to the self) that supports democracy reveals itself to be "care for the world" in the first instance, not care for the self. In short, for Myers it is wishful thinking that care of the self leads automatically to care for a democratic world. Either the aims of care of the self fail to support democracy or, if they do, it is only because they are animated by something beyond concern for oneself.

Yet there is a key assumption in Myers's critique. She seems to believe that political theories based on care of the self proceed in the same manner—that they recommend that an individual attend to him- or herself in the first instance, and only then proceed to care for others. She assumes, in other words, a two-step chronological or sequential model: care for the self first, care for others and the world second. To reach for a metaphor, we could liken this kind of care of the self to the emergency airplane procedure that tells parents to put on their own oxygen mask before helping their child.

This picture of the care of the self is at times warranted by Foucault's remarks. We have heard him insist that the object of the care of the self is the self. "Under no circumstances," he states, "can this activity, this practice of the care of the self, be seen as purely and simply preliminary and introductory to the care of others. . . . In the care of the self one is one's own object and end."[11] Moreover, it is possible to envisage and practice care of the self exactly along the lines of the two-step model Myers portrays. Plato, for example, characteristically does so: the young Alcibiades is urged by Socrates to take care of himself before he can consider taking care of others.[12] And when Foucault comments on Plato and uses him as a point of departure to reflect on the care of the self, he gives voice to this very model: "I think the postulate of this whole morality was that a person who took proper care of himself would, by the same token, be able to conduct himself properly in relation to others and for others."[13]

But, as we will see, not all theories of the care of the self work this way, that is, by starting from the self and then radiating outward. My objection to Myers, then, is that although caring for others is an effect or consequence in the discourse of the care of the self, it is not necessarily a *chronological* effect or consequence. The two can be contemporaneous. And in this book I focus on authors for whom care for the world is undertaken to care for the self. One cares for the self, in other words, by caring for a wider world.

This possibility is not entertained by Myers. For her, care of the self can be only an offshoot, never a driver, of care for a democratic world. Consider her concluding remarks on Foucault, in which she comments on his observation that practices of the self are not invented by individuals but created within a broader culture: "What Foucault seems to recognize in this moment—that the conditions of possibility for the ethical practice of self-care are publicly constituted—allows one to appreciate that practices that aspire to care for the world are potentially enabling of 'new subjectivities.' *Self-constitution can be helpfully conceived of as an indirect enterprise*, one practiced not only by conscious focus on oneself as an object of care, but also through engagement with others that is directed at changing worldly conditions in ways that make them more amenable to individual experimentation and flourishing."[14] Myers says that self-constitution "can be" helpfully conceived of as an "indirect enterprise" accomplished through engagement with others. But that does not convey her critical thrust. I take her real claim to be that self-constitution *must be* conceived in this way—that is, as an "indirect enterprise" and not as the primary focus—if democratic theory is to avoid the pitfalls she had earlier identified: that, on its own, care of the self is not conducive to democracy (or if it is, then it is not care of the self, but care for the world, in the first instance).

This is too sweeping and peremptory a criticism. Care of the self might take self-regarding and antidemocratic forms, granted. But why should it be fated to be so? It depends on the kind of care and instruments in question. Take human rights. Human rights are other-oriented, universal, and declared with the aim of furthering justice worldwide. Yet this origin has not prevented generations of authors and actors from recommending them as an instrument to care for the self. What it has done, however, is color the nature of that care. Human rights are not chosen arbitrarily by the authors I treat. They are adopted as techniques of the self because they are deemed appropriate to administer the kind of self-care required at a particular time and place. Tocqueville, to name only the next author in my sequence, fastens onto human rights because they turn individuals away from themselves—because, to use Myers's phrase, they teach individuals to care for a world. That is what he thinks democrats need to do for their own personal well-being. And this reveals an important potential of caring for oneself more generally: it does not necessarily lead to selfishness or individualism. Care of the self can assume the form of care for others and the world, insofar as that care (of other people, of the world) is undertaken in order to care for the self.[15]

Put it this way: my approach to human rights appears to amplify the most ethically worrisome aspect of the care of the self. It takes a leading institution of global justice and seems to degrade it into another form of self-help for already privileged people. But that is not the direction the human rights authors discussed in this book tend. In caring for the self with human rights, the individual is turned outward, attuned in various ways to others and to a world. For Wollstonecraft, caring for the self makes women into better citizens, mothers, spouses, and friends. For Tocqueville, a better democrat is the product. And for Bergson, Roosevelt, and Malik, it results in more joyful, fearless, and meaningful subjects. Yet all of this, to be crystal clear, is undertaken *for the self*, in the name of caring for oneself. In short, by attending to how human rights cultivate the self it becomes possible to safeguard the care of the self on the point where it seems most suspect and vulnerable: the primacy of caring for oneself.

Critique of Human Rights

Just now I presented objections to the care of the self. Remarkably, though, if I were to substitute the words *care of the self* with *human rights*, the same criticisms could be marshaled just about verbatim. Today it is commonplace to hear human rights disparaged on the grounds that they encourage political retreat, fan ethical self-absorption, diminish critical capacities, and most of all, risk capture by globalization and neoliberalism. As I indicated earlier, there is substantial overlap in the critiques of the care of the self and of human rights.

But there is another overlap to mention. It is between what critics identify as the problems *with* human rights, and the problems that the authors I discuss in this book *call upon* human rights to fix. Surprisingly, many are the same. Not only do my authors not perceive these problems in human rights, but human rights are explicitly identified as a resource to combat several of them, including political withdrawal (Tocqueville), self-absorption (Roosevelt), and acquisitive materialism (Malik).

Now, it would be hasty to straightaway mobilize these human rights authors as counterexamples to contemporary critics. Wollstonecraft and Tocqueville wrote two hundred years ago, after all; Bergson, Roosevelt, and Malik seventy years ago. Much has changed since then and, as recent studies in the history of human rights have made abundantly clear, the aims, institutions, and sentiments behind human rights do not remain constant.[16] We cannot, in other words, presume that what these historical figures meant by "human rights" amounts to what today's critics attack. The two may well be ships in the night, working from vastly different conceptions of human rights.

I take up this question in my chapters on Tocqueville and Bergson, and then again in the chapter 9, which is dedicated to human rights education. There I will consider which elements of our historical authors are compatible with contemporary human rights discourse and practice, either in the sense of already having been integrated into it, or else as providing useful new directions for it. This will enable us to determine if the ways these historical authors propose to care for the self remain viable and are (or can become) part of human rights today. It will also enable us to gain traction on the issue at hand—that is, whether or not these historical authors serve as counterexamples to contemporary critics—not by refuting or challenging them head-on, but by highlighting resources *in* human rights to counteract the pitfalls *of* human rights which they (i.e., the critics) identify.

First, however, I need to present the contemporary critique. As before, I have chosen a specific text to channel my discussion: Wendy Brown's classic indictment of human rights discourse, "The Most We Can Hope For . . ." (2004). Her essay is a critical comment on Michael Ignatieff's 2001 Tanner Lectures at Princeton University, *Human Rights as Politics and Idolatry*. In ten searing pages she anticipates many attacks that subsequent critics will come to make of human rights. She also centers her critique on two issues that correspond to problems that Myers (and others) identify with care of the self. First, human rights promote depoliticization. Second, human rights facilitate the rise of antidemocratic powers (neoliberalism, chiefly).

Brown's essay quarrels with the main idea that Ignatieff advances in *Human Rights as Politics and Idolatry*. In a nutshell, this is that all human rights law and activism seek to do is limit political violence and reduce misery. Ignatieff calls this the "minimalism" of human rights, and for him such minimalism is laudable in that it strives to curtail violence while preserving (indeed, augmenting) personal agency.[17] Here is how Brown paraphrases it: "On [Ignatieff's] view rights simply set people free to make the world as they see fit—they do not have normative or subject-producing dimensions; they do not carry cultural assumptions or aims; they do not prescribe or proscribe anything; they do not configure the political in a particular way or compete with other political possibilities or discourses. They simply expand autonomy and choice."[18]

Brown has spent a career problematizing this kind of argument. In this article she takes human rights to task. But in her wider work she dissects other ideas and discourses that behave the same way—as if they have no entanglements with power and seek only to limit pain and suffering. The liberal idea of tolerance is her paradigm case. As she says in a discussion with Rainier Forst, "tolerance *tends* to operate discursively as if it has nothing to do with power, but both of us [i.e., Forst and herself] have our eye on the extent to which it is always imbricated with power."[19] If we return to her critique of Ignatieff, we see that his conception of human rights commits the same error. In a line that could apply as much to boosters of tolerance as to human rights activists, Brown concludes, "it is an old ruse of liberal reformers, in pursuing agendas that have significant effects in excess of the explicit reform, to insist that all they are going is a bit of good or holding back the dark."[20]

Let's attend to her first criticism of human rights: it is depoliticizing and promotes an antipolitical form of subjectivity. On one issue Brown and Ignatieff are in full agreement: human rights are subject-forming and shape our sense of self. "Rights language," writes Ignatieff and quoted by Brown, "has been central not simply to the protection but also to the production of modern individuals."[21] But what kind of "modern subjects" do human rights produce? For Ignatieff, it is clear. Human rights foster moral agency: the ability of subjects to define and pursue (reasonable) goals free from external interference. Human rights, he says, help people to become self-determining "individuals" by lessening the hold and pressure exerted upon them by groups.[22]

Brown takes this aspect of Ignatieff's theory to task. Tellingly, however, she faults it not simply as the view of a particular thinker (i.e., Ignatieff) but as a feature of human rights discourse more generally.

> To the extent that human rights are understood as the ability to protect oneself against injustice and define one's own ends in life, this is a form of "empowerment" that fully equates empowerment with liberal individualism. . . . As human rights discourse draws a line between the space of the individual to choose how she or he wants to live and the space of politics, what Ignatieff calls "empowerment" is located in the former. In his framing, human rights discourse thus not only aspires to be beyond politics (notwithstanding his own insistence that it is a politics), but carries implicitly antipolitical aspirations for its subjects—that is, cast subjects as yearning to be free of politics and, indeed, of all collective determination of ends.[23]

The word *empowerment* works like a pun here. For Ignatieff, and for mainstream defenders of "human rights discourse" in general, it means what it does in the dictionary: human rights provide safeguards for people to take control of their lives and foster awareness of themselves as moral agents.[24] But for Brown the word takes on a different inflection, which could be hyphenated as "empowered": namely, as invested by power, as constituted within a field of power relations. On the surface, the sense of self produced by human rights is non- or extrapolitical. Agents are led to locate the meaningful part of themselves beyond politics and the collective determination of ends. But this has unmistakable political effects: it anchors a dispensation of economic and political power within the subjectivity and self-understanding of its members. People are "em-powered" as individuals on condition of being "em-powered" by a social, economic, and political order that thrives on their retreat from collective action.

Whether or not this is a fair reading of Ignatieff is beside the point.[25] What matters is that Brown articulates a widely resonant view in the critical literature. We see it in Susan Marks's complaint that human rights individualism erodes awareness of systemic and structural injustice.[26] It inspires Joseph Slaughter's claim that support for human rights by powerful political and economic stakeholders is driven by the desire to dampen enthusiasm for collective political undertakings.[27] And a related message appears in Stephen Hopgood's indictment of the human rights movement as nowadays little more than a free-floating individual lifestyle choice.[28]

This is the first overlap between critiques of care of the self and human rights that I wish to highlight. Both discourses stand accused of promoting retreat from democratic engagement. This brings me to the second overlap. Critics assume that, because care of the self and human rights promote political disengagement, human rights are either, in the softer version of the criticism, vulnerable to co-optation by globalization and neoliberalism, or in the harsher version, active and willing promoters of it.

The relation between human rights and neoliberalism is hotly debated in human rights scholarship. Striking correspondences certainly exist. Human rights and neoliberalism achieved popular and global support at roughly the same time, in the mid- to late 1970s. They prioritize the individual. And perhaps most significantly, they target the activist and interventionist state.[29] Critics build on these similarities to propose a correlation and claim that human rights are an ally (or really, a sidekick) of neoliberalism: institutionally by laying the ground for market and property rights, and ideologically by spreading an ethos of depoliticization.[30]

The first of these two correlations—that human rights promote market and property rights favorable to neoliberalism—is center stage in Brown's article. She zeroes in on the priority Ignatieff assigns to civil and political rights (over and above social and economic rights). The justification Ignatieff gives for this prioritization is that civil and political rights are a condition for social and economic security.[31] But Brown detects a sleight of hand. "What Ignatieff is rehearsing," she states, "is not an ontological account of what human beings need to enjoy life, but rather a political-economic account of what markets need to thrive."[32] Or, as she concludes slightly later on, "Through a tortured historiography and a terribly vulnerable set of ontological claims, Ignatieff argues for human rights as the essential precondition for a free-market order and for the market itself as the vehicle of individual social and economic security."[33] In brief, international human rights law and activism promote a class of rules necessary to the globalization of capitalist production and consumption.

This is an established line of criticism, and it reappears in scholarship that challenges mainstream accounts of human rights.[34] Still, this criticism does not cut to the heart of the matter. It remains confined to an institutional level: human rights spread a class of rules (i.e., individually held civil, political, and property rights) that facilitates the primary institution of neoliberalism (i.e., the market). But in Brown's later work, especially *Undoing the Demos* (2015), she does not treat neoliberalism primarily as a set of institutions. She views it as a "normative order of reason."[35] And it is here, on an ideological and ethical level, that human rights truly lend a helping hand.

What does it mean to call neoliberalism a normative order of reason? On Brown's account, neoliberalism stands for the economization of everything. It sets out to "transmogrify," to use her word, every human domain and endeavor according to a specific picture of the economic. "All conduct is economic conduct," she writes; "all spheres of existence are framed and measured by economic terms and metrics, even when those spheres are not directly monetized. In neoliberal reason and in domains governed by it, we are only and everywhere *homo oeconomicus*."[36] To be clear, this does not refer just to the transformation of institutions, as if only the state, or law, or university were affected. What is really being reworked are human beings themselves: "the soul" is remade.[37] Neoliberal subjects comport and understand themselves as if they were little firms or capitals, such that day-to-day life is spent in continual enhancement of one's own value through practices of entrepreneurialism, self-investment, and by attracting investors. Whether in education, employment, love, fitness, or recreation, neoliberals seek always to strengthen their portfolio—which is nothing more or less than their being. *Homo oeconomicus* takes over the figure of the human.

This is a provocative thesis to be sure. But what does it have to do with human rights? Just this: human rights and neoliberalism both drive out the best potential rival to *Homo oeconomicus*: *Homo politicus*. *Homo politicus* involves a very different normative order of reason, one which cannot be reduced to interest and individual advantage. "This subject," Brown writes of *Homo politicus*, "forms the substance and legitimacy of whatever democracy might mean beyond securing the individual provisioning of individual ends; this 'beyond' includes political equality and freedom, representation, popular sovereignty, and deliberation and judgment about the public good and the common."[38] What is thus tragic for Brown about the eclipse of *Homo politicus* in the late twentieth century, and the reason why it is "*the* most important casualty of the ascendance of neoliberal reason," is not merely that an alternative way of collective and personal life fades away, but that the main weapon against neoliberalism and its governing rationality is lost.[39]

In *Undoing the Demos*, Brown barely mentions human rights. Still, the critical dots are there to connect. In her earlier article, "The Most We Can Hope For . . . ," the demise of *Homo politicus* was already charted. Human rights discourse, you recall, was faulted for carrying "antipolitical aspirations for its subjects" and for casting them as "yearning to be free of politics."[40] Furthermore,

Brown linked the contemporary human rights movement to neoliberalism thanks to its promotion of a particular vision of rights. True, in that article she does not claim that the subject of human rights—*Homo juridicus*, if you like[41]—has become *Homo oeconomicus*. But it surely helps to pave the way. This is an irony to be sure. When triumphant, neoliberalism and *Homo oeconomicus* will not have much place or patience for the *Homo juridicus* of human rights. As she writes of neoliberalism, "no longer are citizens most importantly constituent elements of sovereignty, members of publics, *or even bearers of rights*. Rather, as human capital, they may contribute to or be a drag on economic growth; they may be invested in or divested from depending on their potential for GDP enhancement."[42] That said, *Homo oeconomicus*—being *Homo oeconomicus*, after all—is not above using *Homo juridicus* and human rights discourse in its broader campaign against *Homo politicus*. The *Homo juridicus* of human rights may not be a lapdog of *Homo oeconomicus*, but that does not make it any less of an ally in blotting out *Homo politicus*.

The supremacy of neoliberalism and *Homo oeconomicus* is a disaster, according to Brown. It is definitely so for liberal democracy. Her list of reasons is long and compelling. Neoliberalism intensifies and normalizes inequality. It eliminates the idea of a people. It withers radical collective imaginings. More generally, it causes citizenship to lose its political valence. "*Homo oeconomicus* approaches everything as a market and knows only market conduct," writes Brown. "It cannot think public purposes or common problems in a distinctly political way."[43] In a word, public-mindedness is undermined by neoliberalism's stealth revolution. If the big question in republican and classical liberal democratic theory is how to get citizens to carry out the common good, then neoliberalism deepens the problem. What is now at issue is the future of democracy if the capacity to so much as think the common good is neither valued nor preserved.

To add to this discussion, Brown identifies a final consequence of the ascendance of *Homo oeconomicus*. Of an ethical nature, it is of special interest for us. Her claim is that when neoliberalism carries the day, and when its form of value becomes total, everyday life is impoverished and constrained. Human potentiality is swallowed up by a limited, and frankly ignoble, set of desires and pursuits.

> As economic parameters become the only parameters for all conduct and concern, the limited form of human existence that Aristotle and later Hannah Arendt designated as "mere life" and that Marx called life "confined by necessity"—concern with survival and wealth acquisition—this limited form and imaginary becomes ubiquitous and total *across* classes.

Neoliberal rationality eliminates what these thinkers termed "the good life" (Aristotle) or "the true realm of freedom" (Marx), by which they did not mean luxury, leisure, or indulgence, but rather the cultivation and expression of distinctly human capacities for ethical and political freedom, creativity, unbounded reflection, or invention.[44]

Allow me to put this passage into perspective. In this chapter, I have tried to show how two streams of criticism mesh. Critiques of the care of the self and critiques of human rights do not consciously build off one another. Nevertheless, they meet on several levels. In the first half of the chapter, I described how Myers, together with other political theorists, faults an ethic of the care of the self as damaging to democracy. In the second half, I outlined a similar critique, only this time about human rights. Brown, and those inspired by her, charge a mainstream conception of human rights with producing subjects who are disinclined toward political engagement and hostile to collective action. Moreover, by linking this critique of human rights to her later writings on neoliberalism, it becomes possible to label human rights an accomplice to the evisceration of public-mindedness and the political valence of citizenship.

In the passage I just cited, however, Brown places us in new territory. At issue is not *political* criticism driven by a concern over the welfare of democracy. It is instead an attack on a way of life in and of itself. It is *ethical* criticism. Granted, Brown's target is the ethos of *Homo oeconomicus* (and not *Homo juridicus*). But we know how slippery the slope is. *Homo oeconomicus* and *Homo juridicus* work side by side to clear the landscape of *Homo politicus*, which is the central challenger to a transactional, portfolio-enhancing, and acquisitive way of life.

This kind of ethical indictment puts a finger on something prevalent in criticism of human rights today. If we move beyond Brown's text, it is evident that much contemporary criticism of human rights activism—academic and journalistic—is driven by ethical indictment. Think, for example, of the oft-recurring lament that people (young people, in particular) engaging with human rights issues today are mostly interested in presenting themselves (and more snarkily, their social media profile) in an altruistic, justice-minded light.[45] More to the point, consider the recently coined words to damn this kind of posturing: "slacktivism" and "clicktivism." On Wikipedia, slacktivism is defined as "a pejorative term that describes 'feel-good' measures, in support of an issue or social cause, that have little physical or practical effect other than to make the person doing it feel satisfied that they have contributed."[46] True, a share of the contempt packed into this word stems from political grievance: support of this kind is superficial and ineffective. Yet an equal measure surely has its roots in ethical criticism: that support of this kind only fans the superficiality and ineffectiveness of the supporters themselves. As *Urban Dictionary* tells us, slacktivism "is fun, easy, and builds self esteem in a cheap way."[47]

Whatever we might think of such criticisms, two points should be noted. First, there is a connection proposed between human rights activism and the promotional, neoliberal self. From this perspective, commitment to human rights is as often as not driven by a desire to boost one's own portfolio value and moral capital. Second, this attitude is reproached as a poor way to live and be: it makes for a cheap, shrill, and sanctimonious self. Put differently, in our day and age, the human rights movement is indicted for spawning a veritable devolution of the self, a kind of anti-care of the self.

There is no corresponding criticism in my earlier discussion of care of the self. Myers, for example, does not claim that the discourse of the care of the self is, well, a bad way to care for oneself. Few political theorists do; their concern is with whether or not care of the self is conducive to a flourishing democratic politics.[48] But ethical criticism of the care of the self is made from other quarters. None is more surprising than that of Foucault's mentor for his later work, Pierre Hadot. This is where the next chapter begins. With it I will round out the dual criticism of care of the self and human rights: as bad for the self, and as bad for the social and political world, for exactly the same reasons.

[4]

HUMAN RIGHTS AS SPIRITUAL EXERCISES:
TOCQUEVILLE IN AMERICA

In the previous chapter I outlined dovetailing criticisms made by contemporary critics of human rights and care of the self. One area of overlap had to do with democracy, and specifically with the suspicion that care of the self and human rights are depoliticizing discourses that undermine democratic engagement. As a shorthand, I spoke of this in terms of human rights and care of the self being bad for the world. I also introduced a second criticism, which is, in keeping with my shorthand, that human rights and care of the self are also bad for the self: they lead to an impoverished way of life. The nub of this shortcoming was, ironically, that human rights and care of the self are too centered on the self: they tend to produce self-regarding, self-obsessive, self-indulgent, and self-important people.

Foucault did not view care of the self in this harsh light. He created this concept not only to describe how ancient philosophers understood and practiced morality, but also to offer a model of living for our own times. Yet one of his contemporaries did criticize it this way: Pierre Hadot. What gives this criticism a special sting is that Foucault credits Hadot's work as a guiding light for his own later thought on the care of the self.

Hadot was a colleague of Foucault's at the Collège de France and a specialist of ancient history and philosophy. More than anyone, he tried to define what makes ancient philosophy distinctive in comparison to modern philosophy. In a nutshell, ancient philosophy is a way of life (*une manière de vivre*). It is not primarily a theoretical discourse, which we moderns all too quickly assume philosophy to have always been, but is instead a certain way of living and seeing the world (which theoretical discourse helps in part to bring about).

Hadot laid out this interpretation of ancient philosophy in several places.[1] One essay of his especially marked Foucault: "Spiritual Exercises," published in 1977. Foucault cites it as an inspiration for his books on ancient sexual practices.[2] More generally, it informs Foucault's understanding of ancient morality as comprised of "techniques of the self" designed to modify the relation we have to ourselves.[3]

Hadot never commented on Foucault's work during his lifetime. But at a conference on Foucault in 1988, he delivered "Reflections on the Idea of the 'Cultivation of the Self.'" The tone of the essay is respectful, and Hadot warmly points to areas of agreement between himself and Foucault. But make no mistake, it is a thoroughgoing critique. Most of it is devoted to differences in interpretation of classical texts: it centers on Foucault's too strong emphasis on the "self" in Stoicism and Epicureanism, and exposes his neglect of efforts made by these philosophical schools to transcend the self. This is not the occasion to elaborate on this facet of Hadot's essay.[4] But a second criticism that Hadot makes is significant for us. It is that, apart from any particular interpretation of the ancients, Hadot is wary of Foucault's "philosophical choice" to propose a morality based on care of the self. His reason? It has the potential to be a narrow, insufficient, and perhaps even frivolous way of life.

> [My] preceding remarks are not intended to be relevant only to an historical analysis of ancient philosophy. They are also an attempt at defining an ethical model which modern man can discover in antiquity. What I am slightly afraid of is that, by focusing his interpretation too exclusively on the culture of the self, the care of the self, and conversion toward the self—more generally, by defining his ethical model as an aesthetics of existence—M. Foucault is propounding a culture of the self which is *too* aesthetic. In other words, this may be a new form of Dandyism, late twentieth-century style.[5]

We can now close the loop from the previous chapter. There I established a parallel criticism of human rights and the care of the self from the perspective of democracy and political (dis)engagement. With Hadot's reproach of "dandyism," we have a second parallel criticism—this time one that tackles the care of the self from the perspective of subjectivity and spiritual well-being. Foucault may have discussed the figure of the dandy in an important late essay, but that is not what Hadot has in mind here.[6] "Dandyism," in English as in French, designates personal fastidiousness coupled with affectation. It is exactly the kind of spiritual life that results from an attitude of care for self that lacks any corresponding return outward. For Hadot, such an approach to morality is missing the two most promising lessons we can learn from ancient philosophers on how to lead a better, wiser life: first, to make an effort to live in the service of the human community, and second, to make an effort to become aware of our place in the wider whole of the cosmos.[7]

As I will make clear, this is not a fair criticism: not of Foucault's conception of the care of the self, and certainly not of its potential beyond Foucault's own work on it. In this chapter, however, I nevertheless focus on Hadot. His conception of spiritual exercises informs my interpretation of Alexis de Tocqueville. My thesis is that Tocqueville views universal rights along the lines of a spiritual exercise: it is through the practice of political rights that citizens *in* democracy will be able to counteract the spiritual afflictions *of* democracy. My goal in thus pairing Hadot and Tocqueville is twofold. First, I want to use Hadot's own concept of a spiritual exercise to show how care of the self is not fated to merit the criticism he levels at it. Care of self is not intrinsically self-regarding, and there is no inconsistency in its leading past the self, for the sake of the self. Second, I want to challenge the view introduced in the previous chapter that care of the self is inherently undemocratic and depoliticizing. Tocqueville is a powerful counter-example. He argues that care of the self in democracy must take the form of plunging more fully into democratic engagement. This chapter, then, is a first step in defending care of the self against its ethical and political critics.

The Happy American

To introduce Tocqueville to readers who might be unfamiliar with him, I begin with two vignettes. Tocqueville was born into a very old aristocratic family in Normandy. He studied law in Paris and in 1831, just twenty-six years old, he set sail for America with his friend Gustave de Beaumont. They stayed nearly a year, and the official purpose of their trip was to carry out a study of the American penal system on behalf of the French government (which in fact they did, publishing a report in 1833). But, more generally, they toured the country to observe its culture, politics, and law, with extended stays in New York, Boston and Massachusetts, and visits to the frontier West and to the South.[8]

Of the many things that struck Tocqueville, one he keeps coming back to in his travel journal, as well as in his magnum opus *Democracy in America* (1835/1840), is how *political* Americans are. I do not refer only to high levels of civic engagement (though this too was notable for Tocqueville). I also mean the degree to which Americans *are* political animals, down to their bones, and in the way they carry themselves in day-to-day life. Politics is an ethos over there, and that is what astonishes him. Consider two lighthearted vignettes:

> It is difficult to say what place the cares of politics occupy in the life of a man in the United States. To meddle in the government of society and to speak about it is the greatest business and, so to speak, the only pleasure that an American knows. . . . An American does not know how to converse, but he discusses; he does not discourse, but he holds forth. He always speaks to you as to an assembly; and if he happens by chance to become heated, he will say "Sirs" in addressing his interlocutor.[9]

And,

> The first time I heard it said in the United States that a hundred thousand men publicly engaged not to make use of strong liquors, the thing appeared to me more amusing than serious, and at first I did not see well why such temperate citizens were not content to drink water within their families. In the end I understood that those hundred thousand Americans, frightened by the progress that drunkenness was making around them, wanted to provide their patronage to sobriety. They had acted precisely like a great lord who would dress himself very plainly in order to inspire the scorn of luxury in simple citizens. It is to be believed that if those hundred thousand men had lived in France, each of them would have addressed himself individually to the government, begging it to oversee the cabarets all over the realm. (*DA* 492)

It would be a mistake to think that Tocqueville mocks Americans. He gently and joyfully teases them. Yes, there is an element of the ridiculous in these scenes. But there is also something admirable. Americans may get carried away, and they may bring a political temper to places where it does not quite belong, but that is only because they have accomplished something special and important: to have remained committed citizens at a time when retreat into private life is the easiest and most natural thing to do. Tocqueville looks admiringly on ordinary Americans for having cultivated a "public" or "political" sense of themselves, one able to resist the rampant privatization and individualism of the modern world.

We can say more than this. The citizen who "holds forth" is not just endearing or cute. He is "happy"—"great" even—in the sense that the final paragraphs of *Democracy in America* reclaim those terms: "One must take care in judging the societies being born by ideas one has drawn from those that are no longer. That would be unjust for these societies, differing enormously between themselves, are not comparable. . . . We ought not to strain to make ourselves like our fathers, but strive to attain the kind of greatness and happiness [*l'espèce de grandeur et de bonheur*] that is proper to us" (DA 675). In poking fun at democrats, it may seem as though Tocqueville ignores the advice he gives himself. He says that we should refrain from judging a society or its members by standards that do not belong to it. Yet can't we just picture the young aristocrat smiling at his American host? But that misses the spirit of the earlier vignettes. For if Tocqueville was amused by his encounters with Americans, the whole purpose of *Democracy in America* is to report back to France how felicity can be achieved in democracy. He wants to tell his native country how "*bonheur*"—a more expansive word than "happiness," signifying great satisfaction, plenitude, and well-being—can be realized in democracy at the social and political level and, just as importantly, on a personal and spiritual plane.

This is no small task. As we will see, Tocqueville believes that democracy introduces or amplifies several emotions that afflict individuals. Envy, restlessness, chronic discontent, and loneliness are intrinsic to democracy. So too are mediocrity and conformity. These affects and traits damage people to their core—"degrade their souls," Tocqueville would say (DA 8, 662)[10]—and democrats must strive to minimize their presence in their lives for their own sake. How to do so is the topic of this chapter.

The American Revolution

Tocqueville is my second case study in this book. He stands apart from my other authors in two respects. First, he works at a different scale. Those figures address a more or less punctual moment in history. For Wollstonecraft, it is the Declaration of the Rights of Man and Citizen. Bergson discusses the founding of the League of Nations and the impending crisis of the Second World War. Roosevelt and Malik reflect on the Universal Declaration of Human Rights, which they themselves helped draft. And most recently, human rights educators contribute to a movement only twenty years in the making. Tocqueville, by contrast, works in the *longue durée*. He opens *Democracy in America* with a grand sweep that takes in the history of equality from the Middle Ages to the present. The "great democratic revolution" he writes about is not a revolution that has been centuries in preparation; it is a revolution that has been ongoing for hundreds of years (DA 3, 6, 7, 12). So too with the "American Revolution." For Tocqueville, it refers less to a specific event (say, the War of Independence) than to the stamp that America (colonial and postcolonial) has put on the on-going democratic revolution in Western civilization.[11]

The second difference is significant for us. Today we no longer call the kind of rights that Tocqueville discusses in *Democracy in America* "human rights." We call them "civil" or "political" rights: rights that we have and exercise as citizens of a nation-state. As I argue later, the other authors I discuss do not feel dated in this way. They treat features of human rights in their day that remain recogniz-able features of human rights in our day. Wollstonecraft, for example, contends that individuals must learn to view themselves in light of the universal subject of human rights. This, we will see, remains a core part of contemporary human rights pedagogy. But Tocqueville's account of rights is not like that. The issue is not that the kind of rights he discusses cannot nowadays serve to care for the self. They can; in fact, for the same prescient reasons he gives. The issue is that we no longer classify those kinds of rights as human rights.

Why include Tocqueville then? Here we touch on a paradigm shift that political theorists (such as Hannah Arendt) and historians (such as Richard Tuck and Samuel Moyn) have observed in the 250-year history of human rights. Roughly speaking, it is the following: from the late eighteenth century until the Second World War, human rights were inseparable from the nation-state and were conceived in terms of state-building. As Moyn puts it, at this time "it was universally agreed that those [human or natural] rights were to be achieved through the construction of spaces of citizenship in which rights were ac-corded and protected."[12] But following the Universal Declaration of Human Rights in 1948, and picking up steam in the 1970s, the notion of human rights shifted. Human rights were now cast as an institution and movement designed to check, monitor, and limit the power of the state, particularly with respect to its own citizens. This is a fundamental change. To continue with Moyn, "the central event in human rights history is the recasting of rights as entitlements that might contradict the sovereign nation-state from above and outside rather than serve as its foundation."[13]

Tocqueville belongs to the older tradition that sees universal rights in terms of the construction of spaces of national citizenship and political participation. Nowhere in *Democracy in America* does he use the term *human rights*, and he makes just one passing historical reference to *"les droits de l'homme"* (DA 704). That said, he is intensely relevant for my study on human rights and the care of the self. Why? Because he addresses *the* defining American contribution to the natural or human rights tradition: to have disseminated the idea and practice of civil and political rights down "to the least of its citizens" (DA 228).[14] The United States exemplifies the first great paradigm of human rights, in which natural rights are institutionalized and disseminated in the form of universal civil and political rights. It may not be what we call human rights today, but this paradigm exemplifies how human rights were conceived for the greater part of their history.[15]

This universalization of rights is, for Tocqueville, the hallmark of the American Revolution. And its consequences are illimitable. It determines the entire complexion of the government and administration of the United States. Perhaps more importantly, the exercise of political rights in daily life by ordinary citizens alters their sentiments, desires, and self-perception—so much so, as we will see, that Tocqueville speaks in terms of spiritual change, even of salvation and conversion, to describe the transformative potential of political rights in democracy. As he puts it, "I do not say that it is an easy thing to teach all men to make use of political rights; I say only that when that can be done, the resulting effects are great" (DA 228).

Spiritual Exercises

To bring this transformative dimension of rights to the fore, and to show why Tocqueville thinks personal felicity in democracy hinges on it, I need to reintroduce Hadot at this point. His notion of "spiritual exercises" is key to my interpretation.

As I said earlier, Hadot conceives of ancient philosophy in terms of a "way of life." What philosophy requires for the ancients is a commitment to a mode of being guided by wisdom—a love of wisdom, philo-sophia—that is radically different from "non-philosophers," that is to say, from most everybody else. Thus, while Hadot acknowledges great variation between the major schools of ancient philosophy—Platonic, Cynic, Aristotelian, Stoic, and Epicurean—as to what exactly constitutes a philosophical life, he believes they all concur on the fundamental point of departure: philosophy is a comprehensive way of living, or what Hadot calls "an existential option."[16]

"Spiritual exercises" are techniques and practices by which an individual becomes a philosopher and brings about a comprehensive change in his or her way of living. "I would define spiritual exercises," Hadot says, "as voluntary, personal practices intended to cause a transformation of the self."[17] These can be physical (such as dietary regimes), discursive (such as dialogue and meditation), or intuitive (such as contemplation). For example, a preferred Stoic exercise is the premeditation of evils, which involves daily reflection on the worst possible loss you might suffer, in order to appreciate what you have and to be able to bear what is expected. As Hadot puts it, "these exercises correspond, in fact, to a transformation of our vision of the world and to a metamorphosis of our personality. The word 'spiritual' is quite apt to make us understand that these exercises are the work, not merely of thought, but of the individual's entire psychism."[18] The crux of Hadot's interpretation of ancient philosophy is that philosophical discourse is itself a spiritual exercise—one conducted in dialogue and instruction, as well as through solitary meditation—to reorient one's way of life and become a living, breathing philosopher.[19]

In this chapter I draw two parallels between Hadot and Tocqueville. First, I claim that the concept of "citizen" for Tocqueville operates very much like the term *philosopher* does for Hadot and for the ancients. Tocqueville characteristically uses this term to mark the commitment to a way of life that is significantly different—and according to him, significantly happier and worthier of happiness—from that of a person who does not cultivate a public or a political self. Tocqueville, in other words, uses the concept *citizen* in two interrelated (though not always coextensive) senses: political and legal on the one hand, spiritual and existential on the other. Second, I argue that universal civil and political rights in democracy operate as spiritual exercises for Tocqueville. That is to say, he conceives of the exercise of such rights (in part) as a voluntary personal practice intended to bring about a transformation of the self. Democrats become citizens (in the existential sense) by practicing political rights as spiritual exercises.[20]

Diagnosis of Democracy

Stated in the abstract, these connections between Hadot and Tocqueville may seem forced. For this reason, I proceed directly to the problems, and in particular, to the spiritual problems that Tocqueville diagnoses in democracy. This will give us a clear picture of why he believes it is vital for individuals to cultivate a public self and practice rights as a spiritual exercise.

To list the "problems" Tocqueville identifies in democracy is too immense a task to undertake here. This topic takes up most of *Democracy in America*, and commentators who try to follow all its twists and turns produce books just as large! One reason for its omnipresence is that Tocqueville conceives of himself as a diagnostician of democracy—a kindly one, to be sure—tasked with uncovering its sicknesses and potential cures. "I often say harsh things to the new American and French society but I say them as a friend," he writes in a letter to John Stuart Mill. "It is because I am a friend that I dare to say them and want to say them. Among us, equality has its flatterers of all kinds but hardly any staunch and honest counsellors."[21]

To get a grip on the issue, we could say that Tocqueville diagnoses two scales of problems that plague democracy. Some are macro and threaten the welfare of the social and political order. Others are micro and endanger the personal and psychical wellness of individuals. To be clear, this macro/micro distinction is only heuristic. Tocqueville, as Sheldon Wolin states, "is the first to theorize democracy as the dominant cultural force," affecting (and also imbricating) the most structural and formal features of social and political life together with the most personal and intimate.[22] Still, Tocqueville hints at this kind of distinction in another letter, this time to his friend Louis de Kergolay: "To point out if possible to men what to do to escape tyranny and debasement in becoming democratic [*échapper à la tyrannie et à l'abâtardissement en devenant démocratiques*]. Such is, I think, the general idea by which my book can be summarized and which will appear on every page I am writing at this moment. To work in this direction is, in my eyes, a holy occupation and one for which neither money, nor time, nor life must be spared."[23]

In this letter, Tocqueville names two kinds of misfortunes internal to democracy: tyranny and debasement. Tyranny corresponds to the social and political dangers that lurk in democracy and the new forms of authority and despotism it engenders. This topic receives pride of place in *Democracy in America*. Each of its two volumes concludes with a sketch of a new kind of tyranny made possible by democracy: "Caesarism" at the end of volume 1, and "democratic despotism" at the end of volume 2.

Debasement marks out another kind of danger. *Abâtardissement* (literally, bastardization) means degradation, and specifically diminishment: being sapped of power, originality, or quality. This, we will see, is the line of criticism Tocqueville reserves for the pernicious *spiritual* effects of democracy. This diagnosis of debasement is important as it operates at the scale we are concerned with: the individual, his or her powers, and the potential for happiness and well-being.

At the most general level, Tocqueville's ambition in *Democracy in America* is to understand what kind of subject democracy produces. He wants to observe the "revolution in cognition and sensibility" (as Wolin puts it), the "transformation of man by democracy" (as Pierre Manent puts it), and the production of "certain characteristics in its citizens" (as Leo Damrosch puts it).[24] Some of these transformations can be good and salutary. Broadened sympathy and sociability, personal responsibility, and individual initiative and enterprise have the potential to flourish in democracy. But so do a host of debilitating emotions and traits. Here, from Tocqueville's darkest hour in volume 2, is the worst-case scenario:

I see an innumerable crowd of like and equal men who revolve on themselves without repose, procuring the small and vulgar pleasures with which they fill their souls. Each of them, withdrawn and apart, is like a stranger to the destiny of all the others: his children and his particular friends form the whole species for him; as for dwelling with his fellow citizens, he is beside them, but he does not see them; he touches them and does not feel them; he exists only in himself and for himself alone, and if a family still remains for him, one can at least say that he no longer has a native country. (*DA* 663)

This list of personal failings and sorrows is depressingly long: uniformity, mediocrity, restiveness, isolation, lonesomeness, coldness, and indifference. But what Tocqueville makes clear is that these are not accidental or isolated traits and emotions in democracy. Left to its devices, these are the kinds of subjects that democracy will produce. "That such penchants are not invincible I shall not deny," he admits. "I only maintain that in our day a secret force constantly develops them in the human heart, and that not to stop them is enough for them to fill it up" (*DA* 643).

Why such pessimism? Lucien Jaume provides a helpful perspective. In *Tocqueville: The Aristocratic Sources of Liberty* he devotes two fascinating chapters to "Tocqueville as Moralist" and examines the debt to Jansenism and the theoreticians of self-love. He argues that Tocqueville attributes to *democratic* man in particular the very traits that Pascal applied to human beings in general.

Tocqueville retained the general spirit of [Pascal's *Pensées*]: democratic society is in permanent agitation, uncertain of its bearings and vexed by anxiety. But what Pascal described as characteristic of the human condition in general, Tocqueville transposed to the democratic situation, and this is why he cannot follow Pascal when the author of the *Pensées* [claims], "This being the case, I believe that each man should remain at rest, in the estate in which nature placed him." In democracy, fewer and fewer people would remain at rest ("in a room," as Pascal said), and a man's "social condition" was no longer an "*état*" given, as Pascal believed, by nature: *competition had begun.*[25]

Translated into Foucault's idiom, Jaume describes the attitude of a diagnostician. Tocqueville is not asking, as compared with Pascal, "What, in general, is wrong with human beings?" He is asking something much more specific: "What is wrong with us today?" Or, to persist with Foucault's language, he poses the hallmark question of the diagnostician: "Who are we today? Who are we in our actuality?"[26]

The issue is urgent because at the heart of Tocqueville's analysis of democracy is the observation that it gives rise to spiritual afflictions specific to it. Some are associated with insatiable materialism: with equality of opportunity the pursuit of pleasure, comfort, and consumption becomes a dominant passion. This is the line of argument that Jaume develops: Tocqueville singles out psychological states that Pascal assumed were universal and timeless—disquiet and distraction (*inquiétude* and *divertissement*)—and shows how democracy inflames and intensifies them. Another set of afflictions can be found in the passage I cited earlier from *Democracy in America*: isolation, indifference, coldness, and the like. These states are tied to the tendency in democracy to foster individualism and retreat from collective life. In short, clustered around two of the dominant tendencies in democracy—materialism and individualism—are a series of passions and desires that diminish (*abâtardit*, to use Tocqueville's term) individuals in democracy.

What is the solution? The practice of civil and political rights. To introduce this idea, and how it works for Tocqueville, a contrast with Wollstonecraft is helpful. Earlier on, we saw how Wollstonecraft's great ambition is to close out a social, political, and psychological regime. She pins her hopes on human rights to help individuals surmount any attachment they might have to chivalry. Tocqueville proceeds differently in two respects. First, chivalry and feudalism are for him well and truly over. While he may mourn select aspects of its passing—this is, as Wolin calls it, his streak of "*ancienneté*"[27]—the dangers attached to feudalism are no longer pressing for Tocqueville. It is democracy he is worried about, and he calls on universal rights to address an altogether different set of problems.

The second difference from Wollstonecraft relates to argumentative approach. Wollstonecraft, we might say, frontally opposes an epoch, and she deploys human rights to overturn it both political and psychically. Human rights are not a feature of the private and public world of chivalry, and they pose a head-on challenge to it. Tocqueville proceeds differently. He does not oppose or argue against democracy, in the sense of trying to block or overcome it. That would be fruitless and undesirable. Neither does he counsel individuals to try to escape or take shelter from it. That would be self-defeating, given that private retreat is a signature of democracy. What he advises, instead, is the use of resources internal to democracy to better and more happily inhabit it. He urges individuals to become democratic in the right way.

The letter I cited to Kergolay is revealing. Tocqueville speaks of his ambition "to point out if possible to men what to do to escape tyranny and debasement in becoming democratic [*en devenant démocratiques*]." These words are tellingly ambiguous (and also tellingly ambivalent). On the one hand, he seems to say that tyranny and debasement are part and parcel of becoming democratic. But, on the other hand, the clause "*en devenant démocratiques*" works the other way around as well: that in becoming democratic—that is, in becoming *properly* democratic, democratic *in the right way*—we can hope to escape the new kinds of tyranny and debasement that democracy brings about. In the next two sections I argue that political rights in democracy are precisely this kind of internal or immanent solution: they are a democratic means for democrats to overcome the perils of democracy. For, as Tocqueville exhorts himself in an unpublished note, we must "use Democracy to moderate Democracy. It is the only path open to salvation to us."[28]

The Citizen as Public Self

In his Preface to Hadot's interviews, Arnold Davidson reports, "We had innumerable discussions about, and Hadot was passionately interested in, the ways in which the notions of spiritual exercises and philosophy as a way of life could be applied and extended to unexpected domains."[29] It is in keeping with this spirit that I proposed to borrow two of his ideas. First, I drew an analogy between what it means to be an ancient philosopher according to Hadot and what it means to be a citizen in a democracy according to Tocqueville. Second, I suggested that Tocqueville conceives of rights along the lines of a spiritual exercise.

Let's begin with the comparison between citizen and philosopher, on the grounds that each is what Hadot would call an "existential option" or "comprehensive way of life."[30] What does Tocqueville mean by citizenship and the political rights of the citizen in the United States? In part, voting, of course. American citizens have the right to elect local, state, and federal officials. But it is more than that. When Tocqueville reports on the United States, and especially on the townships of New England, he extols the use that citizens make of their right to self-government at the local level.[31] In the townships, which operate almost as if mini-republics, political participation denotes much more than voting. It involves a web of rights and duties in which citizens deliberate and act together on matters of public concern. In New England, in other words, Tocqueville observes an intensely political mode of existence on the part of ordinary citizens. As Wolin summarizes it, "By inverting what had become the modern priorities of private over public, the Americans had developed a politics that was not restricted to a narrow, bounded domain, but was a way of life."[32] Here is the impressive result:

> Life in the township makes itself felt in a way at each instant. It manifests itself each day by the accomplishment of a duty or by the exercise of a right. . . .
> The inhabitant of New England is *attached* to his township because it is strong and independent; he is *interested* in it because he cooperates in directing it; he *loves* it because he has nothing to complain of in his lot; he places his ambition and his future in it; he *mingles* in each of the incidents of township life: in this restricted sphere that is within his reach he tries to govern society; he habituates himself to the forms without which freedom proceeds only through revolution, permeates himself with their spirit, gets a taste for order, understands the harmony of powers, and finally assembles clear and practical ideas on the nature of his duties as well as the extent of his rights. (*DA* 64–65, emphasis added)

In *Democracy in America* Tocqueville wants to show how the right to popular sovereignty can exist in the routines of everyday life. In part, he hopes to convince skeptics back home in France that popular sovereignty need not lead to revolution and disorder. Hence, in the second part of the passage, the motivation behind Tocqueville's fulsome praise of the temperance and moderation that self-government instils in its citizens.

But Tocqueville has another goal as well. It comes across clearly in the first half of the passage. He wants to show how a public and engaged self—a citizenly life, as it were—fosters personal felicity. Indeed, he chooses his words with great care. In becoming "attached" to and "interested" in the township he or she "mingles in," the citizen counteracts the isolation and egoism of individualism. And in "loving" the township, and by being satisfied with his or her "lot," the citizen calms the restlessness and anxiety of materialism. Point for point, Tocqueville proposes that a political or public self—what he calls a "citizen" in the full sense of the word—cultivates a way of life that checks the main pressures in democracy that threaten psychical wellness. Or, to rephrase the point using the concluding words from *Democracy in America*, becoming a citizen is the best chance in democracy, both politically and personally, to "attain the kind of greatness and happiness that is proper to us" (*DA* 675).

Is this the philosopher in Hadot's sense of the term? It is a comprehensive way of life. And spiritual exercises are integral to it. Yet doubts could be raised on one point. For Hadot, the ancient philosopher is a person out of step—deliberately, some might say willfully, so—with his or her own milieu. He or she chooses to "tear away from the everyday," and for every Crito or Glaucon there exist a thousand ordinary Athenians.[33] The American case is different. The New England township, to take Tocqueville's privileged example, is populated by citizens. In that context, a public or political way of life is more majority opinion (*doxa*) than contrarian choice. This much is true, and we will revisit the objection in the next section. Yet it is important to recognize the scale Tocqueville works on. He does not claim that *individual* American citizens are special or unique within their own context. He says, instead, that America *as a whole* is exceptional because it widely produces individuals who are, in democratic times, almost as rare as philosophers were in the ancient world: citizens.

Only America establishes the institutions, practices, and political culture needed to produce citizens in democracy. Tocqueville's word for it is *liberté*. A passage from his late great work, *The Ancien Régime and the French Revolution*, gives a vivid sense of just how exceptional America is, compared to France and the Old World.

> Only freedom [*liberté*] can effectively combat the faults [*vices*] natural to [democratic societies] and keep them from sliding down a slippery path. Only freedom can rescue citizens from the isolation in which the very independence of their condition puts them in. Only freedom can compel them to come together, to warm one another and reunite each day through mutual exchange and persuasion and joint action in practical affairs. Only freedom can uproot the worship of money and the petty vexations of their private business, enabling them to sense the constant presence of the nation above and alongside them. Only freedom can substitute higher, more powerful passions for the love of material comforts and supply ambition with greater ends than the acquisition of wealth. Only freedom, finally, can create the light by which it is possible to see and judge the vices and virtues of humankind.[34]

Tocqueville's critique of democratic life is just as thoroughgoing as anything we can find in ancient philosophy of the false one. This "democrat" is an absolute wreck of a person: isolated from his or her fellows, cold and indifferent toward them, obsessed by desire for money, frustrated as a consequence of it, and worst of all, unable to tell the bad from the good in either human affairs or their own life. In both *Democracy in America* and *Ancien Régime* Tocqueville has a name for this kind of individual: he or she is a "subject" (worse, an "administered being") and not a citizen.[35]

Here the analogy with Hadot and the philosopher is compelling. In the ancient world, a person might be able to recite every doctrine under the sun, yet if he does not conduct himself in accordance with one of them he is a sophist and not a philosopher.[36] The same holds, *mutatis mutandis*, of Tocqueville and the citizen. In the modern democratic world, Tocqueville says, someone might be granted the full spectrum of civil and political rights; yet if he does not occupy himself with public affairs he is a subject and not a citizen. This point is crucial: in democracy it is possible for the two senses of the term *citizen* to become uncoupled. An individual may be a citizen on paper and endowed with rights, and yet he or she may freely choose to forgo a public self. Worse, this scenario is altogether likely. On Tocqueville's analysis, the tragedy of democracy is that it stokes a desire for withdrawal from public into private life, which thus leads people to disdain their best chance for political and personal felicity: a citizenly way of life.

There is no denying Tocqueville idealizes the New England township. His notion of citizenship as an ethos, moreover, is so exigent that it is unlikely to have been realized even there.[37] Yet the ancients too had an unattainable model: the sage. The sage, Hadot tells us, is the figure whom the philosopher "strives to imitate, by means of an ever-renewed effort, practiced at each instant."[38] The sage was a kind of philosophical hero and imparted not so much a doctrine or intellectual system as a style of life. Tocqueville's figure of the citizen is similarly didactic. It too is uncommon and precious, especially given how democracy tends to produce administered beings (or, more critically, tends to produce beings who want to be administered). It too offers up a lifestyle that highlights the felicities—and by contrast, the miseries—intrinsic to democracy. And it too comes equipped with spiritual exercises to ameliorate those miseries.

Human Rights as Spiritual Exercise

We have just seen why, for Tocqueville, democrats should try to lead a citizenly life: their spiritual wellness depends on it. The question is how to do it. This is where rights come in. In this section, I argue that Tocqueville presents political rights in democracy as a spiritual exercise for subjects to make themselves into citizens. Hadot, recall, defines spiritual exercises as "voluntary, personal practices intended to cause a transformation of the self."[39] This compressed definition has three components, each of which is present in Tocqueville's account of rights: "voluntary," "personal," and "intended to cause a transformation of the self." Taking each in turn, we will see how he conceives of political rights in democracy in terms of personal transformation and care for the self.

Start with the notion of spiritual exercises as "voluntary." On first impression, this seems remote from the reality of rights. Spiritual exercises, such as the premeditation of evils, are voluntarily practiced. No law or authority compels it. Indeed, the voluntary nature of such techniques is one of the three main criteria Foucault establishes for care of the self (see chapter 1). Rights, on the other hand, are quite different: they are prescriptions designed to remove certain actions or behaviors from the realm of individual preference or whim. Tocqueville agrees, of course. But what is at issue for him is not whether specific obligations are binding—they are—but whether individuals in democracy will choose to commit themselves to public or political obligations in the first place. We know Tocqueville's answer: they almost certainly will not. Democracy fosters individualism and withdrawal of time, interest, and energy from public affairs. So much so, in fact, that individual democrats need to be reminded of the simple truth that they exist in society, something they seem to grasp only notionally. That reminder, Tocqueville says, is furnished by the exercise of political rights:

> The free institutions that the inhabitants of the United States possess and the political rights of which they make so much use recall to each citizen constantly and in a thousand ways that he lives in society. At every moment they bring his mind [*son esprit*] back toward the idea that the duty as well as the interest of men is to render themselves useful to those like them; and as he does not see any particular reason to hate them, since he is never either their slave or their master, his heart readily leans to the side of benevolence. One is occupied with the general interest at first by necessity and then by choice; what was calculation becomes instinct; and by dint of working for the good of one's fellow citizen, one finally picks up the habit and taste of serving them. (*DA* 488)

In these lines Tocqueville recreates Pascal's famous idea and spiritual exercise: we do not pray to God because we believe in Him; we believe in Him because we pray to God. "Follow the way by which [the faithful] began," Pascal advises. "They acted as if they believed, took holy water, had masses said, etc. This will make you believe naturally and mechanically."[40] Tocqueville's argument is the same: individuals in democracy are not inclined to public participation; but if they try it, if they agree ever so reluctantly to join in, they will find themselves drawn away "from the midst of their individual interests" and "from the sight of themselves" (*DA* 486). By exercising their political rights democrats are reminded that they live among others, and they may gradually come to absorb and enjoy that truth.[41]

Tocqueville, we could say, presents a catch-22 situation. Democrats are, to their political and spiritual detriment, averse to exercising their political rights in daily life. Yet it is precisely by exercising their political rights that they might find they enjoy doing so and, ultimately, enhance their own well-being. The problem, then, is how to get started, that is, how to convince citizens to cultivate a public self for their own sake. We will address this momentarily. For now, this much should be clear: political rights are "voluntary" in democracy because, far from there being an obligation to practice them, citizens can set them aside in favor of other pursuits. By practicing political rights, a citizen may acquire the taste for it. Still, he or she must take the plunge in the first place. And that takes effort and commitment.

But why make the effort? Why swim against the current of democracy? This brings us to the second criterion of a spiritual exercise: it is a "personal" practice. As with the term *voluntary*, this word also seems like a misnomer in discussing rights. Rights are by definition relational and intersubjective.[42] It rubs against the very grammar of rights to describe them as a personal or an individual practice. Yet that is what Tocqueville sets out to do. Consider his remarks on how best to instill respect for rights in an age when religion can no longer guarantee it:

> Do you not see that religions are weakening and that the divine notion of rights is disappearing? Do you not find that mores are being altered, and that with them the moral notion of rights is being effaced?
>
> Do you not perceive on all sides beliefs that give way to reasoning, and sentiments that give way to calculations? If in the midst of that universal disturbance you do not come to bind the idea of rights to the personal interest that offers itself as the only immobile point in the human heart, what will then remain to you to govern the world, except fear? (*DA* 228)

Tocqueville is explicit that rights in democracy must be grounded in "personal interest." It is difficult to read these lines without hearing Marx's critique of the rights of man as "bourgeois" and "egocentric." Didn't Marx—along with nearly two hundred years of critique inspired by him—say the same thing but in a very different tone? "The so-called rights of man," he thunders, "are nothing but the rights of the member of civil society, i.e., egoistic man, man separated from other men and the community."[43] Do Tocqueville's apology for rights grounded in self-interest and Marx's criticism of rights as bolstering egoism and self-interest amount to the same thing?

It is best to speak plainly. Tocqueville does indeed believe that in democracy self-interest becomes the driver of most things. Disinterested patriotism and civic virtue, altruism and purely other-minded morality, if these were ever realities, are found only in a vanishing past. "The century of blind devotions and instinctive virtues is already fleeing far from us," he says (*DA* 503). But Tocqueville also strenuously distinguishes between two kinds of self-interest, that is, two different forms self-interest can take in democracy. One is cynical and self-centered. The other is wider and potentially public-minded.

Tocqueville's critique of the narrow kind of self-interest is revealing. Yes, he finds it morally and politically reprehensible. More damningly, though, it is stupid and self-defeating: "[It] withers the seed of all the virtues" and, in the end, leads to solitude and unhappiness (*DA* 482–83). The second kind of self-interest, by contrast, is much smarter, and thus also happier. Tocqueville accordingly calls it "the doctrine of self-interest well understood" (*DA* 500–504). This kind of self-interest is "refined," in the sense of polishing a rough substance. And one way to state the purpose of *Democracy in America* is that it attempts to lead individual democrats to recognize what enlightened self-interest really consists of.

It can be boiled down to a practical maxim: get out of yourself! For Tocqueville, the key to happiness (*bonheur*) in democracy is to avoid the egocentrism to which it all too naturally predisposes us. To put it in a paradox: it is basic to self-interest (well understood) to overcome (narrow, egocentric) self-interest. A remark by Hadot is pertinent. In an interview with Davidson he is asked, "in antiquity one could not take care of others if one did not take care of oneself. Do you think this is a necessary relation?" His response applies perfectly to Tocqueville's efforts: "I believe that your phrase should be reversed, at least insofar as it concerns the Stoics. Not, one cannot take care of others if one does not take care of oneself, but on the contrary, as Seneca says, 'Live for others if you want to live for yourself.' For, Seneca adds, one cannot be happy if one considers only oneself. It is true that one could think that in order to take care of others one must first transform oneself, but this self-transformation consists precisely in being attentive to others."[44] Spiritual exercises are, for Hadot, "personal," because they are undertaken by the individual. But that does not mean they are selfish or egoistic. As he says here, the opposite is true: spiritual exercises are practiced in order to free oneself of selfishness and egoism, attitudes that are ignoble and miserable. So too for Tocqueville. Political rights are certainly relational and intersubjective. Through them citizens become involved with one another in shared interests and undertakings. Yet, because of that, citizens learn a truth similar to what Seneca said long ago: "often one's interest is in a way found in forgetting oneself" (*DA* 486). In reality, then, Tocqueville's conclusion is contrary to Marx's. The so-called rights of man—or at least their political aspect—are a means to combat egoism and redress withdrawal, all in the name of (enlightened) self-interest. To use Furet and Mélonio's fine phrase, "there is nothing less independent than a free citizen."[45] It is this lesson that, for Tocqueville, makes the practice of political rights in democracy a personal practice, that is, a practice of the self.

Could the analogy with the ancients be extended? Tocqueville famously calls the New England townships "schools" of democracy (*DA* 57). These are places where democrats participate in public life, learn about rights (their own and those of others), and gain practical political experience. But given what we have said about political rights as spiritual exercises, these schools also initiate individuals into a comprehensive way of citizenly life. The ancient schools of philosophy, of course, served a similar purpose. "The philosophical school," writes Hadot, "corresponds, above all, to the choice of life and an existential option which demands from the individual a total change of lifestyle, a conversion of one's entire being, and ultimately a certain desire to be and to live in a certain way."[46] Men, and in exceptional cases women, would join a school (whether Platonic, Stoic, Epicurean, or any of the others) as a conscious, voluntary decision to transform and ameliorate their way of life.

Here the comparison between Tocqueville and Hadot falters. A philosopher in antiquity enters a school resolved to reform him or herself. The New Englander doesn't do that, or at least not in the same purposive way. This raises the more general issue: is it correct to say that democrats practice political rights with the *intention of* bringing about a transformation in themselves? Recall Hadot's third criterion of spiritual exercises: that they are intended to cause a transformation of the self. Do political rights in democracy meet this requirement?

Yes and no. I imagine Tocqueville would have answered "no" for the Americans he describes, but "yes" for the democrats he hopes to convince. On the one hand, he does not explicitly state that Americans in the township—which is the closest he comes to outlining an ideal or model society in democracy—exercise their political rights in order to care for themselves. It has that effect, but he never claims that New Englanders exercise their political rights for that specific end. Yet there is a simple explanation as to why he doesn't. The New Englanders in question do not have a felt or perceived need to care for the self in the ways Tocqueville describes. These citizens are lucky enough to have been born and raised within a political culture that manages the spiritual pressures of democracy. They do not have to discover the means to work on themselves in order to become citizens. They have already found them. They are great and happy in the manner of democrats.

Sadly, that is not the case for most everyone else. Hence Tocqueville's parting advice in *Democracy in America*:

The political world is changing; henceforth one must seek new remedies for new ills.

To fix extended, but visible and immovable, limits for social power; to give individuals fixed rights [*donner aux particuliers de certains droits*] and to guarantee them the uncontested enjoyment of these rights; to preserve for the individual the little independence, force, and originality that remain to him; to elevate him beside society and to sustain him before it: this appears to me to be the first object of the legislator in the age we are entering. (*DA* 672, translation modified)

[I would very much like you to tell me what makes the greatness of man if it is not man himself.
Who the devil does it concern except each one of us?][47]

It is hard to tell who exactly Tocqueville is speaking to here. He seems to address the "legislator," whom he calls upon to extend full civil and political rights to each member of society. Yet we know that this kind of formal or legal solution is only a first step for Tocqueville, a necessary but not sufficient condition for felicity in democracy. While individuals must be granted rights, it is the actual, on-the-ground exercise of such rights that really matters for well-being. And that, of course, is left up to the individual him- or herself. Perhaps that is how we should understand the two brusque sentences at the end of this passage, which are notes from Tocqueville's draft. The first nominates humanity as responsible for its own greatness. The second hammers home the point that, in democracy, this responsibility belongs to each and every one of us. In this respect, if rights are singled out by Tocqueville to help individuals preserve "independence, force, and originality," it falls on individuals to personally take up these rights for their own sake. That, to use Tocqueville's words, is one of the "new remedies" furnished by democracy to ward off its "new ills."

To return to the question: Do citizens exercise political rights with the intention of changing themselves? In the townships, and at Tocqueville's moment of writing, the answer may be no. But the whole purpose of *Democracy in America* is to extract elements of actually existing democratic practices and put them to use. At the risk of putting words in his mouth, Tocqueville tells his non-American contemporaries that if they hope to achieve the enlightened self-interest of democracy, they need to work on themselves by exercising political rights. Tocqueville encourages democrats in this direction by showing what their own felicity requires, and by demonstrating how it has been achieved, if only partially, in America. Tocqueville knows full well that America offers no automatically transferable lessons. He is at pains to insist that no specific laws or practices from the United States should be exported to France. There is, instead, an opportunity to learn techniques necessary to care for oneself in democracy.

Summary of the Book Thus Far

Let's take stock of where we are. So far we have seen two authors represent the rights declared in the French and American Revolutions in terms of the care of the self. For Wollstonecraft, the "rights of man" help women to overcome any fondness they might have for a culture that enfeebles them. For Tocqueville, the exercise of political rights in democracy is a countermeasure to the spiritual pressures it inflicts. That said, I positioned both authors in relation to different debates. My chapter on Wollstonecraft served to reply to Foucault and his suspicion that care of the self (and ethics-oriented morality more generally) withers in the juridical age. Wollstonecraft, of course, does not upend that thesis in general. No example set by a single author could. What she does, however, is put forward a possibility that Foucault never considered: that the juridical subject could be used by individuals for ethical ends. She picks up a tool that for Foucault works only one way and shows how it can serve a surprisingly different function.

Human rights have no monopoly on the care of the self. Many other codes, religious and secular, together with their attendant practices, can lend themselves to it. Foucault, for example, considered anarchism a promising candidate from which to develop an "aesthetics of the self."[48] Another example is Jochen Hellbeck's fascinating analysis of diary writing practices under Stalinism, in which subjects would reflect upon and remake themselves in line with revolutionary standards of rationality, transparency, and purity.[49] Closer to human rights is the American civil rights movement of the 1960s, and in particular, Martin Luther King Jr.'s vision of civil rights as spiritual transformation, assertive selfhood, and self-healing of oppressed peoples.[50] One more example, this time explicitly adopted by later human rights educationalists, is the combination of Marxism and liberation theology in 1970s Latin America: its call for critical awareness—what Paolo Freire calls "conscientização"[51]—is as much geared to exposing and repairing the contradictions of the self as the contradictions of the social order. Humanitarian work and activism can also be taken on to care for the self.[52] And I would be remiss not to mention that care of the self can have much less distinguished, and certainly much less desirable, origins and outcomes. Chauvinism furnishes resources to enable (certain) people to provide (a certain kind of) care for themselves. To name only one popular example, think of Chuck Palahniuk's *Fight Club* (1996) and David Fincher's movie based on it (1999). Fight club has a code—well, eight rules[53]—and is entirely dedicated to men taking care of themselves. More sinister and comical still is Patrick Bateman's opening voice-over in the film version of *American Psycho* (2000), which begins with the words, "I believe in taking care of myself."

This is not the place to weigh good and bad, or desirable and demeaning, kinds of care of the self. My point is simply that the codes and practices for the care of the self are not invented out of thin air by the individuals practicing it. As Foucault makes clear, people adopt (and sometimes modify) those at hand: "If I am interested in how the subject constitutes itself in an active fashion through practices of the self, these practices are nevertheless not something invented by the individual himself. They are models that he finds in his culture and are proposed, suggested, imposed upon him by his culture, his society, and his social group."[54] Care of the self in human rights is no different. In one form or another, human rights codes and practices have been in circulation for nearly 250 years. My argument is intended to show how different authors and actors avail themselves of human rights as an ethic and technique to care for the self. Wollstonecraft is the first author to have done so. But Bergson, Malik, Roosevelt, and certain contemporary human rights educators, along with figures that I discuss passingly, all lay claim to human rights in the way that Foucault suggests here: as a model, widely available in a culture, for individuals to use in order to constitute themselves. In sum, I use Foucault's concept of the care of the self to highlight a dimension of human rights that our human rights authors raise, and I use the fact that these authors raise this dimension of human rights to question Foucault's assumption that the juridical subject is intrinsically hostile to the care of the self. This is the line of argument that my discussion of Wollstonecraft was intended to flesh out.

My chapter on Tocqueville has a different purpose. It does not take issue with Foucault but, on the contrary, defends the discourse of the care of the self against two challenges: first, the criticism that care of the self is deleterious to democracy (as represented by Myers); and second, the criticism that it is deleterious to the self (as represented by Hadot). Both objections stem from the same complaint: political and personal felicity depends on movement away from the self, which is just what this discourse prevents.

In chapter 3 we heard the critique made by Myers. She envisages care of the self in terms of a two-step model: step one is to care for oneself, and step two is to go on and care for others and for a shared world. The trouble with this picture, however, is that not all theories of the care of the self work that way, that is, by starting from the self and then radiating outward. For example, in the interview with Hadot that I cited earlier, Seneca is explicit that one takes care of oneself *by* caring for others. And the whole purpose of this chapter has been to argue a similar point with Tocqueville. Care for oneself in democracy must take the form of care for a shared world due to the fact that democracy leads us to deadly self-absorption. In other words, the very movement away from the self that Myers believes is blocked by care of the self is precisely the kind of self-care advocated by Tocqueville and also, as we will see, by many others who reach for human rights to cultivate the self. In their hands, care of the self does not tend to selfishness or withdrawal. It powers care for others and care for the world, all the while remaining in service of the self and motivated by care for oneself.

What about Hadot? The reader will recall that he reproaches "the culture of the self, the care of the self, and conversion toward the self" as a "new form of Dandyism, late twentieth-century style."[55] There are two issues here. More narrowly, Hadot might be saying that *Foucault's* concept of the care of the self is dandyistic. This is not a claim I can address here as it would require an extended examination of Hadot's interpretation of Foucault's interpretation of ancient philosophy and culture. Suffice it to say, I am inclined to agree with Edward McGushin's defense. Drawing on Foucault's lectures at the Collège de France, unpublished at the time of Hadot's essay, he writes: "It becomes overwhelmingly clear that Foucault's conception of the culture of the self in no way entails a detachment from relationships with, and responsibilities to, others— quite the contrary, in every form of care of the self Foucault analyzes, the relationship to others is a central component."[56]

The more pressing question Hadot raises is whether the whole notion of caring for the self (and not just Foucault's take on it) is dandyistic. Is care for the self really just a cult of the self? There is no general answer. Care of the self can take that form, sure. In my opinion, dandyism is a good illustration of it. But why should care of the self be reduced to one of its historical instantiations? In chapter 1, I defined care of the self according to three criteria extracted from Foucault's later work: its purpose is to transform the self; its object is the self as an end in itself; and it is voluntarily undertaken. Tocqueville's account of the practice of rights in democracy ticks all these boxes, yet it is as far removed from dandyism as possible. He is talking about Puritans, for heaven's sake! And Tocqueville's vision of care of the self is not unique in this respect. In the next chapter, we will see another version of the care of self that is equally remote from Hadot's charge: it takes the form of Bergson's depiction of human rights as an escape from a self-centered emotional life. In short, care for the self is not intrinsically self-centered, in the narrow sense that Myers and Hadot seem to think. It can lead away from the self, whether toward a political community

(Tocqueville), or the vital impetus of life (Bergson), or other people (Roosevelt), or God (Malik). But make no mistake: in so doing, care of the self does not abandon its vocation. Movement away from the self is undertaken for one's own sake. It is what caring for oneself takes when faced with problems and dangers of a certain kind.

[5]

HUMAN RIGHTS AS A WAY OF LIFE:
BERGSON ON LOVE AND JOY

It may not be apparent from the preceding chapters, but this book is inspired by the author I am about to discuss: Henri Bergson. That may come as a surprise. So far I have mentioned him only as one author among many who see human rights in terms of care of the self. On top of that, he is by far the least famous of the bunch. Wollstonecraft, Tocqueville, Roosevelt, Malik, and Foucault are household names for political theorists and political historians. But although Bergson is the preeminent philosopher of early twentieth-century France, he is virtually unknown in these circles.

That is a shame. I wrote my previous book to improve the situation.[1] To convey the vitality of his political thought I focused on his conception of human rights. Bergson has a timely perspective to offer—one, moreover, that fits nicely with the trend in contemporary human rights education and policy to view human rights "as a way of life." In a nutshell, he says that human rights teach human beings how to love. For him, the purpose of human rights is to initiate human beings into a kind of love that is open, universal, and unalloyed with exclusion or hatred. In hindsight, my earlier book on Bergson was a first attempt to formulate the main idea of my present book: that human rights can be a medium of personal improvement.

In this chapter I revisit Bergson to highlight the role he sees human rights playing in caring for the self. Bergson is a thinker, as we will learn momentarily, who wrote his political philosophy in dark times: early 1930s France. Yet even though he was acutely aware of the looming social and political crisis, he focused much of his attention on the spiritual condition of his world, and in particular on its intensifying bonds of solidarity and fellow-feeling stoked by xenophobia and exclusion of outsiders. It is in response to this spiritual condition that Bergson most often evokes human rights. His reasons for doing so have to do with care of the self. Rather than emphasize the potential for human rights to check the political and military excesses of nationalist populism, he suggests that their real benefit is to help individuals escape from a psychic life that is joyless, hate-ridden, fearful, and flat. To put it positively, he sees human rights as the best resource available in his day and age to infuse life with a loving and joyful sensibility. My goal in this chapter is to give his message on human rights a short, clear form that is accessible to readers unacquainted with him. The result is a vision of the care of the self adapted to ills that look frighteningly like our own today.

Henri Bergson

To introduce Bergson to a wider audience it is best to begin with a bit of biography. He is, it may be surprising to learn, significant to the human rights project not just for his intellectual contribution, but also because he was an important actor in early twentieth-century internationalism.

Our story begins in 1916 when the French government entrusted him with a series of diplomatic assignments, first to Spain and then, much more importantly, to the United States. The purpose of this second assignment was to strike up a personal relationship with President Woodrow Wilson in order to persuade the United States to enter the Great War. Now, on first impression, Bergson would seem to be an odd choice for such a momentous task. At the time he was the world's most renowned philosopher, and he spoke impeccable English, but he had next to no experience in diplomacy or political affairs. And yet his nomination was astute. For what Bergson was able to do, precisely because he was an eminent philosopher, was to reflect the president's own sense of historic mission back to him. Bergson's biographers put it nicely: "In essence, Bergson says to Wilson: 'you are philosopher, prophet, and king. For the first time in human history these three figures are one.' And if Bergson is persuasive, it is because he believes what he says. In this sense, Bergson is truly 'witness to the truth': he presents Wilson the very image he would like to have of himself. He is witness to Wilson's desire; or in other words, he guarantees Wilson's ideal self. Only a philosopher could have provided this guarantee."[2]

Bergson is thus at the heart of a world historic event: the entry of the United States into the First World War. But his foray into politics and diplomacy did not end there. Due to his close relationship with the Wilson administration, his role in the Paris Peace Conference as a negotiator between France and the United States, and his own intellectual stature, Bergson was appointed president of the League of Nations' newly founded Commission for Intellectual Cooperation, the forerunner to UNESCO. The goals of the commission may seem modest. It was created to foster intellectual cooperation between member nations, including student and scholar exchanges, translation of scholarship, dissemination of scientific results, and reports on intellectual life in member countries. By all accounts, Bergson took his responsibilities very seriously. A touching story has him poring over his notes, "like a schoolboy before an exam," prior to a meeting to request a small sum from the League.[3] Yet all this hard work was done with a sense of purpose. In his mind, the commission was nothing less than the spiritual wing of the League of Nations and indispensable to its broader aim of internationalism. As he states in his presidential address, "In asking us to lay the foundation of an organization for international cooperation the League of Nations has set a mainly scientific goal. But at the same time it probably also pursues a moral goal, the very one it has set for itself: to raise a great monument to fraternity, to solidarity and accord between people."[4] Thus, in these two posts— as emissary to the United States during the Great War and as president of the Commission for International Cooperation—Bergson is both a philosopher who influenced the highest levels of policy and also an administrator who labored for a philosophical ideal. He is, to borrow a phrase from Mary Ann Glendon, one of those rare figures who have straddled the forum and the tower.[5]

The circumstances of his last days and death are poignant for a human rights imagination.[6] By 1941 the Nazi occupation of France had begun and the first discriminatory laws introduced. According to several testimonies, the Pétain government had offered Bergson the title of "honorary Aryan," as the Jewish descent of France's greatest living philosopher posed some embarrassment. Bergson not only declined the title but also made a great effort, crippled as he was by arthritis and helped along by nurses, to line up on a cold winter's day and register himself as a Jew—the cruel irony being that it was probably on this occasion that he contracted the bronchitis that eventually killed him. Last, although these letters have been lost, just before he died Bergson is reported to have renounced in writing all honors and titles bestowed on him by France, distinctions that he cherished. A sad end for a man who championed international cooperation in politics and who was often reproached for optimism in his philosophy.

A Contemporary Debate

Bergson's reflections on human rights are found in his last book, *The Two Sources of Morality and Religion*. It was published in 1932, a year that falls between his hopeful work on internationalism and the tragedies of the late 1930s and early 1940s. Now, it would not be accurate to suggest that Bergson has a fleshed-out theory of human rights in *Two Sources*. His discussion consists of a dozen or so pages scattered throughout the book. What he offers instead are flashes of insight in his remarks on human rights, remarks that are embedded within a broader reflection on morality, religion, and politics.

Rather than plunge right into *Two Sources*, I would like to suggest Bergson's relevance for a contemporary audience by way of a present-day debate. No work in recent years has generated more interest or controversy in the field of human rights than Samuel Moyn's *The Last Utopia: Human Rights in History* (2010). Moyn's thesis is that the human rights project as we know and practice it today is of relatively recent vintage, much more so than we typically imagine. Far from coming out of the great political revolutions of the late eighteenth century, Moyn claims that human rights emerged as a viable and popular moral, legal, and political phenomenon only in response to the breakdown of socialist and liberal utopias in the mid-to-late 1970s. The reason it flourished at this time is that it offered a minimalist and moral alternative to failed political paradigms.[7] "In this atmosphere," Moyn explains, "an internationalism revolving around individual rights surged, and it did so because it was defined as a pure alternative in an age of ideological betrayal and political collapse."[8]

As one can imagine, this thesis has sparked much debate. For political theorists it raises issues as to whether socialist and liberal utopias are truly dead, whether the concept of utopia in general remains productive, and whether human rights help to remake our political sensibility and to what end. But the main controversy *The Last Utopia* has stirred up is in the discipline of history, for the good reason that its critical thrust is directed at the historiography of human rights and what Moyn attacks as its progressivism and triumphalism. Here is his indictment:

> Historians in the United States started writing the history of human rights a decade ago. Since that time, a new field has crystallized and burgeoned. Almost unanimously, contemporary historians have adopted a celebratory attitude toward the emergence and progress of human rights, providing recent enthusiasms with uplifting backstories and differing primarily about whether to locate the true breakthrough with the Greeks or

the Jews, medieval Christian or early modern philosophers, democratic revolutionaries or abolitionist heroes, American internationalists, or antiracist visionaries. . . . They have used history to confirm their [i.e., human rights'] inevitable rise rather than register the choices that were made and the accidents that happen.[9]

On Moyn's account, nearly all historians of human rights have fallen into the same trap: teleology. All that really distinguishes them is the date from which they begin to narrate the steady march to our human rights present: whether it be ancient, Christian, early modern, and so forth. But perhaps his main target—or at least a highly representative one—is Lynn Hunt's *Inventing Human Rights* (2008).

Hunt is a leading American historian, and in *Inventing Human Rights* she locates the origins of human rights in a widespread cultural transformation that took place in the eighteenth century. She starts from the premise that human rights require a society at large (or at least its middle and upper classes) to undergo a sentimental education in order to become widely accepted. Her basic claim is that if human rights are to become popular as an ideal and institution, it is necessary for people to learn to empathize more broadly beyond their own narrow group. They must be able, in a word, to step into the shoes of a wide variety of others. "Human rights are not just a doctrine formulated in documents," Hunt states. "They rest on a disposition toward other people, a set of convictions about what people are like and how they know right and wrong in the secular world. Philosophical ideas, legal traditions, and revolutionary politics had to have this kind of inner emotional reference point for human rights to be truly 'self-evident' . . . and these feelings had to be felt by many people, not just the philosophers who wrote about them."[10]

Much of Hunt's book is spent documenting the ways in which sentimental education occurred in the eighteenth century. For example, she turns to the immense popularity of epistolary novels—such as Richardson's *Pamela* (1740) and *Clarissa* (1747–48), and Rousseau's *Julie* (1761)—to argue that this genre prepared a reading public to empathize across more broadly defined boundaries.[11] The reason this kind of sentimental education is so crucial to her argument is that it matches and sustains what she calls the "inner logic" of human rights.[12]

This logic is as follows. Universal rights are declared at a particular point in time (her book focuses on the French Declaration of the Rights of Man and Citizen of 1789). Afterward comes the messy business of deciding to whom and what these rights actually apply. Hunt marshals a wealth of documentary evidence to depict the extension of universal rights as a series of ever-widening inclusions. In France, the first groups to be extended rights were perceived as more or less unobjectionable, such as Protestant males. Then, following in their wake, more marginal groups petitioned for these same rights on the basis of the previous extension. It is from this process that Hunt infers the "inner logic" of human rights:

> The French Revolution, more than any other event, revealed that human rights have an inner logic. As the deputies faced the need to turn their lofty ideals into specific laws, they inadvertently developed a kind of conceivability or thinkability scale. No one knew in advance which groups were going to come up for discussion, when they would come up, or what the resolution of their status would be. But sooner or later, it became clear that granting rights to some groups (Protestants, for example) was more easily imagined than granting them to others (women). The logic of the process determined that as soon as a highly conceivable group came up for discussion (propertied males, Protestants), those in the same kind of category but located lower on the conceivability scale (propertyless males, Jews) would inevitably appear on the horizon.[13]

Hunt is fond of calling this process a "cascade."[14] Another way to picture it is as a series of concentric circles. Rights and sympathy are at first gathered into a small and exclusive core (say, propertied Christian males). Yet, over time, the effects start to ripple outward, growing wider and wider, until eventually such rights and sympathy reach the outer shore of humanity as a whole. Such a process may take years, decades, even centuries. But, according to Hunt, the Enlightenment unleashes an inexorable force of sympathy and fellow human feeling that over time will vanquish prejudice and establish an international human rights culture and regime. To quote the title of her penultimate chapter, which she herself takes from John Adams: "There Will Be No End to It."[15]

This is exactly the kind of history of human rights that Moyn takes to task in *The Last Utopia*. It is entirely too progressive, too laminar, and too triumphant to be creditable. It presupposes that the institutions, sentiments, rivals, and opponents of human rights remain steady over centuries, whether in their first iteration as the rights of man in 1789, or in their relative eclipse in the nineteenth century by nationalism and colonialism, or in their adoption by the League of Nations and the United Nations for state-centric internationalism, or right up until our own contemporary global movement that champions human rights as checks and limits on states. This kind of narrative is not properly historical for Moyn. It is, in his words, "church history."[16]

At this point I reintroduce Bergson. He too would object to Hunt's teleology and progressivism, but for different reasons. His quarrel would not be so much with her depiction of history.[17] It would be with her account of sentiment, and in particular with her account of the nature and spread of sympathy. Hunt thinks that sympathy for other people (which for her underlies human rights) can radiate out indefinitely. Properly cultivated, it can expand from family, to tribe, to country, all the way to humanity. But for Bergson this ignores something essential: morality is not infinitely extendable. It has limits, biologically built-in limits, and to turn a blind eye to these is devastating for the theory and practice of human rights—both from the point of view of human rights as a legal and political institution, and also as a medium to care for the self. I will expand on these criticisms in the following two sections.

The Critique of Human Rights

A key respect in which Bergson remains our contemporary, even seventy-five years after his death, is that he is a naturalist moral philosopher. Whereas many peers of his time thought that human beings were inherently selfish and vicious, he held that we are naturally sociable, cooperative, and other-regarding. His reason is simple: there are tremendous evolutionary advantages to solidarity and cooperation. Thus, rather than see human beings as naturally bad, as "red in tooth and claw," he suggests that we are naturally good. Morality—and all that goes with it, including empathy, cooperation, reciprocity, and solidarity—is not extrinsic to our evolved nature. It is a product of it.

The first thirty pages of *Two Sources* present this argument. But it is at this early stage of his book that Bergson makes a crucial move. If, as he says, morality "is in essence biological," that is, if we instinctively care about and feel for our fellows, it follows that morality has sharp natural limits.[18] He does not mince words: "Who can help seeing that social cohesion is largely due to the necessity of a community to protect itself against others, and that it is primarily as against all other men that we love the men with whom we live? Such is the primitive instinct" (*TS* 33). This, then, is the critical point: if the biological function of morality is to ensure the cohesion and solidarity of groups (and thus to help ensure the survival of the individual), it means that the scope of moral obligation extends no further than the group, however large it may be. To use Bergson's term, to a greater or lesser degree, all societies are constitutively "closed." Underpinned by our natural morality, "their essential characteristic is [to] include at any moment a certain number of individuals and exclude others" (*TS* 30).

This view closely anticipates present-day naturalist accounts of morality. A fine example is the eminent primatologist Frans de Waal. In his 2004 Tanner Lectures on Human Values at Princeton University he argues that morality is the outgrowth of our evolved cooperative tendencies.[19] Just as Bergson does, he observes that this entails an underside. "It should be noted," says de Waal, "that the evolutionary pressures responsible for our moral tendencies may not have all been nice and positive. After all, morality is very much an in-group phenomenon."[20] And in a later lecture he continues, "Morality evolved to deal with [one's] own community first, and has only recently begun to include members of other groups, humanity in general, and non-human animals. While applauding the expansion of the circle, this expansion is constrained by affordability, that is, circles are allowed to expand in times of abundance but will inevitably shrink when resources dwindle. . . . A level playing field, in which all circles count equally, clashes with ancient survival strategies."[21] According to de Waal, then, only in times of abundance are groups able to expand moral concern and consideration to distant others. When times are tough and resources scarce, the circle of morality contracts to a core membership.

On these two issues Bergson and contemporary naturalism are of a mind: first, morality is a product of evolution, and second, as a consequence it has limits as to how far it can extend. This is where we return to Hunt and *Inventing Human Rights*. Moyn's criticism, you recall, is that the historical *progress* of human rights she describes is all too smooth and constant. Bergson would have a related objection, though with a different target: that the *expansion* of sympathy she describes is all too smooth and constant. Hunt believes that sympathy has the capacity to grow until it encompasses all of humanity. All it has to do is overcome prejudice. Yet for Bergson this ignores the very real limit of evolved morality. Sympathy cannot fully shed its origin: it was made for groups and with groups it shall remain.

The bounded nature of sympathy is of fundamental importance to Bergson's understanding of human rights. As we will see, he too believes that such rights can be universal and encompass all of humanity. But he is deeply skeptical that such universality can be achieved by extending sympathy and moral obligation from smaller to bigger groups. Indeed, to think it can be is not just mistaken but mendacious. That is the message of a key critical passage in *Two Sources*:

> When we lay down that the duty of respecting the life and property of others is a fundamental demand of social life, what society are we talking about? To answer we need only consider what happens in time of war. Murder and pillage, as well as perfidy, fraud and lies become not only law-

ful; they are praiseworthy. Just like the witches of *Macbeth*, the belligerents will say: "Fair is foul, and foul is fair." Would this be possible, would the transformation take place so easily, generally and instantaneously, if it were really a certain attitude of man toward man [i.e., of human beings toward human beings] that society had recommended up till then? Oh, I know what society says (it has, I repeat, its reasons for saying so); but to know what it thinks and what it wants, we must not listen too much to what it says, we must look at what it does. It says that the duties it defines are indeed, in principle, duties toward humanity, but that under exceptional circumstances, regrettably unavoidable, they are for the time being suspended in practice [*l'exercice s'en trouve suspendu*]. (TS 31)

Bergson is not an author prone to sarcasm. Here, though, his temper seems pushed to the limit. But we need to be clear about what provokes him. He is not upset that in times of war morality flips its general orientation, such that what was once foul now becomes fair (and vice versa). That's just the nature of morality. Sympathy and obligation are born from evolution and it would be misguided to expect them to lead beyond the mutual preservation of self and society. What infuriates him is the moralism and hypocrisy of pretending to ground universal rights on sympathy and moral obligation. In refusing to acknowledge the inherent closure of morality, moral and political promises are issued that will not be kept in moments of crisis.

This criticism can be put more starkly. Bergson's argument is not just that sympathy and obligation are an inappropriate foundation for human rights. That much is obvious. The real issue is that the purpose of human rights is to defend people *from* sympathy and obligation, that is to say, from sympathy and obligation when they (inevitably) contract back into a narrow group. This is why a theory of human rights such as Hunt's is misguided. Its progressive narrative misdescribes the social, psychological, and affective basis of human rights. Worse, by configuring human rights as an extension of our closed moral nature—of our sympathy and obligation—she links human rights to the very thing they are meant to guard against.

We can bring this criticism home by placing *Two Sources* in its context. Bergson has the ravages of the Great War just behind him, and the explicit anticipation of the Atomic Age just in front (TS 287). It is not for nothing that in a later interview he said, "Hitler proved the truth of the two sources."[22] He is acutely aware that sympathy and obligation are potentially very dangerous. It is by confining duty and sympathy to an exclusive group, to "people like us," that one group of people persecute and attack another. Thus, to return to our problem, we can see why for Bergson it is a terrible mistake to presume that human rights are based on the kind of sympathy and obligation that holds groups together. It makes what should be a shield against closed morality a pillar for it.

The Closed Life

We have just seen one criticism Bergson makes of a conception of human rights such as Hunt's, based on sympathy and moral obligation: when push comes to shove and a group ("society," in the above passage) is threatened by real or perceived attack, support for such rights will evaporate. Here Bergson sounds a social, political, and legal alarm. He warns, first, of a conception of sentiment and obligation that hides the exclusivist core of morality; and second, he cautions against basing human rights—or any institution that aspires to moral and political universality—on this conception. Doing so makes human rights not just ineffective but phony, hitched to the very thing they are meant to guard against. In this section, however, I will focus on a second problem that Bergson identifies with this orthodox conception of human rights. It stems from the fact that closed morality, if unchecked, threatens to enclose human beings—*all* human beings, insiders and outsiders alike—in a stunted emotional and spiritual life. Put in other words, the problem with closed morality is not merely that it has the potential to be socially and politically dangerous, but also that it can enclose people into a narrow, stultified, and joyless existence. And so, as I will argue, what is worrying for Bergson about the assumption that human rights are based in closed morality—in sympathy and obligation for our fellows—is that one of the most promising means (i.e., human rights) to challenge the psychic life of closed morality becomes another support for it.

Let me explain. Closed morality has an unattractive name. Who indeed likes to be called "closed"? But the meaning of this term is more nuanced than meets the eye. Throughout *Two Sources* Bergson identifies its many healthy emotions and virtues. In the early part of the book he lists the best and most prominent, which include discipline and self-sacrifice (*TS* 9), obedience (*TS* 10), solidarity and fellowship (*TS* 15–16), honesty and fairness (*TS* 17), tranquility (*TS* 21), loyalty (*TS* 27), security (*TS* 30), and patriotism (*TS* 30). That said, although a life guided by closed morality may not be awful or even unhappy, it is nevertheless limited. It crowds out a whole range—a whole half, in Bergson's words—of joyful affects and passions. In particular, it closes off emotions and experiences that depend either on dissolving and dissipating the self (such as joy and heroism) or else on leaping beyond a closed community (such as love and charity). And the reason it does so, that is, the reason why certain emotions and experiences are inaccessible to closed morality, is that it is constitutively self-centered. This is the paradox of closed morality: it turns self and society toward one another in a mutually reinforcing and mutually regarding relation of sympathy and obligation. The individual, he states, "is part and parcel of society; he and it are absorbed together in the same task of individual and social preservation. Both are self-centered" (TS 37). And again: "At once individual and social, the soul here moves round in a circle. It is closed" (TS 38).

In and of itself there is nothing wrong with this self-centered nature. Closed morality is a product of evolution, and we should not expect it to behave otherwise. What would be dispiriting, however, is to assume that closed morality exhausts all possible permutations of morality, that is, that closed morality is the foundation not just of exclusive attachments (such as to family or country), but of open and universal ones as well. For what is lost in this assumption—or better, what we lose of ourselves in this assumption—are, in the words of one commentator, "[all] those absurd and useless virtues without which life would lose all its value."[23]

Here, then, is the second criticism Bergson makes of human rights as an extension of sympathy and obligation: We become personally and spiritually trapped in closed morality. Or, to speak more precisely, by basing human rights in closed morality we transform one of the most powerful tools (i.e., human rights) to help us escape from the psychic life of closed morality into just another support for it.

As we will see in the next section, for Bergson the best and most important thing human rights can do is to initiate all human beings into emotions that closed morality knows nothing about: genuinely open love and joy. That is how human rights can serve to care for the self, and it is precisely that potential that is ruined by seeing human rights as nothing but expanded sympathy and obligation. Consider here Vladimir Jankélévitch's depiction of the great gradualist dream of (closed) morality: "In ethics, such a symmetry [between closed and open morality] would not only be economical, it would also be reassuring; to enlarge domestic and corporative solidarity in small doses and to obtain, at the end of this magnificent widening, charity: what a godsend for egoism! Virtue and group interest would finally be reconciled. . . . Charity will appear as the superlative of egoism!"[24] Jankélévitch's tone (and Bergson's as well, as I noted earlier) is contemptuous: he leads us to picture a self-satisfied soul, greedy in spirit and flabby in mind, who wants to have his ethical cake and eat it too. But just as contempt lurks in pity, so too is there pity in contempt. For Bergson (as well as for Jankélévitch) such a person is an object of concern as well as one of criticism. The way in which he tries to clutch at charity—as if openness meant only to broaden the closed—all but ensures that love and joy elude him.

Human Rights as Works of Love

In one respect, Bergson differs slightly from the rest of the human rights authors in this book. Those other authors are what I have called diagnosticians: they address themselves to historically specific forces that threaten the self at a particular moment in time. To an extent, this holds true for Bergson. He writes from a keen awareness that sentiments of (inwardly directed) solidarity and (outwardly directed) xenophobia at his moment in time are being fanned by a historically contingent set of national, colonial, and military factors. On the other hand, it is also true that there is nothing historically contingent about closed morality, given that it is part of our biological makeup. But where Bergson rejoins these other authors, and why he features in this book, is because he portrays human rights in terms of what Foucault might call a "technique of the self," defined as the "reflective and voluntary practices by which men [and women] not only set themselves rules of conduct, but seek to transform themselves, to change themselves in their singular being."[25] The specific form this technique of the self takes in Bergson is that human rights furnish individuals with a "rule of conduct," to use Foucault's term, to cultivate a more loving, joyful, and intrinsically rewarding way of life for themselves. Human rights, in other words, are depicted as a tool to care for the self by helping individuals to turn away from the closed mode of existence described above toward one that is, in his words, "open."

To set out this positive vision, let me suggest that *Two Sources* is a book on love. Or rather, it is a book on two different kinds of love. There is the "closed" love I've described: an intensely felt attachment for a specific person or group. But there is also "open" love: an equally intensely felt attachment that is non-exclusive and universal. What Bergson means exactly by open love is difficult to explain. The closest concept is Christian *agape*. For the moment, let us say that open love refers less to a particular relation to an object or beloved and more to an exalted state or attitude of the soul.

Now, for Bergson, love—closed or open—is not just a feeling or an inner state of mind. It is a creative force capable of crystallizing into a doctrine, a work of art, an institution, and many other forms (*TS* 47–48, 74, 238).[26] For example, as I write, presidential candidates in the United States are debating whether or not to build a wall along the border with Mexico. That wall would be a crystallization—a brutal and literal concretization—of closed love. But open love can crystallize as well. In *Two Sources* Bergson points to several occasions in history where individuals, moved by such love, created lasting works from it. These include "the sages of Greece, the prophets of Israel, the Arahants of Buddhism, and others besides" (*TS* 34). His two privileged examples, however, are Christianity and the Sermon on the Mount, and human rights and the Declaration of the Rights of Man and Citizen. These are the paradigmatic moments in which humankind has sought to overcome the boundaries of the closed society. Bergson writes:

> The morality of the Gospels is essentially that of the open soul: are we not justified in pointing out that it borders upon paradox, and even upon contradiction in its more specific recommendations? If riches are an evil, should we not be injuring the poor in giving them what we possess? . . . But the paradox falls away, the contradiction vanishes, if we consider the intention of these maxims, which is to induce a disposition of the soul [*un état d'âme*]. It is not for the poor, but for his own sake, that the rich man should give up his riches. . . . We should need then, strictly speaking, a direct expression of the movement and the tendency; but if we still want—and we cannot avoid it—to translate [them] into the language of the static and the motionless, we shall have formulas that border on contradiction. (*TS* 59–60, translation modified)

And:

> Of all political systems, [democracy] is indeed the furthest removed from nature, the only one to transcend, at least in intention, the conditions of the "closed society." It confers on man inviolable rights. . . . [Democratic theory] proclaims liberty, demands equality, and reconciles these two hostile sisters by reminding them that they are sisters, by exalting above everything fraternity. Looked at from this angle, the republican motto shows that the third term dispels the oft-noted contradiction between the two others, and that the essential thing is fraternity: a fact which would make it possible to say that democracy is evangelical in essence and that its motive power is love. (*TS* 282)

I juxtapose these passages to make two points about the role of love in human rights. First, as I have said, human rights have their origin in love. To borrow a phrase from Kierkegaard, they are "works of love." And clearly, Bergson does not think that open love reveals itself only once in the history of human rights—as if the French Revolution and its Declaration was the sole occasion when it broke through. Closest to his heart is the League of Nations, the roots of which he traces to love and not tactical or pragmatic motivations. Indeed, it is because he thinks the League of Nations originates in open love that he so bitterly laments its failure: "Thus was lost the sole chance offered to the world, ever since the announcement of the Gospels, to infuse the evangelical spirit into relations between nations. Humanity would have raised itself to un-dreamed of heights. Instead it fell lower than ever. *Corruptio optimi pessima* [the corruption of the best is the worst of all]."[27]

The second point is that human rights have the power to spread love. As he says just above with respect to the Gospels, the intention of these maxims is to "induce a disposition of the soul" (*TS* 59, translation modified). In bringing love into the world, then, the Sermon on the Mount and the Declaration of the Rights of Man have the potential to introduce all human beings to a way of life that is open. *That* is their great purpose. Even if most of us are unable (or initially, unwilling) to create great works of love on our own, contact with such works has the potential to awaken this capacity within us. As Bergson says, "When we bring these great moral leaders [*grands hommes de bien*] to life in our minds, when we hear them speak and watch them act, we feel that they communicate to us something of their fervor, and that they sweep us up in their movement" (*TS* 96, translation modified). Such events and documents "echo" in all human beings and help stir, if only fleetingly, a kind of love distinct from preference and closure (*TS* 35, 100, 214). That is why, for Bergson, the promise of the Sermon on the Mount and the Declaration of the Rights of Man, along with all other creations of love, is to turn each and every human being away from a life in which partiality and exclusion reign. In this respect, then, it is necessary to insert an addendum to a remark by Jankélévitch. "This opening and mobili-zation of the soul has taken place," he states, "thanks to the Prophets first, then with Christianity."[28] For Bergson, this task is today continued by human rights.

Love and Joy

It is fine and well to say that human rights are created by open love. But what does that mean? What is this exalted spiritual condition to which human rights introduce all of us? Bergson never positively defines it. Instead, he offers an uncompromising contrast between open love and the kind of preferential and exclusive love characteristic of closed morality.

> The other attitude is that of the open soul. What, in that case, is allowed in? Suppose we say that it embraces all of humanity, we would not be

going too far, we would not even be going far enough, since its love may extend to animals, to plants, to all nature. And yet no one of these things which would thus fill it would suffice to define the attitude taken by the soul, for it could, strictly speaking, do without all of them. Its form is not dependent on its content. We have just filled it; we could just as easily empty it again. "Charity" would persist in him who possesses "charity," though there be no other living creature on earth. (TS 38, translation modified)

This is an astonishing comment on love. Bergson takes an emotion that, at first glance, seems to be warm and fuzzy and safe, and demonstrates how austere and almost unthinkable it becomes when pushed to its genuine meaning (which, for him, is really its only meaning). For in trying to imagine a truly universal and inclusive kind of love Bergson effectively asks us to conceive of it outside the categories of preference and esteem. And that is deeply counterintuitive. Love is something we ordinarily take to be deserved, gain, and earned. We love something *because* it is worthy of it. Granted, love based on esteem has nice versions (such as friendship and marriage) as well as nasty ones (such as chauvinism). Still, the fact remains that all such kinds of love are inextricably bound up with preference, hence with closure and exclusion.

Open love rubs against all those concepts, practices, and forms of life by which we have come to learn what love is. Perhaps it is better to think of it not as love *for* something but as being *in* love, if we take the preposition to mean the state of being enclosed, engulfed, or surrounded by something. It is a way of being in the world rather than an attachment to any specific thing in it.

Open love is the emotion from which human rights are born, and which they in turn disseminate. It unsettles and breaks through our ordinary way of being in the world, with its familiar orderings of preference and exclusion. But why, to ask a blunt question, is open love so good and desirable? Its appeal at a social and political level is obvious. Love is a bulwark—*the* bulwark—against closed morality. But on a micro scale, that is, at an ethical and existential level, why should people want to experience it firsthand?

There are two good reasons. First, open love is pure: it is unalloyed with preference, exclusion, or hatred. And that, Bergson makes clear, is something only rarely felt and enjoyed. "Who can help seeing," he asks, "that social cohesion is largely due to the necessity of a community to protect itself against others, and that it is primarily as against all other men that we love the men with whom we live? Such is the primitive instinct" (TS 33). Here, then, is the first benefit of open love for individuals: it suspends the emotional life of our species. It holds out a momentary reprieve, necessarily fleeting and fragile, from a psyche naturally given to closure (TS 311). Or, positively speaking, it makes available a gamut of emotions that closed morality blocks access to, such as charity (TS 38), simplicity (TS 54), generosity (TS 232), and joy (TS 230).[29]

The second reason open love is desirable is closely related. It provides an escape from ourselves. Here, one of the oldest known definitions of love is relevant. In *Symposium*, Plato claims that love means that I am not centered in myself.[30] What Bergson does in *Two Sources* is push this idea to its limit. Closed morality, you recall, along with its version of love, is constitutively self-centered. "At once individual and social the soul here moves round in a circle. It is closed" (TS 38). According to Bergson, it is because open love splits this circuit, because it ruptures the mutual reinforcement of self and society, that it alone deserves the name *love*: it transcends the limit of a closed community and, just as crucially, leads the self beyond its social ego. Open love is what biologists might call a saltation, and it is no coincidence that Bergson uses the language of leaping and jumping—"*un saut brusque*" (TS 73)—to describe the kind of movement and effort needed to break from the social self.[31]

Now, from one perspective, the prospect of setting aside the social self is terrifying. As Bergson is the first to admit, closed morality gives our ego a sense of identity and purpose. "Its solidity lies in this solidarity" (TS 15). Yet at the same time, he is clear that a great reward attends the leap. It leads to the best and highest emotion to which human beings can aspire: joy.

Joy is an important—and extraordinarily recurrent[32]—topic in Bergson's work. It is also an emotion that he always ties to a single feature or capacity of human nature: creativity and self-creation. He states this connection in several jubilant passages. For example, "Wherever there is joy, there is creation; the richer the creation, the deeper the joy."[33] Or again, "Philosophy stands to gain in finding some absolute in the moving world of phenomena. But we shall gain also in our feeling greater joy and strength. Greater joy because the reality invented before our eyes will give each one of us, unceasingly, certain of the satisfactions which art now and again procures for the privileged."[34] Or yet again, "The soul that is opening, and before whose eyes material objects vanish, is lost in sheer joy. Pleasure and well-being are something, joy is more" (TS 58).

Love and joy are intimately connected. But we must be precise about the connection Bergson establishes, for it is not the one that common sense leads us to believe. Metaphorically speaking, but *only* metaphorically speaking, open love is "joyful" in that it is free of partiality, indifference, enmity, and exclusion. It is free, in Bergson's words, from the "morality of the city" (TS 58). But love is not joy in and of itself. Neither does love elicit joy by filling our lives with more positive and less hateful affects. Joy is always and only tied to creation. Properly speaking, open love is joyful for Bergson not because it is not hateful, but because it generates the deepest and most comprehensive kind of personal transformation. Closed morality may contain pleasure and comfort, but love and joy remain—conceptually, yet not experientially—separate. Love elicits joy through the creation of a new moral nature.[35]

This relation between love and joy matters for human rights. It is the second key respect in which human rights ameliorate our emotional or spiritual life. By introducing individuals to love, and thus potentially setting a deep personal transformation into motion, human rights elicit joy. By loosening the hold that the "morality of the city" has over us—or, more literally and strikingly, by loosening the hold that our evolved (closed) morality has over us—human rights deliver us to the joy of creation and self-creation.

Human Rights, Love, and Other People

To conclude, I want to step back and place Bergson more directly into relation with my guiding concept of the care of the self. As I said at the end of chapter 1, three criteria need to be met to use it in the sense Foucault gives it. First, care of the self aims at self-transformation. Second, it is a self-sufficient moral end (and not merely preparatory labor for care for others). Third, it is nonprescriptive and allows for individuals to voluntarily adopt a moral code to cultivate the self.

Does Bergson's conception of human rights align with this? Let's take it one criterion at a time. The first is very clearly satisfied: the main purpose of human rights in Bergson's view is personal transformation. In fact, the kind of self-transformation he is talking about—escaping our biological nature—is so emphatic as to leave even a sympathetic reader in doubt whether it could be even momentarily accomplished. Leaving that worry to the side, what about the third criterion? Here too Bergson matches it. Open love—that is, the kind of love radiating out from human rights—is opposed to the morality of the city, which always exacts loyalty, solidarity, and hence exclusion. Recall the witchy words he cites from Macbeth: "fair is foul, and foul is fair" (TS 31). Typically, when we reflect on this line, the second clause draws all the attention, mostly in connection with wartime atrocities. But Bergson is clear that the first clause is just as important: actions that are ordinarily praiseworthy can be condemned as deplorable. Acts of open love such as asylum, aid, or forgiveness to enemies or outsiders can be seen as treacherous and blameworthy. From this point of view, those who love in the manner of human rights can be in breach of their social and moral duty. Far from being prescribed by a social, political, or religious authority, when such open morality is most urgently needed it is taken on in spite of commands to do the opposite.

Here we arrive at what may seem like the sticking point: the second criterion, for which care of the self is a self-sufficient moral end. With respect to human rights, this has always been the trickiest of the three. Intuitively, we resist: it goes without saying, we think, that human rights are about *other* people, especially about providing less fortunate people with an institution to secure basic dignity and justice. But if in this book I have presented voices for whom other people are not the first port of call for human rights, Bergson's position is without a doubt the most strident of them all.

Allow me to explain. In this chapter I positioned Bergson against an orthodoxy in human rights discourse: that care and concern for the whole of humanity is reached by learning to broaden a narrower set of attachments. Lynn Hunt was representative of this view, but in truth, it is widespread in modern and contemporary political thought.[36] As I said, both Hunt (and many others) and Bergson agree that human rights require, and also foster, sympathy and generosity for the whole of humanity. The difference is how they get there. For Hunt, the process is step-by-step. Over time, thanks to a process of sentimental education that begins in the Enlightenment, the ambit of sympathy and moral concern has been able to extend past kith and kin, include ever-larger groups, and gradually encompass distant strangers and humanity as a whole. This, you may recall, is what she called the "inner" or "cascading" logic of human rights.[37]

We know that for Bergson this is doomed to fail. Sympathy cannot indefinitely radiate outward because it was designed to—or rather, because it has evolved in order to—make groups internally cohesive. "The closed society," he says, "is that whose members hold together, caring nothing for the rest of humanity" (TS 264). What, then, does he propose? How can human beings, saddled as we are with evolved morality, love universally?

Bergson's answer is complex and I cannot hope to fully address it here.[38] The condensed version is that he adopts and reworks the Christian conception of *agape*. At the heart of Christianity is the idea that God creates a new relationship with humanity by loving us, in a way that we cannot love each other unaided. In *Two Sources*, Bergson preserves this scheme, but he makes a crucial substitution and addition. Instead of God enabling love, it is what Bergson calls "life," "evolution," or the "*élan vital*" that performs this role. *Love* is the name he gives to the emotion (*sentiment*, in French) that accompanies our power to tap into and realize the essence of life itself: interconnection, mobility, creativity, and movement. "By going deeply into this new aspect of morality," says Bergson in reference to love, "we should find the feeling of a coincidence, real or imaginary, with the generative effort of life" (TS 54). And more succinctly: "[Love's] direction is exactly that of life's *élan*" (TS 235).

Here is the point I wish to make: Open love is exactly the kind of love that Bergson thinks human rights teach, but it is not in the first instance a love we feel for other people. It is not inspired by other people. It is not even exactly directed to other people. Love is Bergson's word for the exaltation and intensity of being that comes through immersion in life (what, in Christianity, was understood as immersion in God).

With this, Bergson turns our normal way of thinking about love for humanity, as well as humanitarian concern, on its head. Love for *other* people—along with the kind of sympathy, attention, solicitude, and care for other people that Hunt describes—is, according to him, a by-product of an altogether different and higher kind of love—one that is essentially unconcerned with any particular object, *including other people*. This is not to say that Bergson downplays love for distant strangers or love for humanity. But, unlike closed and exclusive love, open and universal love cannot be attained by direct attachment to its object. We learn to love all others on condition that we do not set out to love specific others. Or, in Bergson's words, "[Love] has not aimed at an object; it has shot beyond and reached humanity only by passing through it" (TS 39).

Louis Lavelle, an existential philosopher, has a beautiful name for what Bergson describes: sacred indifference. It consists, he says, "in according no preference to any of the beings upon our path, in giving everyone our entire presence, and responding with precise faithfulness to the call they utter to us."[39] Sacred indifference is what human rights strive for. This is true for human rights considered as a moral and political project: the absolute and incommensurable justice it represents depends on an impartiality that closed morality denies itself. This is also true for human rights considered as an ethic and existential option, with its joyous release from partiality and hatred. To care for others (for *all* others) without prejudice, and to also care for oneself by attaining love, joy, and generosity, it is necessary to leap away from direct attachment to other people. Human rights, astonishingly, are a springboard to do just that.

[6]

ON HUMAN RIGHTS CRITICISM

We all know the word *criticism* has two different meanings. It can refer to disapproval of someone or something. It can also denote analysis and judgment (whether positive or negative) of a literary or artistic work, and sometimes goes by the name of appreciation or review. This two-sided quality makes it a rich, but also a tricky, concept. In his now classic *Keywords* (1976), Raymond Williams opens his entry on "Criticism" on just this note: "Criticism has become a very difficult word, because although its general sense is of fault-finding, it has an underlying sense of judgment and a very confusing specialized sense, in relation to art and literature, which depends on assumptions that may now be breaking down."[1]

My question is: Which kind of criticism does human rights discourse deploy? Is it of the fault-finding and censuring variety? Or does it also partake of the other version of criticism, one closely allied with judgment and analysis?

Without a doubt, fault-finding criticism—what might be called "critical criticism"—is more prominent. Think, after all, of two key functions of this discourse. First, international human rights law establishes global standards for domestic political institutions. Second, and here is fault-finding criticism in action, human rights institutions and activism monitor and publicize breaches of these standards in order to promote reform. In this respect, a principal (arguably *the* principal) illocution of human rights discourse is naming and shaming. It is at the heart of organizations such as Amnesty International and Human

Rights Watch, which report and indict the persecution of nonviolent individuals by their own governments.[2] And fault-finding criticism—and also naming and shaming, though in a diplomatic tone[3]—is also central to the United Nations' treaty bodies, which monitor implementation of the core international human rights treaties.

What about the other kind and meaning of criticism? In art and literature, it stands for the act of judging and evaluating works. And in philosophy, "criticism" can take the form of something more fully positive. Kantian and Hegelian criticism, for instance, sets out to define the proper limits of a phenomenon, and to observe what happens when these are exceeded. Hermeneutical criticism is based on charity of interpretation and potential fusion of horizons. Deconstructive criticism is dedicated to showing the nonidentity of a text with itself. And, as we will see, the later Foucault's preferred sense of criticism is also positive: it is poetic criticism, that is to say, criticism through poesis. "I can't help," he says, "but dream of a kind of criticism that would try not to judge but to bring an oeuvre, a book, a sentence, an idea to life; it would light fires, watch the grass grow, listen to the wind, and catch the sea foam in the breeze and scatter it. It would multiply not judgments but signs of existence. . . . It would bear the lightning of possible storms."[4]

Can any of this positive kind of criticism be found in human rights discourse? Yes, it can. In this chapter I sketch the later Foucault's conception of criticism, along with his view of the essentially critical relation of ethics to politics. I do so in order to set up my next two chapters on Roosevelt and Malik, both of whom draft the Universal Declaration of Human Rights with a critical spirit similar to what Foucault describes. But in this chapter I also present a strikingly different interpretation of the critical power—or rather, the absence of critical power—of human rights law and discourse found in Joseph Slaughter's *Human Rights, Inc.* Slaughter claims, in general, that human rights are an uncritical discourse and institution, and in particular that the drafters of the Declaration (Roosevelt and Malik included) exemplify this lack of critical sensibility. As will become clear, I strongly disagree with this position and, in the following two chapters, I argue that human rights can engender, following Foucault, what I call an "ethic of resistance."

Poetic Criticism

The best statement of the later Foucault's conception of criticism is found in his essay, "What Is Enlightenment? [*Qu'est-ce que les Lumières?*]" (1984).[5] This text is a commentary on Immanuel Kant's own short essay, also titled "What

Is Enlightenment? [*Was ist Aufklärung?*]," written two hundred years earlier (1784). One way to summarize Foucault's argument is that he offers a qualified defense of the Enlightenment, or more precisely, a qualified endorsement of Kant's version of it. Kant is unique, says Foucault, in conceiving of the Enlightenment as an attitude rather than as a historical period. What attitude is that? Kant's formulation is almost entirely negative: Enlightenment is an "*Ausgang*," an "exit" or "way out," from our self-incurred immaturity (*Unmündigkeit*), that is, from our tendency to take someone else's direction in areas where our own reason is called for.[6] In this way, the Enlightenment is characterized by Kant not only as an ongoing process, but also as a task and an obligation, and even as an act of courage.

The finer points of Foucault's reading of Kant do not concern us. What does is the connection he draws between this conception of the Enlightenment and the broader critical sensibility he tries to extract from it: the "attitude of modernity." Both, says Foucault, are animated by "a philosophical ethos that could be described as a permanent critique of our historical era."[7] In Kant's version, this ethos takes the form of a critique of that which impedes willingness to employ our own reason. In Foucault's attitude of modernity, critique consists in an orientation "toward the 'contemporary limits of the necessary,' that is, toward what is not or is no longer indispensable for the constitution of ourselves as autonomous subjects."[8] Put differently, the attitude of modernity is an ethos on the lookout to determine what, in our present day, is necessary, and what is adventitious (and especially, what is adventitious in that which presents itself *as* necessary), to the project of making ourselves free and autonomous subjects.

Part of this task involves historical—"archaeological" and "genealogical," Foucault specifies—investigation into the events and discourses that have made us who we are today. But the other, and more significant, part of this task consists in work upon the self in order to move beyond the limits of the present. *This* is what Foucault calls criticism. Importantly, he insists that it is a positive enterprise: "It seems to me that the critical question today must be turned back into a positive one: In what is given to us as universal, necessary, obligatory, what place is occupied by whatever is singular, contingent, and the product of arbitrary constraints? The point, in brief, is to transform the critique conducted in the form of necessary limitation into a practical critique that takes the form of a possible crossing-over [*franchissement*]."[9]

Call this "poetic" criticism. Although not Foucault's term, it captures the essence of the attitude he outlines: namely, criticism in and through poesis. Put it this way: Why does Foucault admire Kant's text? Because it advances Enlightenment as an ethic. Ausgang refers to the transformed relationship a subject has to his or her own reason (and along with it, to spiritual and political authority). The attitude of modernity Foucault proposes is an ethic in just this sense. The limits of the present are scrutinized in order, first, to diagnose who we are today, and second, to move beyond them—to *personally* move beyond them, to overcome these limits in our own person. From this perspective, the self is explicitly seen as an object of elaboration, and that elaboration, or poesis, *is* itself the criticism. That is why the attitude of modernity is at one and the same time criticism *and* creation, diagnosis *and* poesis. It is "a philosophical life in which the critique of what we are is at one and the same time the historical analysis of the limits imposed on us and an experiment with the possibility of going beyond them [*de leur franchissement possible*]."[10]

Many celebrated thinkers and artists embody this attitude. In "What Is Enlightenment?" Foucault singles out Kant, Charles Baudelaire, and Constantin Guys. And though unmentioned, Nietzsche looms in the background. But the authors I treat in this book also exemplify it. What makes them distinctive is that they actualize the attitude of modernity through the medium of human rights. Or, better put, they use human rights to undertake both tasks of the attitude of modernity. On the one hand, human rights serve as a standpoint from which to identify the limits of their present day and age: this is the diagnostic task. On the other hand, human rights are offered up as a means to work upon the self in order to overcome those very limits: this is the poetic task. Just as in Foucault's account, then, they use human rights to advance a type of criticism that is simultaneously censorious and creative, negative and positive, destructive and productive.

Allow me to elaborate the dual nature—as diagnostic and poetic—of human rights criticism, starting with the diagnostic. A point I have emphasized in previous chapters is that my human rights authors write from an acute perception of the limits imposed by their time and place. Now, the ancient philosophers Foucault discusses in his later work do not have this kind of historical consciousness. The ills, temptations, and failings they address are universal and plague humankind everywhere. Seneca, for example, tackles anger and gluttony. Marcus Aurelius obsesses over quick-temperedness. And Epictetus confronts self-pity and partiality for one's own cause. These are not "Roman" problems in the way that chivalry (Wollstonecraft) or individualism (Tocqueville) are specifically Western European and American problems. That is why the authors in this book exemplify the attitude of modernity. They are driven by a version of Foucault's own animating diagnostic question: "Who are we today?" and "Who are we in our actuality?"[11] Or, to put it in terms of my problematic, what these authors do, and where they succeed most brilliantly, is in transposing the key question of the ancients—how do I care for myself?—into the ethos of modernity, that is, into an awareness and critique of who we have become.

Diagnosis through human rights is inevitably an exercise in fault-finding. Human rights norms and practices, after all, furnish a standpoint from which the present state of human existence can be judged and denounced. But for the main authors I discuss in this book, human rights criticism does not stop there. Such criticism has an irreducible, and irreducibly positive, element as well: poesis and autopoesis. Human rights are employed as a medium to cultivate and elaborate the self. Moreover, the poetic element of criticism does not come "after" the diagnosis and fault-finding element. The sequence is not, first, tear the subject down through human rights, and next, build the subject back up through human rights. Rather, the process is simultaneous: the subject builds him- or herself up through human rights, such that he or she is released from a world that now appears limiting and even dangerous. The indictment, we might say, comes through the creation; the diagnosis comes through the poesis. Or, to put it in Foucault's terms, the historical limits imposed on us are never so manifest as when human rights have led an experiment to go beyond them.

A rich thought of Bergson's is illuminating. In an essay on his methodology, he observes that the way we tend to think about the relation between problems and solutions is all wrong. We assume that the nature of problem solving consists in starting from problems and then moving on to find solutions for them. But that is not how it works (or rather, that is only how tests and quizzes work). Problems and solutions are instead given simultaneously. As he says, "the stating and solving of the problem are here very close to being equivalent; the truly great problems are set forth only when they are solved."[12] The same goes for poetic criticism, as exemplified by the human rights authors I have been discussing. They do not start from a problem (e.g., chivalry, individualism, closed morality) and *then* proceed to devise a solution for it (e.g., the equal subject, the engaged subject, the loving subject). Rather, the problem becomes clear, concrete, and urgent once the solution to it has already been devised and achieved. I am not saying that the experience of suffering and lack does not give rise to the aspiration for a different possibility. My claim, instead, is that the appearance of a different possibility is what reveals suffering and lack as intolerable. Thus: the miseries of chivalry are apparent to women who have crafted themselves using the rights of man; the spiritual deficiencies of individualism are disclosed to the engaged political citizen; and the drabness of closed morality is cast into relief by the love and joy human rights impart.

My point is this. As I said at the beginning of this chapter, fault-finding seems to have a monopoly on human rights criticism. That is just what we assume human rights criticism is and does: fault-finding is the image or picture of criticism that pre-reflexively dominates the human rights imagination. I do not mean to challenge that assumption. It is morally and politically indispensable to have global institutions to monitor and indict, to name and shame, national political institutions. That said, human rights criticism operates in other registers as well. To bring these into relief, I drew on Foucault's idea of poetic criticism. That this kind of criticism is practiced by celebrated human rights authors is instructive. It shows, first of all, that a positive conception of criticism can be found at the heart of the tradition, and that negative fault-finding criticism can be derived from it. Second, as I propose in the next section, it suggests an additional way—an ethical way, in Foucault's terminology—for human rights to generate social and political resistance.

An Ethic of Resistance

In the second half of chapter 1, I presented Foucault's case that care of the self is unlikely to be found in modern political thought, underwritten as it is by a strongly categorical and prescriptive understanding of morality. But that should not imply that Foucault believes care of the self and autopoesis (or ethics more generally, understood as the reflexive relation we establish with ourselves in relation to a code) have no political use or value for us today.

Quite the contrary. For proof we need look no further than Foucault's first lecture series on ethics and ancient philosophy at the Collège de France. Midway through *The Hermeneutics of the Subject* (1981–82), he pauses to reflect on the fate of ethics and care of the self in modernity. He starts by noting that it reemerges briefly in the sixteenth century with Montaigne, and then again in the nineteenth century through a series of revivals by Stirner, Schopenhauer, Nietzsche, Baudelaire, and others. Then he proceeds to reflect on what has happened to ethics-based morality in his own time, the late twentieth century. And here Foucault is torn. He acknowledges how vapid and self-serving evocations of "caring for oneself" have become in his milieu. Whether through the efforts of advertising or the platitudes of newfangled spiritualisms—among which he counts the "Californian cult of the self"[13]—Foucault admits to his audience that "we have [nothing] to be proud of in our current efforts to reconstitute an ethic of the self."[14] Still, he isn't willing to throw the baby out with the bathwater. There remains something indispensable, something *politically* indispensable, in a "self-centered" ethic, that is to say, a morality that accords a central place to cultivating the relation the self has to itself.

What I would like to point out is that, after all, when today we see the meaning, or rather the almost total absence of meaning, given to some nonetheless very familiar expressions which continue to permeate our discourse—like getting back to oneself, freeing oneself, being oneself, being authentic, etc.—when we see the absence of meaning and thought in all of these expressions we employ today, then I do not think we have anything to be proud of in our current efforts to reconstitute an ethic of the self. And in this series of undertakings to reconstitute an ethic of the self, in this series of more or less blocked and ossified efforts, and in the movement we now make to refer ourselves constantly to this ethic of the self without ever giving it any content, I think we may have to suspect that we find it impossible today to constitute an ethic of the self, even though it may be an urgent, fundamental, and politically indispensable task, if it is true after all that there is no first or final point of resistance to political power other than in the relationship one has to oneself.[15]

The majority of this passage is given over to disappointment about the contemporary state of ethics and what a "return to" the self has become: empty, vague, indulgent, ossified, and all the rest. Yet Foucault's concluding note is not so much optimistic as it is insistent: any adequate theory of political resistance needs to take an ethic of the self into account. Because no matter how degraded this discourse has become—and no matter how cozily it seems to sit with contemporary forms of social and political power that deploy discourses of individualization and hermeneutics of the self[16]—it remains indisputable for Foucault that ethics marks the point at which subjectivation becomes either a pillar of support for political power, or else, as he suggests, "a final point of resistance" to it.

At this juncture, Foucault's lecture branches off in other directions. But elsewhere he pursues this thought on the salience for politics of an ethic of the self. The best-known example is the preface he wrote for the English edition of Gilles Deleuze and Félix Guattari's *Anti-Oedipus* (1977). He suggests that the importance of *Anti-Oedipus* is to initiate its readers into a way of thinking, or an "art of living," that is resolutely nonfascist. Indeed, because it attempts to root out even the most taken-for-granted forms of fascism, Foucault proposes to read it as a "manual or guide to everyday life."

The major enemy and strategic adversary [of *Anti-Oedipus*] is fascism. . . . And not only historical fascism, the fascism of Hitler and Mussolini— which was able to mobilize and use the desire of the masses so effectively—but also the fascism in us all, in our heads and in our everyday behavior, the fascism that causes us to love power, to desire the very thing that dominates and exploits us.

I would say that *Anti-Oedipus* (may its authors forgive me) is a book of ethics, the first book of ethics to be written in France in quite a long time (perhaps that explains why its success was not limited to a particular "readership": being anti-oedipal has become a lifestyle, a way of thinking and living). How does one keep from being fascist, even (especially) when one believes oneself to be a revolutionary militant? How do we ferret out the fascism that is ingrained in our behavior? . . . Paying a modest tribute to Saint Francis de Sales, one might say that *Anti-Oedipus* is an *Introduction to the Non-Fascist Life*.[17]

"Poetic" criticism is on full display in these lines. As Foucault makes clear, the only kind of criticism that has a fighting chance to overcome fascism consists of working upon the self in order to become free of the love of power that fascism depends on and instills. The critical trick, in other words, is not just to fault or condemn a desire for power. It is to cultivate oneself in such a manner as to no be longer enamored with it. That is the path Foucault praises Deleuze and Guattari for having cleared. And it is the path he sees his later work as also helping to chart: an ethic of the self as a first or final point of resistance to political power.

All of the human rights authors in this book share this conviction. Rather than belabor the point by revisiting Wollstonecraft, Tocqueville, and Bergson, I will make it explicit in my discussion of Roosevelt and Malik in the next two chapters. Roosevelt and Malik work, of course, with a different horizon in view than Foucault. Whereas he is wary of a potential complicity between an ethic of the self and political power, Roosevelt and Malik both criticize a collectivist mind-set that openly threatens to swamp the individual. What all three share, however, is the priority they accord to ethics. As the relay between subject formation and political power, and also as the bridge between psychological and political criticism, ethics is the key site to which Roosevelt and Malik bring human rights to bear.

Human Rights, Incorporated

Before turning to positive, poetic, and politically meaningful criticism in human rights, I must address a work that forcefully denies that such criticism can be found there: Joseph Slaughter's *Human Rights, Inc.* As I said in chapter 2, this is a book at once very near to, and very far from, my own conception of human rights as care of the self. This is an opportune moment to discuss it because Slaughter assumes that Roosevelt and Malik—that is, the very authors in whom I claim human rights inspire an ethic of resistance—exemplify an inherent deficit of criticism in human rights theory and practice.

Let's start with our common ground. Slaughter and I agree that human rights theory and practice are intensely preoccupied with the cultivation of subjects and selfhood. He formulates this idea in terms of a founding "tautology" and "teleology," in that human rights law and discourse seek to produce subjects (i.e., real empirical human beings) in the image of the juridical subject they presuppose human beings already are. Stated as a general proposition, I have no trouble affirming Slaughter's core idea that the human rights project is tied to "the project of becoming a person," and in particular "[to] the development of a human person and personality capable of occupying the place of the 'human' in international human rights law."[18] This is even an elegant way to describe how care of the self works in human rights: to cultivate oneself so as to become the free, equal, open subject that each one of us is already declared to be.

Where Slaughter and I part company is with respect to the implications of this tautology. He argues that human rights law and discourse have an essentially harmonizing and conservative function: to incorporate and reconcile the individual with his or her society.

Slaughter's criticism is founded on the bold and perceptive idea at the heart of *Human Rights, Inc.* He proposes that there is a profound similarity between two historical genres that few would intuitively connect: the nineteenth-century bildungsroman (i.e., a novel dealing with a person's spiritual education) and twentieth-century international human rights law. What links the two genres is that they are centered on the problem of cultivating our humanity, and more specifically, that they both mold individuals according to a shared vision of what it means to be human. "[My] book is about the sociocultural, formal, historical, and ideological conjunctions between human rights and the novel, particularly the coming-of-age genre, the bildungsroman, whose plot we could provisionally gloss as the didactic story of an individual who is socialized in the process of learning for oneself what everyone else (including the reader) already knows."[19] Human rights law and the bildungsroman, he continues, "are mutually enabling fictions: each projects an image of the human personality that ratifies the other's idealistic visions of the proper relations between the individual and society and the formative career of free and full human personality development."[20]

With this correspondence in place between human rights and the bildungsroman, Slaughter begins his attack. He says that both discourses seek to integrate—and ultimately, to reconcile—the subject with his or her social, political, and economic milieu. Here is an early presentation of the argument: "Both human rights and the idealist bildungsroman posit the individual personality as an instance of a universal human personality, as the social expression of an abstract humanity that theoretically achieves its manifest destiny when the egocentric drives of the individual harmonize with the demands of social organization."[21] And the further we go into the book, the more pointed this thesis becomes:

> Human rights law aspires to domesticate the impulse of the revolutionary plot of rebellion into the less-spectacular, reformatory plot of human personality development as the progressive harmonization of the individual and the state. As part of its institutional conservatism, human rights law aspires to normalize, publicize, and disseminate both its plot of personality development and responsibility for it, so that rebellion—as an act of collective self-assertion—might be trans-plotted into socially acceptable modes of narrative protest that make individual claims on the state. . . . The implicit *Bildungsroman* narrative of personality development codified in international law unfolds the plot for transforming personal rebellion into social legitimation with the individual's progressive incorporation into the regime of universal human rights—a plot for keeping the broken promise of the Enlightenment with the individual's reabsorption into universal humanity through the "natural" medium of the nation-state.[22]

I am not competent to judge whether or not this is an accurate depiction of the bildungsroman. But it is of limited application as a theory of human rights. Certain thinkers may see human rights in this way, that is, as seeking to incorporate an asocial and unruly individual into a social order. Émile Durkheim, for example, springs to mind with his vision of human rights as "lifting" an egocentric individual into a national (and eventually, into a cosmopolitan) social order.[23] But, to speak only of the human rights authors I explore in this book, Slaughter's theory misses the problem that drives them. They are not worried about how to reconcile an individual with a social and political body. Their concern is how a reigning social and political order socializes individuals into crippling desires and passions. And here is the critical point: human rights, for them, do not serve to reconcile or harmonize the individual with their milieu. Human rights set the individual at variance with it and furnish a means, if not to escape their own time and place, then at least to gain some critical and therapeutic distance from it.

It is worth dwelling on this point as it will bring us to Roosevelt and Malik, both of whom see their work on human rights as engaged in struggle against their own social and political order. Yet this theme of resistance is present in all the authors I have discussed so far. Wollstonecraft provides a touching example. As we know from chapter 2, she hopes the rights of man (i.e., universal rights to liberty, equality, friendship, and fraternity) can inspire women to a new way of life, one in which they relate to themselves and to others as equal and free human beings. But what I did not stress earlier is her awareness of the toll her advice takes on those who heed it. For in using the rights of man as a perspective from which to cultivate the self, she knows perfectly well that women (and men) will become more fully aware of the violence and degradation their milieu inflicts. So much so, in fact, that the world as it stands won't simply be dismissed as rotten or bad, but will, instead, become a source of acute disappointment and even despair. Just look at the sentiment behind this poignant thought of Wollstonecraft's in contemplating her infant daughter:

> You know that as a female I am particularly attached to [my daughter].— I feel more than a mother's fondness and anxiety, when I reflect on the dependent and oppressed state of her sex. I dread lest she should be forced to sacrifice her heart to her principles, or principles to her heart. With trembling hand I shall cultivate sensibility, and cherish delicacy of sentiment, lest, whilst I lend fresh blushes to the rose, I sharpen the thorns that will wound the breast I would fain guard—I dread to unfold her mind, lest it should render her unfit for the world she is to inhabit— Hapless woman! what a fate is thine![24]

In these terrible lines Wollstonecraft outlines something of a prisoner's dilemma with respect to a woman's prospects for virtue and happiness. It is almost as if she says to her daughter, "Maybe it would be better for you to grow up self-interested and shallow. Because if you don't, and if you really take my principles to heart, this world will pain you to no end." Hence the tragic dilemma: if the kind of virtues acquired through human rights make us sad in an unjust world—and what world isn't unjust by Wollstonecraft's standard?— then one of two fates is possible: to fit in *or* to be virtuous, to be happy *or* to be right, to be at peace with the world *or* to be at peace with yourself. In *Rights of Woman*, Wollstonecraft does her utmost to show the dangers of the first option. If women swim in the culture of chivalry, all will not be well. Even if they are not disgusted by it, dissatisfaction is inevitable. The other option has a different sting. Caring for oneself has its advantages. The rights of man can free us from destructive virtues. They may even lead to the special fulfillment that comes from friendship. Yet caring for oneself comes with costs. Whether it leads us to retreat from the world at large and insulate ourselves from it, or whether it drives us to confront our milieu as Wollstonecraft did, there is a price to pay: the impossibility of settling in a time and place that we are nevertheless fully exposed to. No sweet *ataraxia* is to be found down this road, no imperturbability or freedom from anxiety. To adapt a phrase from Paolo Freire (who in turn takes it from Marx), the rights of man have the potential to make real oppression more oppressive still by adding to it the realization of oppression.[25]

I revisit Wollstonecraft as a counter-example to Slaughter's thesis. Perhaps in the land of ideal political theory human rights could work the way he describes and criticizes. If we assume reasonably favorable social conditions, in which citizens and societies abide by principles of political cooperation and mutual acknowledgment, then human rights could very well be a device to mold individuals into a wider social and political order. But that is not the reality that the authors I discuss—or, I add, that he discusses—are dealing with. They appeal to human rights for reasons opposite to what Slaughter supposes. Human rights are a precious resource because they make the individual out of sync, critical, and resistant to his or her own milieu. Human rights have the power of *égarement* and can help to distance individuals from reigning norms.[26] That is why human rights are upheld as both psychically *and* politically emancipatory.

Another counter-example is Tocqueville. His conception of rights casts doubts on one of Slaughter's more pointed criticisms: "*Bildung* and modern human rights were both technologies of incorporation whose historical social work was to patriate the once politically marginal bourgeois subject as national citizen. As such, they articulated nationalizing projects intended to consolidate and legitimate the emergent bourgeois nation-state and its institutions of citizenship."[27] We know from chapter 3 that this is a popular criticism of human rights: they bolster and ratify a bourgeois, capitalist, and eventually neoliberal order. But it does not fit Tocqueville in the least. He calls on universal political rights to resist an ethos of individualism, and to help citizens to realize the personal and political felicity of other-mindedness and engagement in public life.

My objection to Slaughter is not that his view is wrong per se. Human rights can serve to integrate the individual into society. Human rights can also rationalize capitalism and entrench neoliberalism. But it overreaches to mobilize this critique as a general theory and criticism of human rights. Some of the most powerful expositors in the tradition—such as Tocqueville, as well as Bergson, Roosevelt, and Malik, along with others whom I do not discuss such as Jacques Maritain, Peng Chun Chang, and Martha Nussbaum—call on human rights to resist these trends.

Slaughter does, however, misread two authors in particular: Roosevelt and

Malik, both of whom he dismisses as apologists for the nation-state, modernization, and a new world order. For the sake of brevity, I cite only his criticism of Malik:

> In the writings of the early UN delegates, the founding of the organization and the act of declaring human rights are routinely figured as evidence of humankind's coming of age—the *Bildung* of the species. In this story, the recent crimes against humanity become, retrospectively, temporary crises that make humanity's eventual maturity (in the objective form of the UN) not only necessary but inevitable in a progress narrative still unfolding. Charles Malik, Chair of the Human Rights Commission in the 1950s and one of the primary drafters of the [Universal Declaration of Human Rights], is perhaps the most insistent upon this narrative of modernization; he characterizes human rights as a plot for "*the modernizing of the world*," and he advocates this project, in blustery, Cold War terms, as the moral advantage that "Western, Christian civilization" has over the material, developmental promises of communism in a Manichean struggle for the hearts and minds of the "underdeveloped" Third World.[28]

I have two remarks. First, in this chapter, I distinguished two types of criticism: negative fault-finding on the one hand, and positive "poetic" criticism on the other. I further claimed that, for Foucault, poetic criticism—that is, criticism through autopoesis—is not only a relevant strategy to contest political power but is, in fact, "the first or final point of resistance" to it. What Slaughter does, to couch it in these terms, is fault the autopoesis of human rights as quietist. We might even say that he adopts the principal illocutionary mode of human rights discourse—naming and shaming—to call out the orthodoxy of the mainstream human rights project. Its mission, he believes, is to posit subjects who engender themselves in conformity with the reigning social, political, and economic order. On this account, the autopoesis favored by human rights is unmasked as the first and final point of support for political power.

Which brings me to my second observation. Whatever the merit of Slaughter's indictment of human rights, it is an inaccurate (and not just an ungenerous) reading of two main figures, namely Roosevelt and Malik, at the center of the event he analyzes: the drafting of the Universal Declaration of Human Rights. As a first item of evidence, consider the phrase of Malik's that Slaughter pounces on in this passage: human rights as a plot for "modernizing the world." This phrase comes from the preface of Malik's *Man in the Struggle for Peace* (1963). Yet when we examine that work, it is abundantly clear that Malik means something quite different than what Slaughter has him say. Indeed, if there is anything that Malik hates and opposes with every fiber of his being, it is "modernization"! Here is the original:

> Another notion has gained currency in high places. These peoples (the underdeveloped, the unaligned, the neutral) are in a hurry to "modernize"; so let us carry the banner of modernization for them and help them to modernize fast. With our resources, we can do it better than the Communists; here, then, is a field in which we can excel—*the modernizing of the world*. But this is sheer empty formalism again. Poor man has sunk into the background: only roads and instruments and standards of living and stages of development are meant. It is good to wave the slogan of "modernizing" if this is the language these people understand; but it is one thing to use their term, and it is another thing altogether to be clear in your own mind as to what content you wish to pour into it. The merry modernizers must face these questions: Modernize *from what?* Modernize *into what?* . . . What kind of humanity do I wish to see them develop into, what kind of fundamental values do I hope to see them realize and love, after they have become, through my help, thoroughly "modern"? What may I, from my resources, from my background, from my heritage, from my civilization, hold out to them as a fundamental message? The gay modernizers will become the laughing stock of the world if all they know is how to modernize.[29]

Malik is a controversial thinker, one whom many of us today would have trouble accepting. But it is important to be clear what he is controversial about. He does rank "the Greco-Roman-Christian humane synthesis" above all other religious, philosophical, and cultural traditions.[30] He also believes that human rights are its contemporary standard-bearer. But he most certainly does not think that human rights are in the service of spreading "modernization," which for him is shorthand to depict the joint forces of materialism, secularism, and collectivism that have been rampant in the West (and so too, by consequence, the world) ever since the Enlightenment. In fact, if Malik sets such high hopes for human rights, it is because they can help individuals to reclaim the founding values of Western civilization as a personal ethic and shake off those baleful modern(izing) influences that have eclipsed them. Contrary to Slaughter's reading, and also as an extended counter-example to his thesis that the real ambition behind human rights discourse is to harmonize individuals with their milieu, I propose that Roosevelt and Malik devise a human rights ethic to resist their own social and political world.

[7]

AN ETHIC OF RESISTANCE I: ROOSEVELT AND
THE UNIVERSAL DECLARATION OF HUMAN RIGHTS

As this is a book on human rights and personal transformation, the next stop on our journey will come as no surprise: the drafters and drafting of the Universal Declaration of Human Rights (1948). I say this because today it is commonplace to hear the Declaration spoken of as a spiritual guide. For example, in *Human Rights as Politics and Idolatry*, Michael Ignatieff cites two Nobel Prize winners to that effect: the Declaration is said to be the sacred text of a "world-wide secular religion" (Elie Wiesel) and "the essential document, the touchstone, the creed of humanity that sums up all other creeds directing human behavior" (Nadine Gordimer).[1] A similar sentiment is found in Johannes Morsink's reference to the Declaration as "the secular bible for hundreds of thousands of human rights foot soldiers who are active in the field."[2] Last but not least, several drafters of the Declaration voiced an ambition to produce a spiritual document. P. C. Chang, the Chinese member of the drafting subcommittee, expresses his hope that the "intention and goal [of the Declaration] should be to build up better human beings . . . [and] to promote the best in man."[3] More explicitly, Hernán Santa Cruz of Chile states, "[the Declaration] should not just be a Bill but rather a true spiritual guide for humanity enumerating the rights of man which must be respected everywhere."[4]

This chapter and the next focus on two main drafters of the Declaration: Eleanor Roosevelt and Charles Malik. Roosevelt was the delegate from the United

States to the newly created Human Rights Commission and was elected its first chair in 1946. Malik was the delegate from Lebanon to the Human Rights Commission and chair of the General Assembly's Social and Humanitarian Committee. They share much in common. Both prioritize the rights of individuals in the face of pressure to acknowledge the rights of groups and collectives. Both are guided by Christian faith. But the deepest similarity is a shared conviction that the main goal of the Declaration must be to help individuals overcome any attraction to what they variously call "collectivism," "fascism," and "authoritarianism."

Working as they do in the wake of Nazism and the advance of Soviet collectivism, they have a strong political motivation to view the promise of human rights in this way. These dangerous ideologies will only be well and truly defeated in the absence of attachment to them. But this is not the entire picture. Roosevelt and Malik also champion an ethical cause: attraction to fascism, collectivism, and authoritarianism must be overcome because it leads individuals to spiritual ruin.

My chapters on Roosevelt and Malik are titled "An Ethic of Resistance" to make explicit an aspect of human rights *and* the care of the self that is underappreciated: the potentially deep and internal connection between ethical transformation and political resistance. The reader will recognize this as an idea of Foucault's from the previous chapter. As he puts it, "there is no first or final point of resistance to political power other than in the relationship one has to oneself."[5] To an extent, this insight has been present all along in the human rights authors I have already covered. If patriarchy in law and politics is to be overturned (Wollstonecraft), despotic tendencies in democracy challenged (Tocqueville), xenophobia and rampant nationalism called out and opposed (Bergson), then a prior ethical transformation is all but required. Yet with Roosevelt and Malik this connection between ethics and politics—or more precisely, between using human rights to care for the self and resisting a reigning social and political order—is thematic. Both drafters see human rights as a tool to root out the personal unhappiness and bitterness that fascism and collectivism foster in their subjects and, just as importantly, require from them in order to flourish.

Roosevelt and Malik single out different kinds of unhappiness for human rights to target. For Roosevelt it is debilitating fear and conformity that saps our adventure for living and spirit of dissent. For Malik it is the loss of a sense of ourselves as meaningful individuals and the reticence to assert ourselves as such. Nevertheless, they are both animated by a version of the same problem: How can people keep themselves from becoming collectivist (or fascist, or authoritarian) even, and perhaps especially, when those political orders are thought to be gone and defeated? Their solution takes the form of a Universal Declaration of Human Rights. To borrow a phrase of Foucault's, the Declaration is, for them, an introduction to the art of nonfascist living.[6]

A Shared Enemy: Collectivism

To introduce Roosevelt and Malik, we would do well to begin with the concrete problem they confront: collectivism, that is to say, the subordination of individuals and the rights of individuals to groups and the rights of groups.

A vignette from their early work together is illustrative. On February 4, 1947, the Human Rights Commission met at Lake Success, the temporary home of the United Nations, to discuss the principles that should underlie the Declaration. To put these deliberations into context, I should mention that Malik was a philosopher. He studied briefly under Martin Heidegger at Freiburg in 1932 until the political climate became unbearable, and then completed his doctorate with Alfred North Whitehead at Harvard in 1937.[7] Training aside, however, what really matters is that Malik very much conceived of himself as a philosopher and, in his role as diplomat to the United Nations, took it upon himself to pose fundamental questions.[8] It is in this "philosophical" spirit, so to speak, that he addressed his fellow delegates at Lake Success:

> If I understand the present age correctly, this is our problem: the struggle between the human person and his own personality and freedom on the one hand, and the endless pressure of groups on the other, including, of course, his own nation.
>
> For one must belong to a group today. He must have his identification papers. He must have social loyalties. He must belong to some association.
>
> The claims of groups today—and especially the political group, the nation embodying itself in the institution called the state—are becoming increasingly dominant. These claims have a tendency to dictate to the person what he ought to think, what he ought to do, what even he ought to believe and hope for, concerning himself and the nature of things. The political state is becoming increasingly determinant of the very being of the person, and it does it by its laws, by psychological pressure, by economic pressure, by every possible means of propaganda and social pressure.
>
> In my opinion, there is here involved the deepest danger of the age, namely, the extinction of the human person as such in his own individ-

uality and ultimate inviolability, and therefore, the disappearance of real freedom of choice. Unless our Bill of Rights somehow rejects or embodies a corrective to that danger, I am afraid we will only be expressing in that Bill the dominant forces of the age without sufficient profound reflection on them.[9]

As might be expected, these remarks set off a chain of reactions. The Soviet delegate leapt in with a defense of the primacy of the state to the lives of individuals. The Indian delegate grew irritated by the direction of the debate and urged her colleagues "not to enter into this maze of ideology at this stage." The French and British delegates tried to steer a middle course between affirming the rights of individuals and the rights of society. But it is Roosevelt's response that concerns us. Paired with Malik's comment, it shows that the two drafters held a similar view as to what endangers human rights and why a bill of human rights is indispensable.

> I think perhaps I would like to say a word about what was said by the representative from Lebanon [i.e., Malik]. It seems to me that in much that is before us, the rights of the individual are extremely important. . . . Many of us believe that an organized society in the form of a government exists for the good of the individual; others believe that an organized society in the form of a government, exists for the benefit of a group. We may not have to decide that particular point, but I think we do have to make sure, in writing a bill of human rights, that we safeguard the fundamental freedoms of the individual. If you do not do that, in the long run, it seems to me, that you run the risk of having certain conditions which we have just tried to prevent at great cost in human life, paramount in various groups. So I do think that what the representative from Lebanon said should be very carefully taken into consideration when the drafting committee meets, as well, of course, as every other thing that has been said around this table.[10]

It helps to take a step back to put Malik's and Roosevelt's remarks into perspective. In contemporary human rights scholarship, there is a consensus that the Declaration was drafted with a specific purpose in mind: to oppose and prevent any recurrence of the horrors of Nazi Germany. For example, in his painstaking article-by-article reconstruction of the Declaration, Morsink insists on the centrality of Nazi atrocities to the drafting process: "While [the drafters] often differed on the specific wording to be used, once it was shown that a violation of a certain clause or article had in some way helped create the horrors of the war, the adoption of that clause or article was virtually assured."[11]

I have no wish to dispute that Nazi atrocities weighed heavily in the process of drafting the Declaration. There is even ample support in Roosevelt's and Malik's speeches at the time—specifically (and this is no coincidence) when they speak or act in their capacity as representatives of the Human Rights Commission as a whole.[12] But when we read the exchange I cited above between Malik and Roosevelt at Lake Success, as well as consult their wider oeuvres and drafting records, it is clear that the kind of devastation associated with Nazism is not their foremost concern. Their real worry is at once more general and also, because of the presence of the Soviet Union at the drafting table, more immediate: moral, political, and legal collectivism.

Think of it this way. Nazism is obviously a species of collectivism. Yet it is so shockingly and violently so that it cannot pass itself off as anything other than external and hostile to the very idea of human rights. This is a key reason why it serves as a touchstone and rallying point for the Human Rights Commission: Nazism provides a common enemy for *all* parties to move deliberations along. Collectivism, however, is a broader and more slippery phenomenon. It can present itself in many guises, some of which are not immediately apparent as adversaries of human rights. For Roosevelt and Malik, the Soviet Union is just such an opponent. It notionally supports the drafting of an international human rights document, all the while maintaining that such rights must be subordinate to the laws and needs of the state.[13]

It is this less overt kind of collectivism that Roosevelt and Malik fear as a more insidious—and for that reason, a more real and present—danger to human welfare in general and to drafting a human rights Declaration in particular. Both drafters are alert to the possibility that the meaningful threat to human rights is not a frontal attack from without (as in the case of Nazism). It lies, instead, in a certain priority given to the group and to the rights of groups that threatens to express and amplify what they take to be the most dangerous political and psychical tendencies of the day: collectivism and the desire of individuals to subsume themselves within an omnipresent group. What Malik thus calls "the deepest danger of the age" is a doctrine and worldview willing and able to assert itself within the very Declaration that ought to fend it off. Or, as he puts it in his diary, "those who seek the salvation of man only through economic and social and political input do not know that they are playing straight into the hands of their deadliest enemies."[14]

Were Roosevelt and Malik "Cold War warriors," in the sense of serving primarily as spokespersons for Western powers? The question remains debated (particularly with respect to Roosevelt's legacy).[15] But they were not "anti-Soviet" or "anticommunist" ideologues in any straightforward sense. For example, Roosevelt and Malik were publicly and privately grateful to the Soviet Union for pressing social and economic rights when their own governments (the United States in particular) were hostile to any class of rights beyond civil and political.[16] Moreover, the collectivist tendency they identify is not confined to a particular country or ideology. It is not uniquely "Russian" or "Soviet" or "communist," but widespread in their own countries and "the West" as well. As Malik makes clear, collectivism and the extinction of the individual human person are "the dominant forces of the age" in general. And that, as we will see, is why the stakes of the drafting of the Declaration are so high for Roosevelt and Malik: they must ensure, on the one hand, that human rights are not captured by collectivist states and, on the other, they must work to frame human rights in such a way that they can help root out a desire for collectivism in individuals everywhere.[17]

Fear: The Great Enemy

As with the other authors in this book, Roosevelt and Malik treat human rights from what might be called an "educational" perspective. They hold that the main purpose of the Declaration is to promote personal transformation and what Roosevelt calls "inward" human progress.[18] For example, in an article written during her tenure as chair of the Human Rights Commission, Roosevelt states, "We have put into words some inherent rights. Beyond that, we have found that the conditions of our contemporary world require the enumeration of certain protections which the individual must have if he is to acquire a sense of security and dignity in his own person. The effect of this is frankly educational. Indeed, I like to think that the Declaration will help forward very largely the education of the peoples of the world."[19]

Why do Roosevelt and Malik see the Declaration in this light? The hardheaded answer, of course, is that they had no choice. Given the political and diplomatic constraints at the United Nations, it became apparent early on in the drafting process that the Declaration would be supported only if it were not legally binding. It is thus possible to read a spirit of resignation—or, from another angle, a resourcefulness of the "make lemonade from lemons" variety—in emphasizing the educational vocation of the Declaration.[20]

These constraints did shape Roosevelt's and Malik's ambitions for the Declaration. But the trouble with an exclusively "realist" explanation is that it is unable to credit their words at face value. When, for instance, Malik states, "the morally disturbing or judging is far more important than the legally binding," or when Roosevelt affirms that "court decisions, and laws and government administration are only the results of the way people progress inwardly," it is clear that neither deems the educational role of the Declaration second best.[21] It is primary. It is primary from an instrumental perspective to promote effective legal and political change. It is also primary in and of itself for people to grow spiritually: the Declaration has the potential to be educative, even therapeutic, in that it can be used by individuals to resist and free themselves from debilitating desires that are reinforced by their milieu.

Which desires in particular? Here Roosevelt and Malik part company. For Roosevelt it is the desire to conform and to shirk courage, self-reliance, and the demands of individuality. For Malik it is something akin to a desire for nihilism: a willing abnegation of a sense of ourselves as meaningful beings. These accounts are not incompatible. Roosevelt's and Malik's warm mutual esteem and continued collaboration on the Human Rights Commission are good proof. More importantly, they arrive at the same conclusion: whichever set of desires dominates, both paths lead to collectivism. Even so, Roosevelt's and Malik's assessments of the dangers and desires of their time and place—and hence too the kind of self-care human rights are called upon to provide—are sufficiently distinct to warrant separate examinations.

I begin with Roosevelt. One challenge in addressing her work within the confines of a chapter is that her corpus is enormous. She wrote almost thirty books, more than 550 articles, roughly 8,000 entries for her nationally syndicated column "My Day," another 250 advice pieces for her column "If You Ask Me," and, together with her staff, thousands of letters per year from 1933 to 1962.[22] Faced with an oeuvre of this size, an exercise that Bergson recommends is helpful. In a late essay, he claims that any great thinker has, in all honesty, only one or two "infinitely simple" ideas that he or she elaborates over the course of a lifetime.[23] Taking up the suggestion, what would we say is Roosevelt's "big idea"? What single idea could possibly span a prolific and diverse body of work that treats politics, religion, spirituality, philosophy, diplomacy, self-help, and manners and etiquette?

Fear is the answer. It is the great theme that binds her life and writings: A warning, on the one hand, against the danger and impoverishment of a life dominated by fear. And an exhortation, on the other hand, for grit and determination along with proposals to cultivate courage. But what is most remarkable about Roosevelt's lifelong meditation on fear—and consequently, so too on courage—is how she addresses its personal and sociopolitical effects, and more to the point, how the personal and sociopolitical roots and effects of fear are entwined. Consider an address she gave in 1950 for the Americans for Democratic Action conference:

> We live in a time when every single one of us must realize that what actually is important in a democracy is that sense of individual responsibility. And there are certain things here in our country that I think we must watch very carefully. It is true, as has been said, that there is a sense of insecurity—I might almost say a sense of fear—among many people in this country of ours. With some people it's a fear of the possibility of war; with others it's a fear of what the new weapons of war may mean if we should come to war; with others it's a fear of what may happen to them personally if by chance they offend in any way. That is the fear that bothers me most—the fear of people who are afraid to be themselves, to hold convictions, to stand up for them—because that fear, I think, is the fear which can really hurt our democracy more than any other.[24]

"Freedom from fear" is a phrase most often associated with Eleanor Roosevelt's husband, Franklin Delano. It is one of the Four Freedoms championed in his 1941 State of the Union address.[25] And his message that "the only thing we have to fear is fear itself" continues to be widely remembered today.[26] But when we read a passage such as this, it is clear that a wish for freedom from fear is no less dear to Eleanor. As she states in *Tomorrow Is Now*, a book dictated from her deathbed with urgent need, "man's noblest freedom" is nothing other than "freedom from fear."[27]

Many of the fears Roosevelt grapples with come readily to mind when we think of her Cold War context. In this passage, she names the fear of war and the potential for worldwide annihilation. Elsewhere in her work—in truth, everywhere in her work—she confronts other fears. Most prominent are fear of political others (as evidenced by McCarthyism) and fear of racial others (manifest in the push for segregation).[28] But while each of these fears is distressing in itself, Roosevelt warns that they compound and imperil the judgment and action of a democratic polity. "People who 'view with alarm,'" she warns, "never build anything." And if the United States, or any other democratic nation, is to regain the moral and political stature of a "democratic way of life," it is essential to learn how to "cast out fear."[29]

We will revisit Roosevelt's call for a democratic way of life. At present, though, it is important to address a second kind of fear she names in this passage. It might better be called timidity, conformity, or shyness: "the fear of people who are afraid to be themselves." This kind of fear surely affects all but the most exceptional of us. Even so, it seems to have touched Roosevelt especially deeply and plagued her for most of her life—a period of time she calls her "girlhood," and which lasted well into middle age. "I was afraid," she writes in her autobiography.

> Afraid of almost everything, I think: of mice, of the dark, of imaginary dangers, of my own inadequacy. My chief objective, as a girl, was to do my duty. This had been drilled into me as far back as I could remember. Not my duty as I saw it, but my duty as laid down for me by other people. It never occurred to me to revolt. Anyhow, my one overwhelming need in those days was to be approved, to be loved, and I did whatever was required of me, hoping it would bring me nearer to the approval and love I so much wanted.[30]

When later in life she went on to write books and advice columns devoted to self-improvement, she always spoke from the position of one who had struggled and learned to overcome fear. Maybe it was modesty speaking—or maybe it was an acknowledgment of just how tremendous her achievement was—but she repeatedly claimed that the only lesson she had to offer came from her talent to live as widely and fully as possible in spite of timidity and fear.[31]

Roosevelt is well aware that the pressure to conform to a group or dominant standard is nothing new. Tribes, churches, and tyrants have always exacted it.[32] Yet what she finds unprecedented in her time and place is the degree to which the desire for conformity has become internalized. In her best-known book, *You Learn by Living*, she paints a picture of the individual in her age that is nothing short of tragic.

> We are facing a great danger today—the loss of our individuality. It is besieged on all sides by pressures to conform: to a standardized way of living, to recognized—or required—codes of behavior, to rubber-stamp thinking. But the worst threat comes from within, from a man's or woman's apathy, his willingness to surrender to pressure, to "do it the easy way," to give up the one thing that he is himself, his value and his meaning as a person—his individuality.
>
> It's your life—but only if you make it so. The standards by which you live must be your own standards, your own values, your own convictions in regard to what is right and wrong, what is true and false, what is important and what is trivial. When you adopt the standards and the

values of someone else or a community or a pressure group, you surrender your own integrity. You become, to the extent of your surrender, less
of a human being.[33]

This last clause—"less of a human being"—is not some loose metaphor or
casual way of speaking for Roosevelt. It has the same deadly literalness as when
Wollstonecraft calls women of her time "brutes" in whom "the characteristics
of humanity can scarcely be discerned."[34] But whereas Wollstonecraft's complaint is that women shun a whole range of humanizing virtues, Roosevelt worries that conformity stifles the single most important capacity that makes all of
us human: a "spirit of adventure." This is a key term. It designates a special kind
of attitude or disposition, one in which we take in the world with interest and
curiosity. And it is the ethos she hopes her writings can inspire. Here is how she
describes it in a crucial passage:

> Curiosity, interest, and a longing to know more and more types of expe-
> rience are the qualities that stimulate a desire to know about life and to
> understand it. They provide the zest that makes it possible to meet any
> situation as an adventure. Without that spirit of adventure, life can be a
> dull business. With it, there is no situation, however limiting, physically
> or economically, which cannot be filled to the brim with interest. Indeed,
> without interest, it is almost impossible to continue to learn; certainly, it
> is impossible to continue to grow.[35]

A "spirit of adventure" is a favorite expression of Roosevelt's. It recurs in her
writings on self-improvement and also, tellingly, in her calls for social and
political reform.[36] That said, she never explicitly defines it. I propose that we
think of this spirit of adventure as a theory of experience, or more precisely, as
a conception of a particular (and hard-earned) way of experiencing. For when
we examine her descriptions of it, a spirit of adventure is found to include the
two facets of experience that virtually every modern philosophical tradition
(e.g., empiricist, Kantian, Romantic, pragmatist, or phenomenological) have
made their mainstay: the reception (or intuition) of reality on the one hand,
and the assimilation (or synthesis) of that reality into reflective consciousness
on the other.

Both facets are on display in this passage. A spirit of adventure refers, first
of all, to a specific way to receive or intuit the world. It is a disposition in which
the world presents itself to us *as* adventurous. It is thus no coincidence that
Roosevelt likens a spirit of adventure to a change in perception: that is, with
learning to listen and see anew.[37] "When I began," she writes of her own trans-

formation, "actually to look around me and to try to understand the meaning of what I saw, everything I encountered became more interesting and more valuable. It was like a two-dimensional picture seen in three dimensions, with depth."[38] For Roosevelt, if the world appears to us as vivid and engaging, it is not due to its own intrinsic properties. It is because we have approached it with curiosity and interest. That is why it is fitting to think of a spirit of adventure as a mode of apperception.

But perceiving the world as bright and exciting is only half of what Roosevelt means by a spirit of adventure. Equally important is the ability to reflect upon and assimilate this experience into our consciousness and character. This is the second facet of a spirit of adventure. If we return to the passage above, two phrases from the concluding sentence stand out: a spirit of adventure is what enables us to "continue to learn" and to "continue to grow." Really, these phrases summarize Roosevelt's single most important piece of advice for self-improvement: always put yourself in a position to incorporate and profit from every single one of your encounters and experiences. That is what a spirit of adventure amounts to. It is her term for a readiness to pounce on any situation that might offer an opportunity for personal development. "Learning and living," she asks, "are really the same thing, aren't they? There is no experience from which you can't learn something. When you stop learning you stop living in any vital or meaningful sense. And the purpose of life is to live it, to taste experience to the utmost, to reach out eagerly and without fear for newer and richer experience."[39]

This second facet of a spirit of adventure is pertinent. As a capacity and willingness to use each new experience to enhance ourselves, it is, in essence, a version of the care of the self. This comes across clearly in a key chapter of *You Learn by Living*: "How to Get the Best Out of People." Given its title, we might assume that this chapter is about bringing out the best in other people, that is, how to help them to become better people. But that's not her topic. What Roosevelt is talking about is how to get the best out of *your own* encounters with other people: "If you approach each new person you meet in a spirit of adventure you will find that you become increasingly interested in them and endlessly fascinated by the new channels of thought and experience and personality that you encounter. I do not mean simply the famous people of the world, but people from every walk and condition of life. You will find them a source of inexhaustible surprise because of the unexpected qualities and interests which you will unearth in your search for treasure. But the treasure is there if you will mine for it."[40]

Here, then, is what a spirit of adventure can do: it can make other people come alive. It can tap into what is interesting and worthwhile in them. It can, in a word, bring out their best. But Roosevelt is clear: it does so *for you*. Her choice of words is striking. A spirit of adventure, she says, is in pursuit of hidden "treasure." We greet others in a spirit of openness and interest, and seek out what is singular and valuable in them, so as to be enriched by the encounter. New people—and this includes not just people we meet for the first time, but everyone in whom we mine for treasure—propel us beyond ourselves. Approached in the right way, they hold the key to unknown channels of thought and experience.[41]

It would not be correct to say that a spirit of adventure is selfish or inward looking. That is not how it works. It is thanks to a spirit of adventure that we pay genuine attention to the other and attend to his or her singularity. Moreover, by revealing the other to be fascinating, and by allowing ourselves to be captivated by them, a spirit of adventure leads us away from self-absorption. Last, and most importantly, a spirit of adventure fosters a practical attitude of care for the other. Only if we are able to truly see what the other is can we truly attend to his or her needs and interests. Ultimately, however, the fact remains that genuine attention to the other is elicited by concern for oneself. Other people, Roosevelt tells us in her autobiography, are "grist to *my* mill"; they hold out "something interesting to contribute to *my* education."[42] And so while a spirit of adventure launches the self toward alterity, and while it leads to an acknowledgment of the singularity of the other, it entails an equally powerful return to the self, alterity in hand, so that this new experience can help us to learn, grow, and become better than we currently are.

In a moment we will examine the link between a spirit of adventure, care of the self, and human rights. First, though, I want to return to the question I posed earlier: Why is fear, and in particular fear in the guise of conformity and timidity, so detrimental according to Roosevelt?

One reason is that it makes us bland and mediocre. This is a criticism made famous by authors whom Roosevelt read all her life: J. S. Mill and Ralph Waldo Emerson. The trouble with conformity is less that it forces individuals to actively repress their own inclinations, than that, over time, it erases any trace of individuality within them. In Mill's pithy formulation, "by dint of not following their own nature, they have no nature to follow."[43] This line of criticism is ubiquitous in Roosevelt's writings. Most often it is directed at her fellow Americans, as when she warns that the net result of trying to live like our neighbors—of wrapping ourselves up in the tastes and dreams of "the Joneses"[44]—is the "destruction of the individual and the loss of his integrity."[45] In other places she turns the lens on herself, as when she reflects that as a young mother she went about "absorbing the personalities of those about me and letting their tastes and interests dominate me."[46] But whether she refers to other people or to herself, the conclusion is the same: the repercussion of conformity is a squandered life. "Not to arrive at a clear understanding of one's own values is a tragic waste. You have missed the whole point of what life is for."[47] It is her definition of what it means to be a failure.[48]

That's not even the worst of it. The most terrible consequence of conformity is that it extinguishes a spirit of adventure. Granted, on its face this might not seem like such a catastrophe. It may seem only to redescribe what Mill and Emerson, among others, already said: that if we no longer assert and cultivate our individuality, our zest for it will dry up as well. But we must remember that a spirit of adventure refers to a conception of experience. Only with this in mind can we appreciate that, for Roosevelt, the cost of conformity is not confined to the loss of a desire to develop our own individual nature. More distressingly, by extinguishing a spirit of adventure we also lose the best and most human way to receive and process our own experience. That is why, as I emphasized earlier, Roosevelt states that to surrender our individuality is to become "less of a human being."[49] She does not say a "boring" or "uninteresting" human being, but strictly speaking, a being who has blocked off its access to a spirit that makes us human. Such a person is, in her damning words, a "drudge": a being for whom the world holds no brightness or excitement precisely because he or she does not meet it with an eye to cultivating their particular tastes and talents.[50]

"The world of the happy man," Wittgenstein once wrote, "is a different one from that of the unhappy man."[51] The same goes for Roosevelt: the world of the adventurous soul is not that of the timid soul. And the ambiguity of the word *world* bears notice. The personal and spiritual world of the timid soul will suffer for having surrendered individuality and extinguished a spirit of adventure. But so too will his or her social and political world. This is the link that Roosevelt establishes between ethics and politics, and in particular the worrisome complicity between conformity and collectivism. To return to a passage I cited earlier, Roosevelt is explicit that of all the fears poisoning her milieu, timidity is the most noxious to democracy. "That is the fear that bothers me most—the fear of people who are afraid to be themselves, to hold convictions, to stand up for them—because that fear, I think, is the fear which can really hurt our democracy more than any other."[52]

Roosevelt's criticism of timidity in politics is most often directed at the United States. That is, after all, the audience she hopes to convince. Hence the reason she lists all the harms that a "fear of being oneself" inflicts on the national interest. This includes how timidity breeds a people unlikely to protest injustice;[53] how it makes social and political reform all too cautious and piecemeal;[54] how it degrades American standing and leadership internationally;[55] and, most dangerously, how it leaves citizens and politicians alike incapable of discerning pressing problems.[56]

Yet in her reflections on fear and timidity, Roosevelt often thinks back to her Soviet colleagues on the Human Rights Commission.[57] They made a great impression on her. Sometimes her tone is mixed with exasperation, which is understandable in light of their obstructiveness. Mostly, though, she voices pity. "I sit with people who are representatives of communist countries, and to sit with them is a lesson in what fear can do. Fear can take away from you all the courage to be an individual. You become a mouthpiece for the ideas which you have been told you must give forth. I have no feeling of real antagonism towards these representatives because, poor things, they can do no other."[58] And again: "It's hard even to say you're meeting with people, because they behave exactly like automatons. They are always government representatives."[59] This state of affairs has not come to pass in democratic countries, according to Roosevelt. And she is well aware that Soviet diplomats are held in place by forces more nefarious than timidity. But these diplomats appear in her work as cautionary figures, a kind of *memento mori*, for the spiritual and political ravages that conformity can inflict. Their presence on the Human Rights Commission redoubles her conviction that human rights must be framed so as to oppose collectivism at its root.

Human Rights and a Spirit of Adventure

On December 17, 1947, almost exactly one year before it was adopted by the General Assembly, the first full draft of the Declaration was completed by the Human Rights Commission. Pleased with the work, Roosevelt sent a letter to a friend: "We finished last night and I drove them hard but they are glad now it's over and all the men are proud of their accomplishment."[60] The next day she dedicated her weekly newspaper column to reviewing the commission's progress with the public. Once again she expresses her view that the main ambition of the Declaration is educational: "There will be provisions which will entail a change of attitude toward the value of the human being as such, and this may require considerable education among our people—but it's a step forward in the conception of civilization throughout the world."[61]

The Declaration, Roosevelt says, "entails a change of attitude toward the value of the human being." But for whom? Who or what is doing the changing?

The standard answer in human rights scholarship is that human rights seek to change the attitude and actions of governments and state institutions and officials, particularly with respect to their own people. Andrew Clapham, for example, states this familiar view in the opening paragraphs of *Human Rights: A Very Short Introduction*: "Human Rights come into play to stop governments and other actors from pursuing expedient policies at the expense of the well-being of certain individuals and the proper functioning of a democratic society under the rule of law."[62]

This is perfectly true. Yet we must add that human rights speak to us on a personal level as well. They are personal, first of all, in the sense that human rights address individuals (i.e., individual and private persons) and not just officials and institutions. And they are personal in the broader sense of touching our inner or emotional life, our "personality," as it were. This is the thread that links all of the historic authors in this book: a belief that human rights can be used by individuals to work upon and transform themselves. In this section I present Roosevelt's version of this thesis. But, before diving back into her work, it is useful to examine the text of the Declaration itself, especially its title and preamble. As scholars have noted, if not in these exact terms, it is a document that addresses the individual and enjoins personal transformation.[63]

Take the title. It is well known that the Universal Declaration of Human Rights was not always called "The Universal Declaration of Human Rights." When the Human Rights Commission first convened in 1946 it had various working titles: "The International Declaration of Human Rights," "The International Bill of Human Rights," and simply, "The Bill of Human Rights." But beginning late in 1947, and then consistently in 1948, it acquired its official name. The reason behind the change was that human rights were held to address individuals as well states and institutions. "The new title," Mary Ann Glendon explains, "had been in casual use for some time, but [René] Cassin, who proposed the official change, rightly considered the name to be of the utmost significance. The title 'Universal,' he later wrote, meant that the Declaration was morally binding on everyone, not only on the governments that voted for its adoption. The Universal Declaration, in other words, was not an 'international' or 'intergovernmental' document; it was addressed to all humanity and founded on a unified conception of the human being."[64]

In the Preamble, we see the "universal" scope restated and confirmed. It is made explicit that the Declaration is addressed to each and every individual: "The GENERAL ASSEMBLY proclaims THIS UNIVERSAL DECLARATION OF HUMAN RIGHTS as a common standard of achievement for all peoples and all nations, *to the end that every individual and every organ of society, keeping this*

Declaration constantly in mind, shall strive by teaching and education to promote respect for these rights and freedoms and by progressive measures, national and international, to secure their universal and effective recognition and observance, both among the people of Member States themselves and among the peoples of territories under this jurisdiction."[65] This section of the Declaration is what lawyers would call its "operative" clause: it brings into existence—it performatively proclaims—the articles that the document enumerates. But we all know this isn't just any clause: this proclamation has acquired the status of a Genesis 1:1 for the global human rights movement. For this reason, it is significant that it foregrounds the educative and transformative role of human rights.

First, as I said, the Preamble reaffirms what the title of the Declaration had only implied: human rights are, in fact, universal and addressed to "every individual" (as well as to "every organ of society"). Second, and this is crucial, this section of the Preamble explicitly presents human rights in terms of personal transformation. This feature can be gleaned from the little phrase, "keeping this Declaration constantly in mind."[66] Indeed, this phrase makes the Declaration into something akin to a spiritual exercise.[67] The reader will recall from chapter 4 that a "spiritual exercise" is defined by Pierre Hadot as a "voluntary, personal practice intended to cause a transformation of the self."[68] With its demand to be kept "constantly in mind," the Declaration satisfies each element of this definition in letter and spirit. It is "personal" in that it addresses individuals. It is "voluntary" in that it is a nonbinding document.[69] It is a "practice" in that its injunction to be kept constantly in mind is a repetitive spiritual discipline, almost like a mantra. Most importantly, it is "transformative" in that it seeks to steep each and every human being in the articles that it enumerates. Personal transformation is what the phrase "keeping this Declaration constantly in mind" is all about: to inscribe the principles and articles of this document in the hearts and minds of individuals.[70] To borrow a genre from ancient philosophy, the Declaration is a modern-day *hupomnēmata* (notebook): a written reminder of a dogma or rule of life that must always be ready to hand.

Roosevelt is an eloquent spokesperson for this vision of the Declaration as educative and transformative. It shines through in her best-known observation on human rights: "Where, after all, do universal human rights begin? In small places, close to home—so close and so small that they cannot be seen on any maps of the world. Yet they are the world of the individual person; the neighborhood he lives in; the school or college he attends; the factory, farm or office where he works. Such are the places where every man, woman and child seeks equal justice, equal opportunity, equal dignity without discrimination. Unless these rights have meaning there, they have little meaning anywhere."[71]

Roosevelt always thinks and works at the scale of everyday life. That is where everything happens, where big ideas can really take hold of institutions and individuals. She treats religion and Christianity from this perspective, that is, as a concrete way of life to develop the spirit.[72] She approaches democracy in the same way: it "must be something you live day by day, and that enters into everything you do."[73] And gauging by the passage above, her approach to human rights is no different. To be more than fine words, human rights must become "the world of the individual person." This means that human rights must do more than find a place in everyday life, in the sense of subsisting alongside it, or simply being compatible with it. They must become its fabric.

Roosevelt is explicit that human rights can and must become a way of life. But my interpretation goes further. I claim that for her human rights also serve to care for the self. She does not say so in so many words. Nor does she directly state the connection between human rights and the spirit of adventure that I will propose. What she does, however, is identify the same ethos as underlying a spirit of adventure and a commitment to human rights: an assertion of one's own individuality on the one hand, and an openness and receptivity to other people on the other hand. This connection is the key to my interpretation. If a spirit of adventure and a commitment to human rights foster the same ethos, and if, as I argued in the previous section, the ethos of a spirit of adventure is Roosevelt's version of the care of the self, then it follows that a commitment to human rights also entails care of the self.

To set out this argument, let's begin with a key similarity between a commitment to human rights and a spirit of adventure. They fight the same enemy: collectivism. Now I admit that it might seem doubtful that the same kind of collectivism is at issue. We know that the kind of collectivism that most afflicts a spirit of adventure is conformity. But when Roosevelt discusses collectivism in the context of human rights, she is not usually thinking of a willing or lazy abnegation of one's own individuality. She refers to the forcible attack on individual freedom by hostile governments. For example, in a debate with the Soviet delegate at the United Nations, Roosevelt claims, "[we] are trying to develop ideas which will be broader in outlook, which will consider first the rights of man, which will consider what makes man more free: not governments, but man."[74] In light of such a statement, it may seem spurious to compare the kind of individuality asserted by a spirit of adventure and the kind of individuality upheld by human rights. They look like apples and oranges: one calls for the moral courage to be oneself, the other establishes protections for that courage to be safely practiced in the first place.

Yet it is essential to remember that human rights are more than a legal or constitutional device. They are a way of life; or more exactly, they are a tool with which to craft a way of life. That is the crux of a major address she gave on human rights at the Sorbonne in 1948.

> The basic problem confronting the world today, as I said in the beginning, is the preservation of human freedom for the individual and consequently for the society of which he is a part. We are fighting this battle again today as it was fought at the time of the French Revolution and at the time of the American Revolution. The issue of human liberty is as decisive now as it was then. I want to give you my conception of what is meant in my country by freedom of the individual.
>
> Long ago in London during a discussion with [my Russian colleague] Mr. Vyshinky, he told me that there was no such thing as freedom for the individual in the world. All freedom of the individual was conditioned by the rights of other individuals. That, of course, I granted. I said: "We approach the question from a different point of view; we here in the United Nations are trying to develop ideals which will be broader in outlook, which will consider first the rights of man, which will consider what makes man more free: not governments, but man. . . .
>
> Freedom for our peoples is not only a right, but also a tool. Freedom of speech, freedom of the press, freedom of information, freedom of assembly—these are not just abstract ideals to us; they are tools with which we create a way of life in which we can enjoy freedom.[75]

These are difficult remarks to interpret. A helpful starting point is the dispute Roosevelt mentions between herself and Andrey Vyshinky, the Soviet diplomat and jurist. The criticism he makes of human rights is as old as Edmund Burke: human rights are a nonsensical idea because the absolute freedom of the individual is incompatible with the rights of others and hence with social life. Roosevelt's reply is at once polite and withering. She agrees with Vyshinky given his definition of human rights; the trouble, however, is that his definition is misguided. What is at stake in human rights—and in her case, in framing a declaration of human rights—is not how to assert or to limit the absolute freedom of individuals. It is, instead, how to create a way of life based on the preservation of individual freedom. And that, she says, is why it is necessary to "consider first the rights of man." Not because such rights trump other people's claims, as Vyshinky seems to think. And not primarily in order to set up a legal framework so that the freedom of many individuals can coexist. Her reason is that human rights are a tool to establish a way of life in which "human freedom for the individual" is enjoyed.

What does this grand vision look like? When Roosevelt advocates "human freedom for the individual," what is she talking about? In the final paragraph she lists a series of specific freedoms to give it substance: of speech, of the press, of information, and of assembly. But here is the crucial point: these freedoms are not distinct from human rights. These freedoms *are* human rights. They are the core civil and political rights of the Declaration that Roosevelt was in the process of drafting. Thus, when Roosevelt states that "freedom for our peoples is not only a right, but also a tool," it must be taken with a grain of salt. She is not setting up an opposition between concrete freedoms on the one hand and abstract human rights on the other. That would be incomprehensible in light of her repeatedly stated view that human rights are meaningful and powerful only to the extent that they become a way of life. The purpose of this statement, rather, is to urge us to see human rights from a wider perspective. Human rights are more than laws and rules—more than just "rights" in the sense of legal entitlements. They are even more than constitutional principles to safeguard freedom for the individual. They are a living, breathing way of life. To recall Roosevelt's emphatic words, human rights *are* the world of the individual: "the neighborhood he lives in; the school or college he attends; the factory, farm or office where he works."[76]

A direct link emerges here between a spirit of adventure and human rights. A "way of life" built upon human rights is not just any old way of life. Its content is neither neutral nor indifferent. It is ethically and existentially thick. It is, for Roosevelt, a comprehensive way of life in which the actual exercise of individual freedoms—that is, the real practice of individual freedoms, as opposed to their mere availability—constitutes everyday existence. It is a way of life, in other words, in which self-determination in the broadest sense, as the exercise of personal freedoms of speech, press, information, and assembly, exists not merely in the sense of being enshrined and respected by constitutions, laws, and courts, but *is* a reality asserted and lived by the individual in his or her everyday life.

What is this but a spirit of adventure? It is a way of life that is constitutively independent, self-determining, and individual. More to the point, it is a way of life that counteracts the great scourge of her age: conformity and collectivism, the difficulty of the individual "to remember that he is himself a unique human being."[77] To be clear, Roosevelt is not forcing anyone down a particular path of human flourishing. No one is obliged to put his or her human rights into practice as a way of life. It is perfectly possible—and in an age of conformity, perfectly likely—for human rights to remain legal or constitutional norms and mechanisms that don't become integrated into an ethic and mode of existence.

All Roosevelt says is that if human rights are genuinely made into a way of life, then *this* is what such a life looks like. It is a style of existence that repudiates collectivism in all of its guises: not just in terms of fighting against external repression of our rights, but also of overcoming a personal reluctance—call it timidity—to make our individuality (i.e., our freedom and self-determination) known.

Perhaps it is this similarity between human rights as a way of life and a spirit of adventure that leads Roosevelt to title the bleakest chapter of her oeuvre, the one in which the individual is most mired by his or her own desire for conformity, "The Right to Be an Individual."[78] On first impression, this seems like an odd choice for a chapter that makes no mention of legal or political rights. And yet, if we keep in mind her reflections on the purpose and value of human rights "as a way of life," this title and chapter is one more assertion of her belief that individuality (and most importantly, the desire for individuality) can be reclaimed by right, that is to say, through rights. To borrow a term from that chapter, a person who crafts a way of life based on freedoms enshrined in human rights will truly be what she calls a "success": someone who has developed him or herself to the utmost and who contributes to a broader shared world.[79]

Human rights as a way of life satisfies one half of a spirit of adventure: the assertion of one's own individuality and self-determination as an end in itself. What about the other half—openness and receptivity to other people? On this point, the link is less direct: a commitment to human rights matches the letter but not the spirit, as it were, of a spirit of adventure. Both involve learning to "see" and to honor the other person in his or her own singularity, but for different reasons. With a spirit of adventure, the aim is to profit from the encounter: to use it as an opportunity for you yourself to learn and grow. But when Roosevelt discusses human rights, along with principles of universal dignity, equality, and respect for the other, she does not highlight this goal of personal enhancement. Her focus is on the need to acknowledge the equal legal and moral status of the other, and to recognize his or her individuality. These are the concerns that drive her appeals for universal respect and dignity. Here are two representative passages:

> [Respect], I think, is a noble word, an indication of a certain attitude
> toward one's fellow men. Used too often in a subservient sense, it is more
> properly a token of equality. To respect one's fellow men is perhaps more
> difficult than to "love" them in a wide, vague sense. In fact, it is possible
> that to feel respect for mankind is better than to feel love for it. Love
> can be misguided and do as much harm as good, but respect can do only

good. It assumes that the other person's stature is as large as one's own, his rights as reasonable, his needs as important.[80]

And:

What is needed is really not a self-conscious virtue which makes us treat our neighbors as we want to be treated, but an acceptance of the fact that all human beings have dignity and the potentiality of development into the same kind of people we ourselves are. When we look at each individual without thinking of him as a Jew or as a Negro, but only as a person, then we may get to like him or we may dislike him, but he stands on his own feet as an individual and we stand with him on an equal basis.[81]

According to Roosevelt, there are excellent reasons why all human beings should be accorded equal legal and moral respect. It will make the world a better and kinder place. It will also make the world a safer place by giving shining examples as to how democracy and decency can flourish. Yet she does not claim that according universal respect for the other through human rights is ultimately in service of the self and of cultivating the self. When Roosevelt says of the Declaration, "there will be provisions which will entail a change of attitude toward the value of the individual," it is a statement of respect for the other for the sake of the other.[82] She gives voice to a change of attitude—moral initially, but potentially also legal and political—that the world desperately needs.

That said, here too we find a striking congruence between human rights and a spirit of adventure. We might even say that the universal dignity and respect for the other enshrined by human rights is an essential condition, a sort of propaedeutic, for a spirit of adventure. For proof we need only continue the passage from *You Learn by Living* I cited earlier, in which Roosevelt explains "how to get the best out of people" in terms of searching for hidden "treasure," that is, for material you can use to learn and grow. As she makes clear, success in this search does not depend on an intrinsically captivating other person. What is required is a talent for sifting out what is unique and valuable in any given interlocutor. For that you need two special skills: "If such a search [for treasure] is to be successful, you will need two qualities which you can develop by practice. One is the ability to be a good listener. The other is the imaginative ability to put yourself in the other person's place; to try to discover what he is thinking and feeling; to understand as far as you can the background from which he came, the soil out of which his roots have grown, the customs and beliefs and ideas which have shaped his thinking."[83] A message Roosevelt repeats time and again is that people graced with a spirit of adventure are made and not just born. It takes training and—a watchword of hers—"self-discipline."[84] You need to learn how to listen, which signifies an ability to hear the distinctive voice of the other person. You must also become able to "put yourself in the other person's place" and to imagine how they are, as Richard Rorty might put it, "people like us."[85]

Commitment to human rights is not some magical path to a spirit of adventure. But it does remove the main obstacles to it. First, human rights teach us to see the other person not as a type—for example, not as a "Jew" or a "Negro," to use Roosevelt's categories—but as a person: someone to whom we can listen (and like or dislike, as the case may be) rather than fear or ignore in blanket fashion. Second, by affirming the equal moral and legal status of all human beings, human rights open a horizon for empathetic awareness, that is, an ability to project ourselves into the shoes of the other person, and to potentially come to see and care about vulnerabilities unlike our own. In short, human rights impart the two crucial virtues (listening and empathetic awareness) needed to encounter other people in a spirit of adventure.

If we are thus to cultivate a spirit of adventure—and remember that for Roosevelt this is single best way to care for ourselves in the face of conformity and collectivism—it is necessary for human rights to become a way of life. Human rights prepare or train a subject able to appreciate—that is, to really see and listen to—what is individual and irreplaceable in other people. It is the sine qua non of a spirit of adventure.

A remark from Roosevelt's speech at the Sorbonne gives us a nice place to conclude. On first impression, it seems like a commonplace. In drafting the Declaration, she says, "we have put down the rights that we consider basic for individual beings the world over to have. Without them, we feel that the full development of individual personality is impossible."[86] Her plain meaning is that the Declaration sets out to provide a framework of rights in which the full development of the individual person is possible. The Declaration would, in this respect, establish a protected space, that is, a kind of legal and political structure or shelter, for people to live and grow under. But there is another interpretation of her remark, fully compatible with this one. Read in the context of her writings on personal development and a spirit of adventure, and also her persistent attempts to instill human rights as a way of life, Roosevelt could also be seen to say that the "full development of the individual personality" is possible only if the rights laid out in the Declaration are adopted as a personal ethic. In this respect, the Declaration offers more to individuals than a space to flourish. Flourishing hinges on the degree to which the rights proclaimed by the Declaration are assimilated into a desire to be and to live a certain way.

[8]

AN ETHIC OF RESISTANCE II: MALIK AND
THE UNIVERSAL DECLARATION OF HUMAN RIGHTS

Charles Malik is widely acknowledged as a central figure—by some accounts, *the* central figure—in the drafting of the Universal Declaration of Human Rights. Johannes Morsink places him in the "inner core" of the Human Rights Commission.[1] Mary Ann Glendon credits Roosevelt and Malik as co-responsible for the triumph of the Declaration.[2] Samuel Moyn calls him "perhaps the key figure in the negotiations."[3] And Glenn Mitoma writes, "With the possible exception of John Humphrey, no individual contributed more" to the UN's human rights program.[4] Part of this reputation is due to Malik being seen as the intellectual heavyweight of the Human Rights Commission. But just as important is his extraordinary institutional placement in the United Nations, which allowed him to shepherd the Declaration through virtually every stage. Within a two-year span, he was a member of the small committee that prepared the early draft of the Declaration, rapporteur of the Human Rights Commission that debated it, president of the Economic and Social Council that revised it, and chairman of the UN's Third Committee on Social, Humanitarian, and Cultural Affairs that presented it to the General Assembly. All of these positions interlocked, and no one was more astonished than Malik himself: "Nothing has been odder than for me, as Commission rapporteur, to submit the Commission's draft Declaration to myself, as Economic and Social Council president, at its summer session in Geneva, and then to find myself, as Economic and Social

Council president again submitting to myself as the General Assembly's Third Committee chairman, the draft text the General Assembly passed on to the Economic and Social Council. Thus, the rapporteur of the Commission, the president of the Council, and the chairman of the Third Commission were all one and the same person."[5]

For all his skill and success we might get the impression that Malik was a born and bred diplomat. But that is far from true. He was an academic by training and disposition, and his diary from this period tells of a sense of himself as badly out of place in the world of politics and diplomacy. "I do not belong in this crowd of unreality and untruth," he wrote after his first big soirée with political and economic leaders in 1944.[6] And these were not just early misgivings. It seems, in fact, that his time on the Human Rights Commission only amplified them. Consider a diary entry from 1948. If we close our eyes to the context, it seems almost to come straight out of a novel by Sartre!

> I went to the Council room this morning in the car alone. I sat there at the Council table alone. I almost sat at lunch alone, but for the kindness of the Yugoslav delegate who asked me to sit with him. Last evening I was all alone back at the hotel. When I returned this afternoon I returned in the car alone. I am now all alone eating at the restaurant of the hotel. A feeling of void and blankness overtakes me. I must bear my loneliness. Drink and sex can never relieve it. On the contrary, they cover it up, for a time only. Then it comes back with added force. It cannot be evaded, it must be faced.[7]

As an interpretive strategy, it would be risky to make too much of Malik's state of mind at the time. One observation, though, strikes me as pertinent. It is that Malik does not set aside his malaise when he goes to work on the Human Rights Commission. He does not put on a "diplomatic face," so to speak, and restrict his sense of alienation, even of anomie, to private life—as if these were things to be confided only to friends or scribbled into a diary. His disenchantment is central to his vision of the Declaration and his contribution in drafting it.

I do not mean that Malik held himself aloof from his colleagues or viewed his solitude as having anything to do with them. By all accounts he was a model colleague and effective collaborator.[8] I mean that his malaise stems from his assessment of his contemporary world, and that it is this assessment (and its resultant malaise) that inspires his diplomatic and philosophical work on the Declaration. Malik, we will see, believes that the modern age as a whole (and not just his present moment, which is only its culmination) has gone awry. Gripped as it is by the combined forces of materialism, secularism, and collectivism, modernity has led to spiritual, political, and humanitarian crisis. And if Malik has great aspirations for the Declaration, and if he argues so tenaciously to guide it in certain directions, it is because he believes that it offers the best chance for humanity to right itself—to "reboot" itself, to use a metaphor that would have made him cringe—by redefining what the human being truly is and needs. Put this way, the sensibility that apparently makes Malik unsuited to the world of politics and diplomacy, and which causes him almost visceral revulsion for it, is the source of his intellectual and moral energy in drafting the Declaration.

Malik the Unmodern

Malik is a decidedly "unmodern" philosopher of human rights. My claim in this chapter is that he conceives of human rights as a spiritual and political antidote to modernity. But he is also unmodern in another respect, one that he could not have anticipated. A prominent approach in the contemporary philosophy of human rights, as well as in political philosophy more generally, is resolutely "post-metaphysical." This line of argument spans thinkers as diverse as John Rawls, Michael Ignatieff, Martha Nussbaum, Jürgen Habermas, Claude Lefort, and Richard Rorty, who argue that it is both unnecessary and undesirable to search for the source of human rights.[9] In this view, human rights are purely a political instrument devised to protect human beings, and attempts to find a deeper and more secure foundation for them are controversial, ineffective, and potentially a symbolic violence. Rorty gives a nice summary in his criticism of attempts to identify a deep ground for human rights:

> As I see it, one important intellectual advance that has been made in our century is the steady decline in interest in this quarrel [among philosophers] about what we are really like. There is growing willingness to neglect the question "What is our nature?" and to substitute the question "What can we make of ourselves?" We are much less inclined than our ancestors were to take "theories of human nature" seriously, much less inclined to take ontology or history or ethology as a guide to life. We are much less inclined to pose the ontological question "What *are* we?" because we have come to see that the main lesson of both history and anthropology is our extraordinary malleability. We are coming to think of ourselves as the flexible, protean, self-shaping animal rather than as the rational animal or the cruel animal.[10]

In short, contemporary post-metaphysical perspectives urge us to refrain from searching for an ahistorical, transcultural source of human rights. Questions like "What is our nature?" or "What is really the foundation of human rights?" get us nowhere. Worse, they saddle human rights law and theory with an ethnocentrism that vitiates any aspiration to universality and legitimacy they might have.[11]

If this is the state of one major branch of the contemporary philosophy of human rights, Malik could not be further from it. More to the point, he would have regarded it as another symptom of our all too modern tendency to avoid real issues. And perhaps one reason Malik is so little read today—beyond, that is, by scholars of the mid-century history of human rights—is that he treats human rights from a maximally "metaphysical" perspective. The cornerstone of his philosophy is that human rights must be grounded in the unchanging nature of human beings. And the cornerstone of his diplomacy is that it is up to the Human Rights Commission to define what that nature is.

Malik expresses his stance with admirable directness in several places. One occasion is a meeting of the Economic and Social Council on March 14, 1947, to review an early draft of the Declaration:

[This Bill of Human Rights] will elaborate what are called human rights, or rights of man. Obviously, the very phrase means that man in his own essence has certain rights; that therefore, what we are going to elaborate must answer to the nature and essence of man. Therefore, it must not be accidental. It certainly must not be changing with time and place. The Bill of Rights must define the nature and essence of man. It will reflect what we regard human nature to be. It will, in essence, be an answer to the question: "What is man?" It will be the United Nations' answer to this question. It will, in short, give meaning to the phrase, "worth and dignity of man," which is found in the Preamble of the Charter.[12]

Listening to Malik it is hard to miss that he sees himself at the center of a world historic event—of that rarest type of event that combines philosophical and political significance. But we must be clear. Malik does not think that the drafting of the Declaration is momentous in and of itself: as if this event was destined for greatness in advance and that he and his colleagues, luckily or not, happen to find themselves in it. It is the other way around: the drafting of the Declaration will be a world historic event only if he and his colleagues take it upon themselves to make it so. And how do they do that? By asking the right kinds of deep philosophical or "metaphysical" questions.

Malik's retrospectives on the Declaration can make it seem as if this happened of its own accord—as if such questions were brought forth by the sheer necessity of the moment. Writing in 1949 with the comfort of hindsight, he states: "Nothing is more repaying to the thoughtful student of the present ideological situation than to read and ponder, in all their prolonged, dramatic richness, the records of our debates in subcommittee, in commission, in council, in committee and in plenary. Here you have the exciting drama of man seeking to grasp himself."[13] But, as anyone who has read the transcripts of these meetings can attest, this retrospection obscures what actually happened in session. Big philosophical questions did not ask themselves. Malik himself insisted on posing them. It was Malik, in other words, who was determined to see particular fundamental questions—"What is man?" "What does the worth and dignity of man consist in?"—debated on a world stage.[14]

To be frank, his colleagues were not always game. Like contemporary philosophers, they too shied away from asking "What is man?" on the ground that it is unanswerable or else that any attempt to answer it would be divisive and counterproductive. At times they tried to steer Malik toward less controversial and less speculative shores.[15] On other occasions they met his proposals with indifference or silence.[16] They also more or less explicitly rebuffed the approach he favored. For proof we need only consult a widely cited anecdote from the drafting of the Declaration. It does not directly concern Malik, yet it shows the atmosphere he was up against. One fine day in 1947, the story goes, Jacques Maritain, the eminent philosopher who headed UNESCO's Committee on the Theoretical Bases of Human Rights, was asked how it was possible for so many opposed ideologies to agree on a single list of fundamental rights. His reply has become a parable for post-metaphysical thinking: "Yes, we agree about the rights, *providing we are not asked why.*"[17] It would seem a post-metaphysical attitude is thus not strictly a contemporary artifact. Seventy years ago, at the birth of the international human rights movement, theorists and practitioners were mindful to set such concerns to the side.

The question for us is, why can't Malik? Why does he insist on the issue of human nature being front and center in the drafting of the Declaration? Why, moreover, is it so important that the Human Rights Commission define human nature?

The one-word answer, in equal parts true and misleading, is: communism. A claim I made in the previous chapter is that for Malik, as well as for Roosevelt, the major threat to human rights in his day is communism and its subordination of individuals and the rights of individuals to groups and the rights of groups. Malik, the reader will recall, was wary of the Soviet Union's participation on the Human Rights Commission because he believed it used the cause of social and economic rights as a vehicle to assert and to disguise the predominance of the state over the individual.

However, when we look to the drafting records, as well as to Malik's many retrospectives on the Declaration, it is evident that his dispute with communism over the priority of social and economic rights has deeper roots. It concerns the very nature and definition of the human being. To use terms I will need to clarify, Malik holds that communism conceives of the human being as "animal," whereas he conceives of the human being as "spiritual." This is the thrust of an important remark he makes in the same March 14 meeting of the Economic and Social Council I cited above:

> There will be lots of talk, Mr. President, about houses and housing, about instruments and tools, and automobiles and standards of living, about wages, and all that sort of thing. There will be lots of talk also about the needs of our subhuman existence, about our impulses and our instincts, our bodies and our bodily functions, about our health, and even about our dreams, as in the case of a shady school of thought.
>
> We believe, Mr. President, that there is a real danger that the subhuman in man and outside man may be confused with what man is in himself. It may be that the subhuman was submerged in the past. It may be that we must now put it in its proper place. It may be that attention was not sufficiently given to things, instruments and conditions, namely to empty stomachs, comfortable chairs and fast automobiles. But this does not mean, in our view, Mr. President, that these things and conditions of life should be allowed to overwhelm what is distinctly human in man. We believe every effort must be made to check this rise of the lower, the subhuman, the merely instrumental, and therefore to enshrine man in his proper place, especially in the formulation of the Bill of Human Rights.[18]

The word *subhuman* appears four times in these lines. Malik uses it to designate our biological or animal needs and comforts. And the prefix *sub* leaves little doubt as to the value he assigns it: it is the "lower," "merely instrumental" condition of human existence which must not, under any circumstances, be confused with "what is distinctly human in man." Yet it is precisely this confusion that he worries many of his fellow delegates at the United Nations are guilty of. They do not, of course, come right out and say that humans are first and foremost biological beings. But for Malik they don't have to. The priority they assign to economic and social rights speaks volumes. For as I said above, Malik believes that privileging this class of rights—for example, to a fair wage, decent housing, and adequate standards of living—works as a Trojan horse to sneak into the Declaration, and hence into the preeminent moral and aspirational document of his (and our) time, a conception of the human being as nothing more than a bundle of biologically satisfiable needs.

With this in mind, the purpose of his remarks at the Economic and Social Council is thrown into relief. In effect, he throws down the gauntlet to his colleagues at the United Nations and asks, "Do you really think that this is what human nature is? Are we no more than that?!" His point is not, as he makes plain, that material needs are unimportant and can be left out of the Declaration. It is, instead, that prioritizing this class of rights, as if it represented the core of the Declaration they are in the midst of drafting, assumes and advances an inverted notion of human nature. And that is exactly what he thinks communists and their sympathizers do.

Communism, however, is just the tip of the iceberg. That is why I suggested it is as misleading as it is true to identify communism as the reason why Malik insists on defining human nature in the Declaration. To put the issue in these terms does not do justice to the scope of the problem he perceives. Communism is merely epiphenomenal. It is the latest, if the most strident and militant, version of psychological and political forces that have been at work for centuries. And only when we register this fact (i.e., only when we appreciate that communism is the culmination of defining tendencies of modernity), can we understand why it is imperative for Malik to define human nature in the Declaration—one way or the other. For if he wins, and if his definition prevails, then the Declaration will have installed a subject to counteract the forces he identifies. But even if he loses, and human nature ends up defined in explicitly materialist terms, then at least he will have succeeded in forcing the issue into the open. In this scenario the Declaration would stand as the emblem for all that Malik opposes. Still, defeat would not be without a silver lining. It would make the modern fly its true colors and lose the advantage of being subterranean. It would, to borrow a term from Carl Schmitt, reveal Malik's enemy for all to see.[19]

Malik makes these connections between communism, modernity, human rights, and the Declaration explicit in an important speech, given only months after the Declaration was ratified by the General Assembly:

> Materialism is much deeper than Marxism. It is man's natural tendency to flee his personal responsibility and to seek his rest in the guarantee of external things, whether they are his bank account, or his property, or the guarantee of his society or his government. It is flight from the creator, in whom alone there is security, in the direction of creatures and things. I submit that this flight is universal today, and that Russia is only carrying

it to its absolute logical conclusion. People everywhere seek their liveli-
hood rather than the source of their life; they want to secure for themselves the endless variety of material comforts rather than the simple few
virtues of the mind and spirit. The Charter speaks of "higher standards
of living": it never speaks of higher standards of feeling, or valuation, or
thinking, or spiritual perception. There is a tendency then to interpret
man in terms of material and economic conditions. The meaning of the
old choice between gaining the whole world and losing one's own soul is
practically lost. The concupiscence of things has overwhelmed the soul.
In the genesis of the Declaration we had to resist the seductiveness of
security at every turn. I believe we ought to have resisted it more. But
the Declaration does retain, I think, as much of the original integrity and
freedom of man as is humanly possible under the terrific materialistic
pressures of the age.[20]

If I had to select a single passage to represent Malik's philosophical and practical approach to human rights, this would be it. It encapsulates two key features
of his thought. First is the magnitude of his problématique: it is materialism,
and not merely Marxism or communism, that human rights must counteract.
Second is the object of his critique: the danger materialism poses to the spiritual wellness of individual human beings. I will treat each feature in turn as it
brings us to how Malik envisages human rights in terms of care for the self—
and indeed, as I will come to call it, care for the soul.

It is best to begin with the basic question: What does Malik mean by "materialism"? Many things, as is plain from this passage. This word marks out a
preference for material comforts and possessions rather than spiritual values:
"the concupiscence of things." It also designates secularism: "flight from the
creator." And last, though less prominently in this specific passage, it refers to
collectivism: an urge to seek our "rest," that is to say, our peace and well-being,
in "society" or "government." Materialism is thus a many-headed beast. It includes the dictionary definition of the word, namely a tendency to consider
material possessions and physical comfort as more important than spiritual
values. But Malik draws two additional components into its orbit: secularism
and collectivism. And it is precisely this unholy trinity—of materialism, secularism, and collectivism—that he elsewhere identifies as the essence of the
modern age. Consider the opening lines of a speech he gave in 1961:

The Communist tide has been rising for 43 years. Having regard to the
prepared antecedent situation which occasioned its rise we must say that
this phenomenon has been tracing itself on the horizon of history for at

least two centuries. The spiritual climate without which Communism could not arise, and if it arose it could not prosper, includes three elements: secularism, materialism, and collectivism. The complete secularization of human affairs, since the breakdown of the Middle Ages, the radical divorce of history from anything above and beyond history, the relativization of all values, the exultant affirmation of the death of God and of the absolute self-sufficiency of man, the bewitching lure of science and progress and all that is visible and sensible and sensuous, the pride of culture and civilization and human achievement—all these things, without which there can be no Communism and certainly no Communist movement, can be clearly traced to the Age of the Enlightenment in the eighteenth century.[21]

Taking his cue perhaps from Kierkegaard, Malik often makes reference in his work to "the age" in which he lives and writes. Here we see the full scope of this term. "The age" in question isn't communist, exactly. It is modern. "The Age of Enlightenment," as he says above, is centuries old and continues to this day. Thus, when at the end of the previous passage, Malik observes that the Declaration was drafted "under the terrific materialistic pressures of the age," we need to keep this vast historical scale in mind. "The age" comprises more than Marxism, and its "terrific materialism" goes beyond a hunger for material possessions and physical comforts. In reality, the Declaration is drafted in and against an atmosphere of materialism, secularism, and collectivism that has been pervasive ever since the Enlightenment. Consider too another remark from that same passage, when Malik says that in in drafting the Declaration "we had to resist the seductiveness of security at every turn." Here again he speaks and operates at the grand level of "the age." More is meant by the "seductiveness of security" than the social and economic security demanded by communist delegates on the Human Rights Commission. This phrase, rather, names an epochal tendency to interpret human welfare "in terms"—and I add, only in terms—"of material and economic conditions." It is Malik's criticism of an age that wants only to secure "higher standards of living" rather than strive for "higher standards of feeling, or valuation, or thinking, or spiritual perception."

With this critique of his age in mind, it becomes clear why Malik insists that human nature be defined in the Declaration, even if many of his colleagues would prefer to leave the question alone. He does not do so, as contemporary post-metaphysical philosophers might assume, in order to gain a solid epistemic foundation for human rights. The stakes are higher than simply "knowing" the essence of human beings so as to recognize which inherent rights flow from it. Malik's true concerns, if I can put it this way, are ethical and ontological. He is convinced that his fellow drafters will not succeed in remaining neutral and open-minded about the definition of human nature simply by refusing to talk about it. On the contrary, they will be oriented by the unspoken definition of man as secular, collectivist, and materialist that the modern age takes for granted. Wittingly or not, they will have played right into the hands of the forces that Malik seeks to use human rights to protect us from.

This point bears repeating. According to Malik, the split dividing the drafters of the Declaration is not between a "pro-human rights" camp and an "anti-human rights" camp. It is between two rival visions of human rights, and ultimately, of humanity. The task of the Human Rights Commission is to determine the relative weight of these visions in the document.

Allow me to state this as simply as possible. For Malik, there are two classes of human rights. To use the conventional categories, there are civil and political rights, and there are social and economic rights. Malik wants both classes to be included in the Declaration.[22] But he also thinks they address different dimensions of the human being. Civil and political rights protect our spiritual nature. This includes freedom to worship, to think and express oneself, to vote, to take part in political life, and to have access to information. Social and economic rights protect our material (or animal) nature. This includes our right to work, the right to an adequate standard of living, the right to health and security, and the right to education. And herein lies the challenge Malik poses to his fellow drafters. They must, of course, include both classes of rights in the Declaration and craft a single, unified document. Doing so, however, requires that they balance and codify the great split in the human personality as a spiritual and animal being. They must, in other words, give proper expression to the duality of human nature. And this, in sum, is Malik's great ambition: to acknowledge in the Declaration, and yet also to subordinate, the material dimension of human nature that the modern age mistakes for the whole.

Did he succeed? Yes and no. Judging from "The Challenge of Human Rights," Malik seems pleased with the efforts of the Human Rights Commission. The Declaration manages to retain "as much of the original integrity and freedom of man as is humanly possible under the terrific materialistic pressures of the age." Compromises were made, naturally. No explicit definition of human nature— that is, of the "Man is x, y, z" variety—was included. Moreover, a special disappointment for Malik was the deletion late in the drafting process of the words *by nature* in Article 1, which had initially stated that all human beings were "endowed by nature with reason and conscience."[23] As Malik told Philippe de la Chapelle in a later interview, he had hoped to preserve this reference as an allusion to Christian natural law theory and thus reintroduce an implicit definition of humankind.[24]

Yet Malik also had victories. He felt vindicated by the mention in the Preamble of the "recognition of the inherent dignity" and "inalienable rights of mankind," which for him recuperated the loss of the term *by nature* in Article 1.[25] He was also instrumental in drafting two articles close to his heart. Article 18 upholds freedom of thought and, at his insistence, explicitly "includes the freedom to change [one's] religion or belief." For him this article was a crucial bulwark against collectivism and state-sponsored religions and ideologies.[26] And in Article 16 he was able to add a crucial description of the family as "the natural and fundamental group unit of society." For Malik this phrase was another key buffer that could defend the individual from state pressure, in this case by fortifying and naturalizing the family as the core institution of civil society.[27]

This is not the place to detail Malik's specific contributions to the Declaration. That has already been expertly done.[28] I would like instead to address the second key feature of Malik's thought on human rights that I flagged earlier: his critique of the spiritual and existential distress caused by modernity. Here our earlier passage on materialism is exemplary. In it Malik makes no mention of the social or political cost of materialism. Every single one of his criticisms is leveled at the spiritual damage it inflicts. He worries that we seek our happiness in things and groups, where it cannot be fulfilled (this is the danger of collectivism); that we turn away from God, in whom alone there is security and peace (this is the danger of secularism); and that we distract ourselves with material comforts instead of cultivating real virtues (this is the danger of materialism). Summing up all three dangers, Malik laments that modern individuals can no longer even register the choice they should make between gaining the world and gaining their soul. "The concupiscence of things" has settled it for them.

This is just one passage, granted. And elsewhere Malik does not fail to criticize materialism and communism for disastrous social and political consequences. He dedicated books, such as *Man in the Struggle for Peace*, as well as occasional pamphlets, such as *War and Peace* (1949) and *Survival in the Age of Revolution* (1972), to exposing the militaristic and undemocratic nature of the age. That said, the fact remains that Malik's critique of modernity, materialism, and communism is overwhelmingly spiritualist. This orientation can be detected in virtually every aspect of his writing. It comes across in his admiration of texts that attack modernity from an existential angle—his favorites being Heidegger's dissection of *das Man* and Dostoevsky's Grand Inquisitor.[29] It is expressed by his rhetorical preference for the second person singular, in which

Malik addresses "you," the reader, on a one-to-one (and quasi-pastoral) basis.[30] It is explicit in his characterization of modernity as "a total outlook on life" rather than as an economic or political doctrine.[31] And, most of all, it is revealed in the great ambition he sets for his work: to "roll back" the "profound spiritual maladies of secularism, materialism, and collectivism" with which Western civilization and "the Western soul" have been afflicted for centuries.[32]

How can this be done? How can the Western soul cure itself of the "spiritual maladies" which have taken hold of it? Such a massive task has no one solution. Yet human rights have an outsized role to play. In the next section I explain how Malik conceives of human rights as an aid for individuals to "roll back"—in themselves and for themselves, so to speak—all three modern spiritual afflictions. Human rights fight collectivism by reminding each human being that he or she is irreducibly individual. Human rights fight materialism by offering individuals a criterion to best rank the values on offer in the modern world. Last, human rights fight secularism by intimating to all those prepared to listen the prospect of a transcendent reality that not even modernity can eclipse. In short, human rights are dear to Malik because they have the potential to turn individuals against their own time and place.

With this in mind we can revisit my criticism of Joseph Slaughter from chapter 6. In *Human Rights, Inc.*, he claims that Malik deploys human rights "as a plot for 'the modernizing of the world.'"[33] We now see how mistaken that is. If anything, Malik hopes that human rights can assist individuals to loosen the grip of the modern age, and to challenge those degrading forms of life that had either gone unnoticed or were merely tolerated. He hopes, if I may drive home the title of this chapter, that human rights can engender an ethic of resistance against the modernization of self and world.

Human Rights and the Care of the Soul

One commentator describes Malik's desire to remake the modern world as "almost millennial."[34] That word is exactly right. *Millennial* captures his scope of centuries and ages. It denotes his desire for comprehensive political and psychical change. Most importantly, it conveys the defining feature of Malik's life and work: his Christianity.

If Malik's "metaphysical" approach is disfavored in human rights scholarship today, so too is his strongly Christian characterization of human rights. Samuel Moyn's *Christian Human Rights* (2015) is a good guide to this issue. In excavating the close connection between Christianity and human rights in the mid-twentieth century—or rather, the sudden appropriation by Christianity of a human rights discourse that it had historically kept at arm's length—Moyn observes how surprising and even unsavory this history is for secular, liberal, and generally left-wing devotees of human rights today. "Almost unfailingly," he writes, "the annunciation of human rights in the 1940s is now viewed by the general public and professional scholars as the uncomplicated triumph of liberal democracy. But the thesis of *Christian Human Rights* is that through this lost and misremembered transwar era, it is equally if not more viable to regard human rights as a project of the Christian right, not the secular left. Their creation brought about a break with the revolutionary tradition and its rights of man—or better put—a successful capture of that language by forces reformulating their conservatism."[35]

Malik does not feature prominently in *Christian Human Rights*. He falls slightly outside the interwar period Moyn examines. Also, Moyn focuses mainly on Catholicism, which was not, for all his indebtedness to Saint Thomas, Malik's own church.[36] But Moyn's book is handy to get a sense of the spirit of the times that immediately precedes the drafting of the Declaration.

Two features are relevant. The first is no great revelation but is nicely summarized by Moyn: the critique of materialism—in particular, the critique of the ubiquity of materialism—made by Christians in the early to mid-twentieth century. What is special about the Christian version of this critique is that it crosses political and ideological lines. Earlier we considered Malik's objection: materialism is not a specifically Marxist or communist disorder so much as a modern one that also encompasses liberal democracies. Moyn demonstrates that this very sentiment was a staple for the ascendant Christian movement of the time, personalism, and served as a common denominator for its many streams. "Personalists," he states, were united in the view "that capitalism and communism, apparent foes, deserved each other, and canceled each other out, in their common materialism."[37] A Christian critique of the ubiquity of materialism (in democracy *and* communism, in the West *and* the East) was thus already well in place within Malik's own religious and intellectual circles.

The second feature Moyn helps us to appreciate is the centerpiece of his book: the unexpected turn by Christians to human rights in the late 1930s and early 1940s. This turn is surprising because the Catholic Church had for the previous century and a half associated "the rights of man" with secularism, liberalism, and revolution—that is to say, with everything it sought to repudiate, or at least to contain. The turn was also unexpected because of the eminence of these new Christian defenders of human rights. Moyn begins his book with Pope Pius XII's Christmas Day message of 1942, in which he delivered five Peace Points, the first of which reads:

Dignity of the Human Person. He who would have the Star of Peace shine out and stand over society should cooperate, for his part, in giving back to the human person the dignity given to it by God from the very beginning. . . . He should uphold respect for and the practical realization of fundamental personal rights. The cure of this situation becomes feasible when we awaken again the consciousness of a juridical order resting on the supreme dominion of God, and safeguarded from all human whims; a consciousness of an order which stretches forth its arm, in protection or punishment, over the unforgettable rights of man and protects them against the attacks of every human power.[38]

Why the Catholic Church reaches for human rights in the late 1930s and early 1940s is a complicated story. A one-sentence summary of Moyn's answer is that the Church evokes human rights only once it has elevated the notions of human dignity and human personhood to the center of its theology and mission. Naturally, this answer commits him to explain why "dignity" and "personhood" became prominent at this moment in time. But this is not the place to retrace his steps. I want only to extract the following point: in the interwar period the Church (not to mention a great many lay Christians) began to appeal to human rights in order to safeguard human dignity.

Here we return to Malik. He puts his own twist on this Christian appeal to human rights to secure human dignity. Rather than focus on how human rights protect human dignity from outside attacks (by communist and fascist states, for example), Malik examines how human rights can help individuals to recover a human dignity they have willingly relinquished. Human rights help individuals to fight against themselves (*intra*-subjectively, as it were) by challenging their attachment to forces—materialism, collectivism, and secularism being the most prominent—that smother the human with the subhuman, the spiritual with the animal.

Put differently, Moyn's *Christian Human Rights* highlights two features of the interwar period that inform Malik's approach to human rights. The first is the Christian critique of the ubiquity of materialism. The second is the Christian appeal to human rights to protect dignity. Malik combines them in the following way: human rights protect human dignity by leading individuals to confront and resist a materialism that has, tragically, become ubiquitous in their own person. He takes human rights to be the best placed institution to remind all human beings of their own humanity—that is, of their dignity and personhood—from within an age designed to tempt it away. That is why this philosopher and theologian devotes a lifetime to the legal, diplomatic, and political advancement of the international human rights movement.

I have titled this section "Human Rights and the Care of the Soul" to reflect the Christian stamp Malik gives to the relation between human rights and care of the self. But before diving into how human rights specifically combat materialism, collectivism, and secularism, I need to establish that Malik conceives of human rights in terms of care of the self.

The reader will recall that I identified three criteria for the care of the self in chapter 1. First, care of the self prioritizes personal transformation and the cultivation of the self (a "poetics of the self," in Foucault's words). Second, care of the self is nonprescriptive in that people care for themselves because they choose to, not on pain of an externally applied penalty. Third, care for the self is a stand-alone moral end: it is not merely preparatory labor for the care of others.

Malik, like Roosevelt, never wrote a dedicated treatise on human rights. That is why I have had to reconstruct the connection they establish between human rights and care of the self by focusing on choice passages. Fortunately, Malik left us a virtual microcosm of all three criteria of care of the self. It is from his essay "The Challenge of Human Rights," in which, once again, he formulates the promise of human rights in terms of spiritual redemption.

> Under this external social and material pressure, man is about to be completely lost. What is needed therefore is to reaffirm for him his essential humanity. He needs to be reminded that he is born free and equal in dignity and rights with his fellow men. He needs to know that he is endowed by nature with reason and conscience. He must know that he cannot be held in slavery or servitude, that he cannot be subjected to arbitrary arrest, and that he is presumed innocent until proven guilty. He must remember that his person is inviolable, that he has the natural right to freedom of thought, conscience, religion, and expression, and so on down the list of proclaimed rights. This reaffirmation, if only he heeds it, might still save him from being dehumanized. Society and the state under modern conditions can take perfect care of themselves: they have advocates and sponsors on every side: their rights are in good hands. It is man, the real, existing, anxious, laughing, free and dying man, who is in danger of becoming extinct. It is man who is the unprotected orphan, the neglected ward, and the forgotten treasure. Therefore, it is good that the Declaration has not lost sight of its main objective: to proclaim man's

irreducible humanity to the end that he may yet recover his creative sense of dignity and reestablish his faith in himself.[39]

The first criterion for care of the self—personal transformation—shines through in this passage. Consider Malik's trio of R words: the Declaration "reaffirms" our humanity, it "reminds" us of our dignity, and it helps us to "remember" our inviolability. His message is not that the Declaration tells people anything new or informs them of anything they do not already know. Its purpose is instead to lead individuals to recognize that they already hold these truths—or better, to recognize that they already *are* these truths—and, through this recognition, transform their self-understanding and way of life.[40] Put differently, this passage depicts the mission of human rights as the performative and personal realization of our humanity. The goal of the Declaration is to transform the relation we have to the knowledge of our own dignity and humanity: from a notional assent that sits comfortably alongside the life we currently lead to a real assent that prompts a genuine transformation of our own existence.

Moving to the second criterion, Malik depicts the Declaration in nonprescriptive terms: as a document that individuals may, if they so choose, incorporate as a way of life. Now, there is no question for Malik that human rights must commit governments. He was an early and avid proponent on the Human Rights Commission for a detailed and binding implementation mechanism.[41] But the need to prescribe rules and norms for governments is not at issue in this passage. What is at stake is whether or not individuals will turn to the Declaration in order to reaffirm their humanity. And his conclusion? They probably won't. His laconic little phrase says it all: "This reaffirmation, *if only he heeds it,* might still save him from being dehumanized." In an age of tremendous materialism, Malik is nothing if not clear-eyed. He knows that the truths of human rights will remain unseized by those he thinks of as "completely lost." And so even if the Declaration is a tonic for the age, one "prescribed" by Dr. Malik, in the end it is up to individuals whether or not they will take their medicine.

And why should they? Here we come to the third criterion of care of the self: it is a self-sufficient moral end and not preparatory labor for care of other people. The key sentence here is the one in which Malik names his true subject, the subject he hopes human rights can recuperate: "It is man, the real, existing, anxious, laughing, free and dying man, who is in danger of becoming extinct." Now, Malik uses versions of this formula—of man as "free," "anxious," "laughing," and all the rest—fairly often.[42] His idea is that these qualities and moods are not given or coextensive with human nature itself. Not everyone in our day and age "laughs," for example. These qualities and moods are achievements.

Malik wants people to become able to exist, to laugh, even to be anxious (he is a student of Heidegger, after all). Anxiety, for example, is a self-finding (*Befindlichkeit*), a mood in which we discover something essential about ourselves.

That is what human rights do. Human rights are therapeutic, a form and practice of self-care, because they work to restore "man" to his or her own full humanity. And for Malik this is far from a theoretical exercise, as if the "humanity" human rights protected were just some abstract essence or quality. The humanity at stake, rather, consists of personal, concrete, joyful, and what Malik (again, following Heidegger) calls "authentic" ways of being in the world. Thus, when the Declaration sets out to "proclaim man's irreducible humanity" so that "he may yet recover his creative sense of dignity and reestablish faith in himself," it is for the sake of man himself—and not "man" in general but men, that is, people, and people in their everyday life and innermost being. It is to care for ourselves that Malik recommends human rights to all human beings.

I can be more precise. Malik warns that joyful and authentic ways of being— or joyful and authentic beings, full stop—are "in danger of becoming extinct." We know why: collectivism, materialism, and secularism. It will thus come as no surprise that, for Malik, human rights fight for our soul on all three fronts.

I will be brief on the topic of collectivism as it has been prominent in this chapter and the last. But consider the following statement. At a meeting of the Human Rights Commission, Malik expresses a point of view which, coming from almost anyone else, would seem like boilerplate liberalism. "I am asking this question," he says to his fellow delegates: "Which is for the sake of the other? Is the state for the sake of the human person or is the human person for the sake of the state? That, to me, is the ultimate question of the present day. I believe the state is for the sake of the person, and therefore our Bill of Rights must express that for the sake of which everything also exists, including the state."[43] These lines suggest an opposition between state and individual, in the sense of distinct and potential antagonistic entities. This most certainly appears to capture something of Malik's meaning if we are mindful of his numerous arguments with delegates from the Soviet Union. But as our discussion reveals, his problem is far more complicated. For he is just as worried about our own personal attraction to collectivism, and about the resulting subsumption of personal identity to the identity and appetites of the mass, as he is about infringements by the state.[44] These worries are why he emphasizes the need for people "to overcome and control *in their own lives*," and not just in society at large, the "endless rise of the lower, the dark, the elemental, the infernal, the material, and the massive."[45]

Malik champions human rights as a means to release us from our own attraction to the massive, that is, to the mass. Our earlier passage underscores this point: human rights are vital to "remind" individuals that they are free and to help them "remember" that their person is inviolable. Malik presents human rights and the Declaration in terms of modifying the perception we have of ourselves, very much in the manner of Wollstonecraft, though to my knowledge without having read her. Human rights encourage us to view ourselves in the light of our personhood, dignity, and individuality. Keeping this in mind, we can perceive different inflections in Malik's question to the Human Rights Commission: "Is the state for the sake of the human person or is the human person for the sake of the state?" The question is as much psychological as it is social and political. The pressures of the age make us all too devoted to the great collective of our time, the state. But Malik's aspiration for the Declaration is that it can reorient us. With it we can learn to reclaim—and learn to *want to* reclaim—the priority of our own personhood. As he puts it, "the international work of human rights and fundamental freedoms is a faint effort to recover this lost individuality, to the end that the individual human person should realize his own natural dignity."[46]

What about materialism? On this subject Malik thinks our confusion is total. We moderns have inverted the rightful order of value. "Nothing is more pathetic today," he laments, "than the spectacle of a man seeking his happiness in the abundance and determination of material things, and forgetting that joy, satisfaction, rest and salvation are all questions of the spirit."[47] Obviously, this inversion has deadly spiritual consequences: we seek fulfillment in a realm where it cannot be found. But we also know it has repercussions for human rights. "Certain rights," Malik says, "are assuming exaggerated importance: it is hard to keep them in their place. Who is not clamoring today for his economic rights, for what is called a decent standard of living? . . . But there is a deadly danger that in our enthusiasm for economic and social justice we forget that man cannot live by bread alone."[48]

What is his solution? Its breadth and ambition is astonishing. He proposes to kill two birds with one stone and have the Human Rights Commission explicitly rank, within the text of the Declaration itself, the value of the spiritual and material: both in and of themselves, and also with respect to their corollary classes of human rights. Here are remarks he made as reported by the Human Rights Commission, along with two later reflections.

> It was easy to fall into the error of over-simplification, and to consider that such things as non-discrimination and universal employment, guaranteed by the State, represented the most important factors in human

life. For his part, Mr. Malik thought that the most fundamental human rights and freedoms were spiritual, intellectual and moral; he would not be satisfied with mere social security and lack of discrimination except as a means to a higher end, namely the spirit of freedom. The various contributions in the field of human rights made by the diverse cultures in the world must be taken into account, and the crucial part of the Commission's task would be the determination of the hierarchy of values.[49]

Surely, economic and social injustice is a grievous thing, but there is such a thing as intellectual injustice, spiritual injustice, moral injustice, where people live in darkness and rebellion and falsehood. *This* injustice, *this* violation of one's own humanity, whether perpetrated by oneself or by one's fellows, is infinitely more grievous. The establishment of the proper hierarchy in human rights, the determination of those rights for the sake of which other rights, if need be, must be joyfully sacrificed, this task is as urgent today as the mere enumeration of human rights as a whole.[50]

If my fundamental rights and freedoms belong to me by nature, then they are not a chance assemblage of items: they must constitute an ordered whole. Responsible enquiry must then exhibit their inner articulation, for it may be that some are more ultimate than others are. It may be that a spiritually free but economically insecure person is better off than the richest millionaire who knows nothing of spiritual freedom is.[51]

To put these remarks into perspective, a comparison is illuminating. René Cassin, another of the main drafters of the Declaration, famously compared the document to the portico of a temple. The pillars represent four ideas, around each of which is clustered a set of articles that together make up the Declaration: dignity (Articles 1–2), liberty (Articles 3–19), equality (Articles 20–26), and brotherhood (Articles 27–28).[52] The key feature of this portico is that its pillars stand on equal footing. This fact was important enough for Cassin to emphasize in a plenary meeting of the General Assembly: "It should be pointed out that the four pillars of the Declaration were all of equal importance, and no hierarchy of rights could be established in the Declaration."[53]

With all due respect to Cassin, Malik is having none of this. Human rights are not all created equal. There is no portico or pillars. And if there is a temple, it is of very different construction. It is a pyramid. A solid base of social and economic rights is called for, certainly. But that base is there to support a summit: spiritual, intellectual, and moral freedoms. Naturally, this summit is supreme. Yet it is endangered. It is under siege by states (communist ones, especially) that would "joyfully sacrifice"—or really, joyfully dispense with—individual freedoms in favor of collective well-being. More generally, it is fundamentally threatened by a modern age that inverts material and spiritual value. That is why, for Malik, it is imperative that the Declaration be drafted as an explicitly hierarchical document. It must, on the one hand, signal the preeminence of the class of rights most at risk. And, on the other hand, it must provide its addressee—which, of course, is each and every human being—with a reminder of what is valuable and ultimate.

Think of his response in the following terms. At root, materialism draws its power from a refusal to judge. It takes an attitude of nondiscrimination with respect to value: a "denial that there is a lower and a higher in life and that the higher is completely independent of the lower and can never be reduced to it."[54] For Malik many things are wrong with this attitude. It is distasteful and ignoble. It is impious. It is also depressing for materialists themselves. By convincing themselves that there is no higher or lower nature, they starve out the best in themselves. Moreover, Malik is certain that materialists are never fully convinced of their own position. An intuition of a higher nature, faint though it may be, gnaws away at them—so much so that it becomes impossible to cheerfully, or even placidly, inhabit materialism. It is thus with a mix of solicitude and glee that Malik makes overtures to his reader: "Are you perplexed? Do you 'feel' the crisis? Do you 'feel' something profoundly wrong, both in your life and in the affairs of the world? Do you as it were 'hold your heart in your hand,' fearing that almost the next moment something terrible is going to break out—both in you and in the world?"[55]

The materialist, in short, is caught in a double bind: he represses his own higher nature, yet remains ill at ease because that repression can never be fully accomplished. And here is where the Declaration—or any properly ordered whole of human rights—comes to his rescue. How? By seeking to heighten, and thereby to bring to a head and resolve, the materialist's own sense of anxiety and internal struggle. A remark Malik makes in his most speculative work is on point. In *The Wonder of Being* he writes, "There goes on in the soul of each one of us a most fateful struggle between these two men—the man of being and the man of not-being. Which has the upper hand at any given moment is the deepest question that can be asked about us at that moment. What is it that calls forth the man of not-being in us, and what is it that calls forth the man of being?"[56] Whether or not the Declaration succeeds in calling forth the "man of being" is, in a sense, secondary. What matters is whether it makes explicit for the materialist what he had only vaguely intuited: that there is an irrepressible struggle between his higher and lower nature. If the Declaration can so much as raise that question it will have opened a path to care for oneself. It will, in other words, have put anxiety to existential use and disclosed the rank and conflict of our higher and lower natures. To return to the earlier passage, we might say that this disclosure is the ambition behind all of the R-verbs Malik uses to describe the work of the Declaration. By serving to personally "remind" us—to "remember," "recover," "recollect," and "reaffirm" for us—that dignity, humanity, and personhood reside in our higher nature, it seeks to roll back the second great scourge of the modern age: materialism.

That leaves secularism. In the previous chapter I claimed that Roosevelt and Malik identify Christianity as the source and motive power of the Declaration. In her "My Day" column, for example, Roosevelt writes, "I think the spirit of the Declaration was inspired by Christianity and it never would have been written if there had not been people behind it who were motivated by the Christian spirit."[57] But while both drafters would have dearly wished for a mention of God in the document, they were mindful of the pragmatic constraints of pluralism. So it was in the same column that Roosevelt jokes, "there were many men around the table who would violently be opposed to naming God, and I did not want it put to a vote because I thought for those of us who are Christians it would be rather difficult to have God defeated in a vote."[58]

Malik feels the same way. He recognizes that any explicit reference to God would be unacceptable at the drafting table. Yet he insists, with more or less success, on religious ciphers and watchwords being inserted into the document: "inherent," "inalienable," "endowed," and so on. Such terms are allies in his campaign against collectivism and materialism. But they primarily challenge secularism, and in particular a phenomenon that today Charles Taylor calls "exclusive humanism."[59]

Exclusive humanism is a worldview able to account for meaning and significance without appeal to the divine or transcendence. It expresses what Malik takes to be the atmosphere of the modern age. "Man and the world between themselves," he writes, "are absolutely self-sufficient; man needs absolutely nothing outside his possibilities to master the world, including of course himself and others."[60] As we have seen, Malik positions the Declaration as a bulwark against self-sufficiency and pridefulness. Even so, the Declaration risks capture by exclusive humanism. On this topic, Malik is at his most derisive. He sneers at colleagues who would transform the best defense against secularism into just another of its instruments.

> You should see and hear modern man argue about his rights! Can you
> suggest to him that he is originally and by nature possessed of his funda-

mental rights? The merest suggestion that there is nature, reality, truth, peace and rest, an unchanging order of things which it is our supreme destiny to know and conform to, is anathema to modern man. He seeks his rights not in and from that order, but from his government, from the United Nations, from what he calls the "existing world situation" and the "last stage in evolution." Destitute and desolate, he goes about begging for his rights at the feet of the world, and when the Commission votes an article by 10 to 8, he rejoices that there, there he is granted a right! Having lost his hold on God, or more accurately, having blinded himself to God's constant hold on him, he seeks for his rights elsewhere in vain. The spectacle of a human being having lost his proper being—can there be anything more tragic?[61]

These remarks were published on July 1, 1948, in the home stretch of the drafting process. By this time the Human Rights Commission had submitted its final draft (the so-called "Lake Success" draft) for debate and revision by the Third Committee. Yet the frustration in this passage tells of Malik's sense that much remains in play. The main lines of the document may have been set, its Preamble in place, and the order of its articles decided. Still, what really matters remains unsettled: How will the Declaration position itself vis-à-vis natural and positive law? Will it inch toward a secular vision—as it did, for example, when the Third Committee vetoed the words *by nature* in Article 1? Or will it leave open the possibility of a transcendent origin and nature?

This is not an abstract or even a "philosophical" issue for Malik. It concerns efficacy and ethics. In terms of whether the Declaration will be effective in protecting people from harm, Malik is of the Dostoevsky school of thought in that everything is permitted if God does not exist. "It is very well to speak of human rights," Malik says, "but may it not be that these rights have of late been disturbed or disregarded precisely because man—modern man, clever man, proud man, sensuous man, self-sufficient man—has ceased to stand in fear and awe before what is above him?"[62] If the secularist drafters carry the day and purge all religious traces from the Declaration, Malik thinks they would contribute to the same ethos that made modern atrocities possible.

It is, however, on the subject of ethics that I conclude. Malik accepts that the Declaration will not include any overt references to God. Even so, the drafting process holds out a unique opportunity: to write an (ostensibly) secular document that opens onto transcendence. With a word here, a clause there, the Declaration could become a chink in the armor of exclusive humanism. Hence the tremendous significance Malik places on the first noun of the document: recognition. "A careful examination of the Preamble and of Article 1 will reveal that the doctrine of natural law is woven at least into the intent of the Declaration. Thus it is not an accident that the very first substantive word in the text is the word 'recognition'—'whereas *recognition* of the inherent dignity and of the equal and inalienable rights.' Now you can 'recognize' only what must have been already there."[63] Malik places a lot of weight—a lot of faith and hope—on a single word. But perhaps one word is all that is needed. It might provide the finest thread to lead out of exclusive humanism.

An observation Malik makes in *The Wonder of Being* is pertinent: "The world is so full of wonder and excitement, thanks to God, that you could literally get lost in it—lost in the sense of resting in it and worshipping it and considering it self-sufficient. This is idolatry of one form or another. It is imperative therefore to debunk the world and everything in it—to restore to its essential non-self-sufficiency. The Bible does this superbly for us, and if we come back to ourselves and consider in our own lives the deceitfulness of the world and everything in it, we find the Bible, as always, eminently true."[64] Now, in his epilogue to *Christian Human Rights*, Moyn doubts whether human rights can be an effective stand-in for religion. "Unlike Christianity," he says, "human rights do not give much of a chance for spiritual transfiguration for the rare authentic seeker of transcendence."[65] But let's give Malik the last word. He knows full well that the Universal Declaration of Human Rights is not the Bible. Yet for him the two differ by degree, not kind. The Bible radiates transcendence in every line and verse. The Declaration, by contrast, sprinkles a few redolent terms here and there, which may (or may not) be read in that spirit. Yet both texts share a power that Malik wants us moderns to realize we desperately need: to debunk the world and restore its essential non-self-sufficiency. This is a third way in which human rights work to care for the soul.

[9]

HUMAN RIGHTS EDUCATION

A remark by Upendra Baxi has been at the back of my mind while writing this book. At the beginning of *The Future of Human Rights* (2008), he states that human rights are valuable inasmuch as they protect people from serious social, political, and legal abuse. "I take it as axiomatic," he states, "that the historic mission of 'contemporary' human rights is to give voice to human suffering, to make it visible, and to ameliorate it." But what he says next has nagged at me. It seems almost as if he had anticipated my own premise and dismissed it out of hand. "The notion that human rights regimes may, or ought to, contribute to the 'pursuit of happiness' remains the privilege of a miniscule of human-ity. For the hundreds of millions of the 'wretched of the earth,' human rights enunciations matter, if at all, as and when they provide, even if contingently, shields against torture and tyranny, deprivation and destitution, pauperization and powerlessness, desexualization and degradation."[1]

Baxi does not elaborate on his comment and I am not entirely sure what he means by it. But what he belittles is not, it seems to me, a poor or inaccurate slogan for my own book. I am looking at how human rights contribute to the "pursuit of happiness," and indeed, of a privileged "miniscule of humanity." To speak colloquially, the problems that our historical authors use human rights to address are by and large "First World problems." In part, that is due to the fact that they inhabit relatively well-off and privileged places. But mainly it is because they position human rights less against capital C catastrophes—that is, of the kind Baxi lists—than against everyday violence, or rather, against the violence of the everyday. And this, I believe, is deeply significant. After all, they do not write from worlds unacquainted with Catastrophe. It looms over their respective horizons, whether in the form of abuse of women (Wollstonecraft), democracy's slide into tyranny (Tocqueville), war (Bergson), or fascism and totalitarianism (Roosevelt and Malik). Yet these are not the contexts in which they characteristically invoke human rights. Rather, they address the blocks or obstacles to the pursuit of happiness (to continue with Baxi's language) that people around them have internalized and that cripple them from within. It is frivolity and emptiness (Wollstonecraft), loneliness and restiveness (Tocqueville), joylessness and lovelessness (Bergson), and conformity and meaninglessness (Roosevelt and Malik) that human rights are reliably called upon to counteract.

The phrase isn't perfect, I admit. "The pursuit of happiness" carries too much American historical freight. Plus, it risks sounding far too glib to capture the intentions of the authors I have singled out: as if they suggest that by caring for the self with human rights all will be well, pleasant, and fine. That would be seriously misleading in light of their shared awareness that caring for the self with human rights means engaging in something difficult and demanding, not least because it involves struggle against the dominant ideologies and practices of one's own time and place. Still, there is something to be said for it. "Pursuit of happiness" captures the therapeutic register of our authors, in that they use human rights to build up a self able to experience a range of affective states that, while not reducible to happiness, are allied with it, such as fulfillment (Wollstonecraft and Malik), *bonheur* (Tocqueville), love and joy (Bergson), and exuberance (Roosevelt). It also conveys, as I mentioned a moment ago, the appropriate scope and pitch of their efforts: less to prevent enormities than to highlight and combat the unhappiness of the everyday and the violence of the ordinary.

I should make clear that attention to Catastrophe is not necessarily siphoned off by concerns over the pursuit of happiness. By conceiving of human rights in terms of care of the self, many authors and activists seek to ward off Catastrophe (through what, in the previous three chapters, I called a human rights–inspired "ethic of resistance"). That said, if priority is given to care of the self (or to, again roughly speaking, the pursuit of happiness), a different picture of human rights emerges than the one typically associated with the project of shielding innocent people from Catastrophe. In the preceding chapters I marked three shifts to match the criteria I identified for the care of the self at the end of chapter 1. In purpose: personal transformation becomes just as important as protection. In object: care of the self is put on equal footing with care of others. And in mode: human rights are voluntarily applied to the self in addition to being prescribed by and for others.

As the reader knows, most of my book is devoted to tracking down permutations of the care of the self in historical human rights authors and events. In this concluding chapter I ask whether anything comparable exists in contemporary theory and practice. More to the point, is there a movement or trend today that could resonate with this history, and perhaps be inspired or instructed by it?

My answer is a qualified "yes." Care of the self is observable in parts of present-day human rights education (HRE). In a sense, this is a natural home for it. The purpose of HRE is to work in tandem with human rights law and policy in order to promote attitudinal and behavioral changes to end systemic violations and abuses. This means, generally speaking, that it is nonlegalistic. Human rights education treats human rights laws and norms less as prescriptive rules than as a basis from which to create a worldwide culture. Moreover, it explicitly aims at personal transformation and the incorporation of human rights principles as a comprehensive way of life. In this respect, HRE satisfies two of the three criteria of the care of the self: namely, purpose (personal transformation) and mode (voluntary and nonprescriptive).

Things are tricky and interesting when it comes to the remaining criterion. Does HRE advance the care of the self as an end in itself (and not merely as preliminary to the care and protection of others)? From one point of view, it seems amenable. An HRE watchword is that it seeks to "empower" individual learners in their day-to-day lives. Studies on HRE also state that it can actually succeed in doing so: learners report increased personal capacities, confidence, and valuing of the self as a result of HRE.[2] And yet, despite these aims and results, HRE does not explicitly represent itself in terms of enhancing, cultivating, or caring for oneself. To return to Baxi's phrase, it does not see its purpose as advancing the pursuit of happiness of individual learners.

In this final chapter I will not be able to flesh out or "operationalize" care of the self for contemporary HRE. Valuable though this may be, it would require a separate study to extract and systematize techniques of the self in and for HRE. My goal is more modest: to propose that HRE could benefit from presenting itself—and frankly, promoting itself—in terms of the care of the self.

This chapter differs from the preceding ones. When writing on historical human rights authors, my goals were broadly descriptive: to show how they already conceive of human rights in terms of care of the self. This chapter on HRE is normative by comparison. Not strongly so, as if human rights *ought* to be taken up as a form of care of the self. I envisage a pragmatic move. The notion of "caring for oneself" could be used by HRE to foreground a task it already claims to be doing: empowering individuals by building personal capacities and by transforming attitudes and behaviors. In a sense, then, care of the self is not such a great departure for HRE. But it does add something new and important. It engages a crucial yet often ignored problem in human rights pedagogy: how to motivate individual learners to adopt human rights as a way of life. As we will see, HRE is virtually silent as to what needs and desires human rights are poised to satisfy in the actual day-to-day lives of its diverse audiences. Care of the self is not the only solution to this problem. It is not appropriate to many target groups of HRE. And there is more than one way to motivate commitment to human rights. Yet the fact that it has been deployed by so many key authors and actors in the history of human rights suggests it is a resource worth considering. It may be that linking HRE to the "pursuit of happiness" is a more viable strategy to foster a worldwide human rights culture than it initially seems.

The HRE Movement

Several good summaries of the contemporary HRE movement are available.[3] For my purposes a brief overview of its purpose and history will suffice. From there I will address what role care of the self might play within it.

Over the past twenty-five years, HRE has emerged as a key feature of the international human rights landscape. Its rise is due in large measure to a recognition that legal mechanisms alone are insufficient to bring about deep attitudinal and behavioral changes, much less a worldwide human rights culture.[4] The most widely accepted definition of HRE is the United Nations Declaration on Human Rights Education and Training (2011). I cite it at length as it addresses both the substance and recommended pedagogy of HRE.

Article 2

1   Human rights education and training comprises all educational, training, information, awareness-raising and learning activities aimed at promoting universal respect for and observance of all human rights and fundamental freedoms and thus contributing, inter alia, to the prevention of human rights violations and abuses by providing persons with knowledge, skills and understanding and developing their attitudes and behaviors, to empower them to contribute to the building and promotion of a universal culture of human rights.
2   Human rights education and training encompasses:

(a) Education *about* human rights, which includes providing knowledge and understanding of human rights norms and principles, the values that underpin them and the mechanisms for their protection;

(b) Education *through* human rights, which includes learning and teaching in a way that respects the rights of both educators and learners;

(c) Education *for* human rights, which includes empowering persons to enjoy and exercise their rights and to respect and uphold the rights of others.

Article 3

1 Human rights education and training is *a lifelong process that concerns all ages.*

2 Human rights education and training concerns *all parts of society*, at all levels, including preschool, primary, secondary and higher education, taking into account academic freedom where applicable, and all forms of education, training and learning, whether in a public or private, formal, informal or non-formal setting. It includes, inter alia, vocational training, particularly the training of trainers, teachers and State officials, continuing education, popular education, and public information and awareness activities.

3 Human rights education and training should *use languages and methods suited to target groups*, taking into account their specific needs and conditions.[5]

This definition captures several features and ambitions of the HRE movement as a whole. As it makes for a handy overview, I will take them one by one. Article 2.1 states the goal of HRE: to prevent human rights abuses by building a universal human rights culture and by providing people with knowledge and skills to transform existing attitudes and behaviors. Article 2.2—with its triptych of education "about," "through," and "for" human rights[6]—elaborates the pedagogy to which HRE should aspire: to convey the norms and principles of human rights ("about"), in a respectful teaching style that mirrors human rights values ("through"), in order to empower people to enjoy and exercise their human rights ("for"). Article 3 sets out three additional features. It specifies the duration of HRE as a lifelong process (Article 3.1). It affirms that HRE covers all forms of education, including formal and informal schooling, as well as professional training (Article 3.2). And it insists on the importance of context and the need to adapt HRE to the needs and conditions of target groups (Article 3.3).

I will return to this definition later on. My sense is that seeing HRE in terms of care of the self advances key elements of it. For the moment, however, let me continue my survey by turning to the history of HRE. Now, some form of teaching about human rights is as old as human rights themselves. But an organized movement is of recent vintage. The institutional history of HRE dates back to 1974. This is the first official mention of the importance of education for international human rights law, made by the United Nations Educational, Scientific and Cultural Organization (UNESCO).[7] The HRE movement gained momentum two decades later, at the World Conference on Human Rights held in Vienna in 1993. This event led the United Nations to proclaim the Decade for Human Rights Education (1995–2004), which called on member states to incorporate human rights, humanitarian law, democracy, and the rule of law in the curriculum of all educational institutions.[8] In 2005, at the conclusion of the Decade for Human Rights Education, the United Nations launched the ongoing World Programme with a Plan of Action for Human Rights Education. The core of this program is to continue the work of the Decade for Human Rights and better integrate HRE within the primary and secondary schooling sector of member countries. In 2014, the Office of the United Nations High Commissioner for Human Rights proposed that learning about human rights is sufficiently essential to the human rights system that HRE should itself be considered a fundamental right.[9] Last, alongside these intergovernmental initiatives is a profusion of nongovernmental organizations (NGOs) dedicated to HRE, whether in the form of stand-alone NGOs (such as the Human Rights Education Associates [HREA], Democracy and Human Rights Education in Europe [DARE], and the People's Movement for Human Rights Learning [PDHRE]), or else as semi-independent wings of established organizations such as Amnesty International and People's Watch. Recently, several HRE NGOs collectively founded the Global Coalition for Human Rights Education in order to strengthen implementation of international commitments to human rights education.[10]

To this bare-bones summary I would like to add one more development in HRE: the trend by governmental bodies and NGOs to call on human rights to become "a way of life." The reader will recall from my introduction to this book that Eleanor Roosevelt coined this phrase in 1948. But only in the past twenty years has it widely taken off in human rights advocacy and education. In official circles it began with a 1995 Resolution by the United Nations General Assembly, which urged that HRE "constitute a comprehensive lifelong process by which people at all levels of development and all societies learn respect for the dignity of others and the means and methods of ensuring that respect in all societies."[11] Since then, it has been echoed many times over: By the General Assembly, which announced that "human rights learning should contribute to the fulfilment of the Universal Declaration of Human Rights as a way of life for people everywhere."[12] By the United Nations Development Programme, which defines human rights culture as "a way of life based on human rights, where respect for the fundamental dignity of each individual is recognized as essential to the functioning and advancement of society."[13] By UNESCO in its HRE initiatives.[14] By the UN Chronicle, which devoted an article to "Human Rights as a Way of Life."[15] By NGOs such as PDHRE, with its mandate to teach all men and women to claim human rights as a way of life.[16] And by distinguished human rights educationalists, such as Betty Reardon (who calls on human rights education to reconstruct "the psychosocial DNA of a person or society"),[17] Nancy Flowers (who claims that human rights educators "aim at the heart as well as the head"),[18] and Shulamith Koenig (who makes the phrase *human rights as a way of life* central to her activism).[19]

At one level, it is fairly obvious why human rights need to be incorporated as "a way of life." This phrase draws attention to the fact that, to be truly effective, human rights principles and practices need to become integrated into the day-to-day of ordinary people. As a former director of UNESCO puts it, "those who have 'inwardly digested' these principles will have no trouble in reconciling individual development and happiness with social peace, dialogue, and conviviality."[20] It is thus understandable why international bodies, governments, NGOs, activists, and academics advance human rights in this manner. They presume that only as a way of life can human rights really sink in.

At another level, however, that of the individual human rights learner, it is less clear why human rights need to be incorporated in this manner. Why should *a person* do so? How will it help *him* or *her*? What advantages will *he* or *she* draw at an individual and personal level, especially given that not everyone in their personal and professional circles can be counted upon to do the same? Human rights education policy and literature is close to silent on this question. Sometimes it seems even to assume that simply by virtue of learning about— even just hearing about—human rights, individual people will want to adopt it as a lifestyle. This strikes me as wishful thinking. More pointedly, it strikes me as magical thinking that elides the pivotal issue on which the success of HRE depends: how to make human rights enticing as a way of life to individual learners. Its attractiveness cannot be taken for granted, and neither can the interest or desire of learners.

My question is this: Why would a person want to adopt human rights as a basis for their own way of life? Why, to use language from previous chapters, would an individual learner presented with HRE affirm human rights as an existential option for him or herself, that is, as a comprehensive way of living and seeing the world?

Human rights education policy and literature tend to skirt the issue. Consider, for example, Monisha Bajaj's assessment of the field: "Previous literature on global HRE has been largely prescriptive. Human rights education is presented in UN documents as a moral imperative grounded in appeals to the conscience of policymakers. In [NGO definitions]—directed primarily at targets of rights abuses—human rights education is thought to appeal to victims as an instrumental or necessary form of knowledge for the reclamation of rights that have been violated."[21] Bajaj is a rare exception to the state of affairs she describes in that she advances a sophisticated "persuasive pragmatism" to account for the diverse motivations that generate and support interest for human rights.[22] In the context she studies—HRE for school teachers in rural India—such motivations run the gamut of better pedagogical and behavioral outcomes in the classroom, using HRE as a means to promote their own interests in education, enhanced professional status through affiliation with international NGOs, and opportunities for travel.[23] On top of that, she provides testimonies from teachers and students alike who credit HRE with having drastically transformed their own personal and professional lives.[24] Yet Bajaj's indictment stands. Either, as in the case of official documents, HRE is prescribed as a moral imperative by faraway policymakers, or else, as in the case of prominent NGOs, victims are taught how to use human rights as legal instruments to redress violations. Either way, HRE sets to the side what should be a basic issue: how to make a human rights culture, and a way of life based on human rights, viable and attractive to diverse publics made up of individual learners.

This lacuna translates into practice. Critics have noted that HRE often proceeds on the assumption that transmitting information about human rights laws and values is enough to modify attitudes and behaviors.[25] This assumption can even be exaggerated into what I call magical thinking: a belief that, upon learning what human rights are and do, people will immediately want to embrace them as a way of life.

A prominent HRE activist exemplifies this kind of thinking. Shulamith Koenig is founder of the People's Movement for Human Rights Learning, an HRE NGO. She also received the United Nations Human Rights Award in 2003.

Adopting the mantle of human rights "evangelist," she claims that the ambition of her work is to "communicate learning about human rights, the promise of human rights, to all women, men, youth, and children around the world."[26] Throughout her speeches and writings lies a conviction that informing people about human rights is potentially transformative. In answer to the question "What should we do about human rights?" she is fond of citing a reply that she attributes to Voltaire: "Let the people know them."[27] Speaking on her own behalf, she states, "I [act] on the firm belief that people on the ground level can—as women have been doing—change the world if they only know human rights as a way of life and act upon it."[28] Here I quote an episode Koenig often recounts. It is from an HRE workshop she helped organize.

> In 1991, in Nairobi, Kenya, an important event gave a more succinct direction to our work. A policeman was sent to observe a learning session of 25 diverse development organizations that were being introduced to Economic Social and Cultural Human Rights related to their issues and concerns. As discussion and interrogation were going on, the policeman called out emphatically at the bewildered participants: "Stop it! Stop it! If this is human rights, come and teach it in my village." We at the People's Movement for Human Rights Learning (PDHRE) have been answering this policeman's request in many villages around the world. We continue to facilitate learning with local community leaders to have them become mentors of human rights.[29]

To state my criticism, I need to take a step back from this scene. Training targeted at police and military personnel is understandably a priority for HRE. After all, the security sector can be either a main perpetrator or a main preventer of human rights abuses. Success is often limited, however. Some argue this is because HRE is inappropriate to this sector, and that reform comes not through convincing actual or potential perpetrators of the value of human rights, but by modifying structures, orders, and hierarchies.[30] Other critics are more open to the potential for HRE to impact security personnel, but are wary of its unwarranted and even dangerous reliance on commonsense thinking.[31]

I am not competent to choose between these competing views. But clearly more is required for HRE to achieve its goals than simply spreading the message of human rights. In the scene Koenig recounts, it is almost as if that were sufficient—indeed, as if that were educational. The policeman hears about human rights, and then the policeman—who is a monitoring agent of the state, no less—wants human rights in his world. It is a standard image of conversion. But really, it is a stereotypical image of conversion: one in which personal transformation is achieved through sudden and decisive illumination. Perhaps it was the case that the policeman felt that the material presented in the human rights seminar would mesh with the professed ambitions and practices of his profession. Or maybe he sensed that this human rights training could be embedded in the everyday realities of his village. Koenig does not tell us, and that is not the point of the story. The implication is that he received a truth so powerful as to overwhelm his preexisting values, interests, and frameworks. Human rights education had knocked him off his horse.[32]

Several objections can be made of this kind of depiction of HRE. It is idealistic, implausible, and potentially moralistic. Most of all, it is facile and flies in the face of a widely shared aspiration held by human rights educators: to ensure that HRE is responsive and adapted to local contexts. As the United Nations Decade Plan of Action for Human Rights Education makes clear in its General Guiding Principles, "In order to enhance their effectiveness, human rights efforts for the Decade shall be shaped in such a way as to be relevant for the daily lives of learners, and shall seek to engage learners in a dialogue about the ways and means of transforming human rights from the expression of abstract norms to the reality for their social, economic, cultural, and political conditions."[33] I do not know if the HRE practiced by Koenig was, in fact, tailored to the daily lives of the learners in question. Presumably it was. How else to explain this willingness to embrace human rights as a way of life? But on the basis of her many accounts—which are how a prominent practitioner represents HRE—we can't be certain. And that is a problem. For it remains mysterious as to how and why human rights are able to hook people from within their everyday realities.

The Care of the Self as Non-Magical Thinking

This is where care of the self has a role to play. Why? Because it is uniquely resistant to magical thinking. First, it tackles head-on the problem of motivation. To the question "Why should I make human rights my way of life?" it offers a direct answer: "to care for yourself." Second, and this is crucial, it tackles the problem of motivation *immanently*, that is to say, from within the lived reality and context of people for whom human rights might have appeal as a way of life.

Let me explain. In this book we have encountered many thinkers who exhort us to care for the self. More precisely, we have encountered many thinkers who exhort us to care for the self *in relation to* a danger or pressure endemic to their own milieu. This is what I have called their diagnostic sensibility: each author reacts to historically specific (or historically exacerbated) forces that threaten the self at a particular moment in time. To recall a few main examples, women need to care for themselves *because of* chivalry (Wollstonecraft), democrats need to care for themselves *because of* individualism (Tocqueville), and Americans need to care for themselves *because of* rampant conformity (Roosevelt). And here is my point: when these authors propose human rights as a means to care for the self, it is always in response to problems that are widespread in their world and suffered by those living in it. Hence the reason their call for human rights to become a way of life is distinctly non-magical. They present human rights as a technique for people to work on themselves to better cope with and resist the real and present sources of distress in their own lives. That is how they build motivation and context—or better: contextually generated motivation—directly into adoption of human rights as a way of life.

I will put this approach into dialogue with HRE in a moment. But first, I would like to share a final example of how care of the self embeds what seem like universal and placeless norms into deeply felt needs and desires arising from a specific context. It is a work by an anthropologist, Liisa Malkki's *The Need to Help* (2015). Like mine, her book is on the care of the self—not in human rights but in a cognate field: humanitarianism. In part, I mention Malkki because she examines care of the self in a contemporary context, and thus helps to bridge the gap between the historical human rights authors I discuss and present-day HRE. More generally, though, I cite her work as close and companionable to my own. Using different methods (ethnography rather than textual interpretation), and treating a related yet distinct topic (humanitarianism rather than human rights), she captures the essence of what I have tried to say through a compelling, empirically rich study of humanitarianism and internationalism.

Malkki's *The Need to Help* makes a unique contribution to humanitarian studies. Rather than attend to aid recipients (which is where scholarship tends to focus), she turns to aid workers. Her question is: "*Who are these people?* Who wants to work in humanitarian aid and emergency relief, and why? What are their motivations and aims? Who wants to help?"[34] What she finds, through interviews with Finnish aid workers at home and abroad, is that they—the benefactors, the "helpers"—are needy people. They throw themselves into demanding, time-consuming, and often dangerous humanitarian work in order to fill a lack or need in their own lives. "For them," Malkki observes, "there was a *need to help* (*tarve auttaa* [in Finnish]). Taking the observation seriously meant revising some basic assumptions about who 'the needy' are in the humanitarian encounter."[35]

This is relevant to the issue I raised at the beginning of this section: namely, how care of the self guards against magical thinking by linking human rights (or in this case, humanitarianism) to motivations that are meaningful to people in their everyday lives. For what Malkki comes to learn through her interviews is that the needs that drive these humanitarians—that is, the needs that prompt them to work for global social justice and to participate in a cosmopolitan order—are highly specific to their domestic (i.e., national) situation, and in the context of her investigation, to lacks and longings that come from living in Finland. Commitment to a global humanitarian project arises in response to problems at home just as much as to problems in the wider world.

I cannot hope to reproduce Malkki's analysis. But to anticipate my concluding remarks on HRE it is useful to sketch the two kinds of humanitarian workers she studies. The first are nurses and doctors in the Finnish Red Cross who work abroad in post-conflict countries such as Burundi, Rwanda, Congo, Somalia, Chechnya, and Afghanistan. When Malkki began her interviews, she had expected to hear about a "humanitarian sensibility," which is to say, "an aspirationally selfless, generic calling to help a distant 'suffering humanity'" on the part of aid workers.[36] Suffice it to say, this expectation did not play out: her respondents were either annoyed or embarrassed by questions phrased in those terms. They spoke, instead, of two sets of motivations. At one end are professional and political obligations to the international community and a desire to give something of one's own abundance to those in need. At the other end is another spectrum of reasons: "a 'longing for the faraway' (kaukokaipuu), a neediness for the world and human contact, and an ever-present tension between solitude and conviviality."[37] And here is the discovery Malkki makes: these motivations—particularly the second set, the longing for faraway places and human contact—arise from within the specificity of Finnish society. These people are attracted to humanitarian work by a desire to leave behind their mundane, workaday selves, and to experience a break from what they felt was a predictable, yet constraining and emotionally cold, national society. What Malkki draws attention to, in other words, is that these humanitarians "always set out from a social and existential position both specific and precarious."[38] Far from being generically cosmopolitan, and far from operating from a straightforward position of strength and power in relation to aid recipients, they express a palpable and urgent neediness to which their own humanitarian work responds.

Malkki's second group of humanitarian workers is quite different from these nurses and doctors. They are knitters—specifically, knitters in Finland who volunteer to make and donate "Aid Bunnies" (handcrafted soft toy bunnies) to comfort children in post-conflict and post-disaster situations. In 2007, the

Finnish Red Cross launched an Aid Bunny campaign, with the hope of collecting 10,000 bunnies by the end of the year. The response was extraordinary. By December, 25,000 had been made and donated. As one volunteer put it, "we're *drowning* in bunnies!"[39] And to repeat, these crafts are handmade, not bought or mass-manufactured. Volunteers purchase wool themselves, and the knitting is labor intensive. Here again Malkki asks: Who are these people and why did they participate so enthusiastically? Well, by and large they are elderly women, many of whom live alone. They suffer from social isolation, silence, and a sense of not being useful, which, while often a condition of old age in general, Malkki reports is acute and well-documented in Finland. It is in this context that knitting aid bunnies is attractive and fulfilling: as a way to feel connected to a wider world, to be useful and needed, and to organize and fill time. The knitting, Malkki explains, "is not just an entertaining pleasure or casual choice but a response to a sharper kind of need—managing time as a way of keeping dead time at bay. The social connections forged in this way may be fragile and temporary, but they are, for many, a vitally meaningful 'care of the self.'"[40] And later on, "It was a giving of one's skill, of time, and of oneself *in aid of* others, and linking it with others' skills and giving. It was a way of imagining oneself as *a member of the lively world*, and of something greater than oneself. One could think of this simultaneously generous and self-interested practice as a *self-humanizing practice*—again, a care of the self."[41]

I dwell on Malkki's study for two reasons. First, by way of summary and extension, it fits nicely with our own historical human rights authors. Just as she is suspicious of the idea of a generic "global citizen" or "humanitarian subject," so too (*mutatis mutandis*) are they, and for the same reasons. They do not conceive of human rights and the subject of human rights as monolithic, abstract, or universal, as if human rights presuppose or impose a selfsame subject no matter what the circumstances. They are interested, rather, in the production of human rights subjects (in the plural), or, to use the indefinite article, in the production of *a* (as opposed to *the*) human rights subject: real, singular, flesh-and-blood people who use human rights to modify the relation they have with themselves in relation to contextual—"home-grown," Malkki would say[42]—needs, cares, and concerns. Underlying their diverse investigations and proposals is a shared method: an immanent and reflexive appeal to human rights from within the complexity and contingency of a problematic situation. In their hands, it is not so much that "universal" rights must adapt themselves to "local" contexts. The goal, rather, is for individuals to use human rights to devise better ways to live within a locality: not by escaping or transcending it, but by cultivating the self in response to it. In other words, and just as Malkki describes in modern-day humanitarianism, human rights interface with a milieu in order for individuals to make themselves into people better able to bear *that* milieu. Hopefully, they will achieve some therapeutic relief from it; perhaps they will modify and reform it to some degree; but they never simply leave it behind, for the reason that they remain tied to it in the way that solutions remain essentially tied to their problems.

The second reason I discuss Malkki concerns HRE. Earlier I claimed that it is prone to magical thinking: an assumption—in truth, a hope or wish—that learning about human rights will lead people to want to modify their way of life. The trouble with this, you recall, is that it ignores the question of motivation (*why* people would want to make such deep transformations) and thereby also downplays the importance of context (because the motivations HRE needs to contend with are always generated from within particular contexts).[43] By now I hope it is clear why care of the self as Malkki and I describe it avoids these shortcomings. First, it is anchored in personal motivation: human rights (and humanitarianism) are adopted as a way of life in order to ameliorate and cultivate the self. Second, it is responsive to context: cultivation of the self by human rights (and by humanitarianism) occurs in reaction to harms and deficiencies imposed by a particular milieu. And so, when I recommend that HRE adopt care of the self as one strategy to instill human rights "as a way of life," this is what I have in mind. The goal is certainly not to tie human rights to "self-interest" in a narrowly self-serving way. It is, instead, to devise a pedagogical strategy to promote human rights as a way of life that is mindful of motivation, sensitive to context, and thus attractive and relevant to learners in their everyday lives.

I can put this another way. At the beginning of this chapter, I cited the United Nations' definition of HRE. It includes two components that care of the self is well-positioned to advance. The United Nations calls for HRE to be a "lifelong process that concerns all ages." It also urges HRE to "use languages and methods suited to target groups, taking into account their specific needs and conditions."[44] With reference to HRE being a "lifelong process," the examples of care of the self in this book have precisely that duration. One reason is that, like contemporary calls by HRE for human rights to become "a way of life," a care-of-the-self approach seeks to embed human rights as principles to live by and become coextensive with the lives of individual subjects. Yet there is a deeper reason why care of the self through human rights has the potential to be a lifelong process. Bluntly put, the problems we have seen human rights called upon to counteract aren't going anywhere. Historically specific though they may be, they have tremendous staying power: chivalry (Wollstonecraft), individualism (Tocqueville), nationalism and xenophobia (Bergson), conformity (Roosevelt), meaninglessness (Malik), and isolation in old age (Malkki) remain in one form or another fixtures of our contemporary world. The struggle against them never ends—not just in the sense that we can't collectively, as a species or even as a country, move beyond them, but that for the foreseeable future such forces will not cease to tempt and harm the selves and souls of individual people who live in their wake. This is something the originators of the idea of the care of the self saw very clearly. For the ancients, care of the self (*epimeleia heautou* and *cura sui*) was not something that was done once and for all. It had to be ever-renewed in order to bring about a state of being that will inevitably be dispersed and diluted by the routines and pressures of living. The same holds true for us moderns. We—you and I—will not outlive any of the problems in this book. Neither will caring for the self with human rights defeat the ones we choose to struggle against, either at large or in us. At best, and this is not nothing, caring for the self with human rights will help us to manage (and manage our own attraction to) those problems we feel impinge upon our chances to live well. And that is what makes the duration of HRE—of learning to live by the principles of human rights—nothing short of a lifelong process.

Moving to the second component of the United Nations' definition—its appeal for HRE to adopt "languages and methods suited to target groups"—we have already seen why care of the self is apt to advance it. Strictly speaking, it should do so automatically: HRE conducted in terms of the care of the self must, by theoretical and practical necessity, adapt its languages and methods to target groups in order to meet the motivations and preoccupations of learners. After all, if the goal of HRE practiced through care of the self is to encourage people to voluntarily adopt human rights norms and practices as techniques of the self, then these norms and practices must be presented in such a way as to address the most pressing concerns of their own lives. My point is not that care of the self alone can meaningfully engage human rights with local contexts and concrete motivations, and thus ride to the rescue of HRE. It is, rather, that care of the self tends toward such engagement and, as such, is positioned to carry forward the ambitions and self-conception that human rights educators set for themselves.

Two Lessons for HRE

In this chapter I have not listed general techniques for HRE to extract from the care of the self. I couldn't even if I wanted to: no such techniques are to be had if we take seriously the fact that care of the self embeds human rights as a way of life only in relation to the needs and desires of specific learners. Short, then, of plunging into a target audience, does care of the self have any parting lessons for HRE? It has two. The first is methodological: care of the self can model responsive and critical pedagogy for HRE. The second is substantive: care of the self can redescribe and reinforce existing HRE goals and approaches.

The first lesson is an occasion to make something plain. Care of the self is not, nor should it be, relevant or appropriate for many target audiences of HRE. Human rights education is avowedly plural, and its best theoreticians and practitioners start from that fact. It is directed toward many different audiences (e.g., primary, secondary, and tertiary school students, teachers, police officers, military personnel, and government officials). On top of that, these audiences are situated in vastly different social, political, economic, and spiritual worlds (e.g., global north and south, secular, nonsecular, and post-conflict countries). It goes without saying, then, that care of the self will not be appropriate everywhere. In post-conflict countries, for example, HRE rightly stresses the interpersonal and intergroup aspects of human rights (and not primarily the intrapersonal dimension highlighted by care of the self).[45] In addressing highly vulnerable populations, HRE instructs learners in the first instance how to use human rights to identify, report, and redress abuses.[46] And nowhere in the literature on HRE in the security sector have I seen it suggested that police and military personnel should be taught human rights as a means to cultivate and care for themselves.

All of this is well and good. No single approach to HRE should apply to the entire field. But what I want to say is that a perspective based on care of the self ought to be more fully cognizant of its own limitedness than any other. I argued a version of this claim in the previous section: HRE conducted through care of the self cannot but be tailored to—and hence, limited to—the needs of a specific audience. Pushing this argument a step further, it is possible to say that care of the self in human rights not only leads to an intrinsically responsive pedagogy, but also to an intrinsically *critical* pedagogy (in the Kantian sense).[47] By nature it should remain aware of the limits of its relevance and usefulness, and strive to remain within them.

Responsive and critical pedagogy are sides of the same coin. Both center on discernment. The question responsive pedagogy asks itself is: "How do I adapt to this situation?" The question critical pedagogy asks itself is a step prior: "Do I apply to this situation in the first place?" Quite clearly, a care-of-the-self approach will not always answer in the affirmative. Just look at the historical authors in this book. Up until now, I have stressed that they bring human rights to bear on irreducibly different problems. But, if I can bracket that fact for a moment, it is apparent that there is also an underlying unity in that they bring human rights—or more precisely, care of the self though human rights—to bear on similar *kinds of* problems. Roughly speaking, these problems share two features. First, the authors treat problems that attack the spiritual well-being of subjects. Second, they recognize that those subjects are, in some deep manner, attracted and attached to those very problems. That is what problems as diverse as chivalry, individualism, closed morality, conformity, and nihilism all have in common: they harm the psychic life of subjects, yet these subjects desire the very problems that dominate and exploit them, to the extent that they seek their sense of self from within them. And here is the essential point: the authors I have singled out do not apply care of the self to problems that lack these two features. Or, positively put, only problems of a certain kind call forward care of the self in human rights. Such problems are, at one and the same time, an occasion and a limit for care of the self.

There is a lesson here for HRE. Care of the self cannot claim to tackle any and every problem that arises in connection with human rights. At its most compelling—and as represented by the authors in this book—care of the self conducted through human rights acknowledges the array of problems facing human rights, limits itself to a section of them, and adapts its pedagogy accordingly. In this regard, it models critical as well as responsive pedagogy. As a critical method, it reminds HRE that no single approach to teaching human rights is applicable to every context. As a responsive method, it instructs HRE to adapt human rights instruction to the needs and conditions of target groups on the ground. And in offering these lessons, care of the self does not depart from the image HRE already has of itself. As I said earlier, HRE affirms its own plurality. "The mutability of HRE is its strength," Bajaj writes. "That different organizations with distinct social bases and worldviews ground themselves in this discourse suggests the richness and possibility of HRE."[48] Thus, if care of the self confirms the fact that no one pedagogy suffices to treat all problems that arise in HRE, and if it also demonstrates that any particular pedagogy of HRE must adapt itself to the specific cases of problems it is competent to treat, then its value for HRE lies not in proposing a radically new direction, but in reinforcing the plurality and mutability it already claims for itself.

There is one more lesson for care of the self to offer HRE. It concerns substance, rather than method. To date, I have not found any HRE that describes itself explicitly in terms of care of the self. Yet some characterizations come close. Consider, for example, a study by Felisa Tibbitts on the long-term and transformative effects of HRE on the trainers of HRE themselves. Tibbitts is a leading scholar of HRE and founder of the NGO Human Rights Education Associates. She surveyed and interviewed eighty-eight HRE trainers in Turkey engaged in a training program sponsored by a women's human rights group. The purpose of the program is to provide legal literacy for adult women by teaching them how to know and claim their rights in the private and public spheres. What Tibbitts discovers is that in addition to the impact this training had on its target audience, it also profoundly affected the trainers. "The vast majority of trainers," she writes, "indicated that because of their engagement with [HRE training] they were more self-confident and courageous; had increased solidarity with other women; and had gained skills that would increase their capacity to claim their rights, including the ability to communicate effectively, to make decisions, and to recognize and address problems."[49] Moreover, in response to survey questions, 95 percent of trainers reported that the training had helped them to achieve their own potential and to value themselves more.[50] According to Tibbitts, these results reveal something significant yet underacknowledged about how HRE can be empowering. It can, of course, address itself to relations of power *between* individuals and see empowerment in terms of conferring power on people with less control over the situation.[51] But HRE can also address itself to the relation people have to *themselves* and foster empowerment in terms of "internal changes at the individual level."[52] This is the kind of empowerment Tibbitts tries to pinpoint in HRE. It consists in what she elsewhere calls "intrinsic empowerment": an enhanced critical consciousness of oneself and one's environment aimed at reducing human rights violations that are being experienced personally.[53]

Is this not a version of care of the self? If HRE can impart increased self-confidence and efficacy, critical awareness of legal and cultural norms, psychological resilience, and the capacity to work with others, does it not satisfy the criteria of the care of the self? It is transformative, to be sure. It urges learners to apply human rights norms to themselves. And it does so for them to become intrinsically empowered. I hasten to add that Tibbitts is not the only representative of such a perspective. Flashes of it exist elsewhere in the HRE literature. Murray Print and colleagues, for example, state that "education in human rights can help a student discover the intrinsic goodness of the constitutive values of a dignified life, such as freedom, autonomy and personal responsibility, as well as respect for equality and personal differences."[54] Upendra Baxi too—who, you recall, was skeptical that human rights are in the service of advancing the "pursuit of happiness"—presents similar formulations. Human rights learning is, he says, "a continual collective search for the plenitude of life, for meaning that confirms individual and collective dignity, and for the resources of human coexistences."[55] And he goes on to state: "[HRE] has to transform all human beings into *human rights beings*, that is, persons who do not just claim these rights for their individual existence but who also affirm, and practice, humanity as a vibrant community of human rights."[56]

Here, then, is the lesson. Care of the self reflects back to HRE a magnified version of an aspiration it has for itself: the transformation and enhancement of individual learners for their own personal betterment. At present, this goal is not exactly unstated, yet it remains unformalized. When it does occur—as in Tibbitts's account, for example—it seems more like a welcome surprise and an indirect effect of HRE rather than as the outcome of a planned and delivered pedagogy. Care of the self has a distinguished lineage in the human rights tradition. This book was meant to show its impressive iteration by celebrated authors and activists. If HRE were to avail itself of this history, it would be in excellent company. More than that, it would gain a useful resource to pursue the goal announced by Roosevelt many years ago: to impart human rights as a way of life.

Conclusion

In this book I have set out to accomplish two goals: First, to show that care of the self is a recurrent feature in and of the history of human rights. Second, to propose that modern political thought is not as inhospitable to the care of the self as Foucault seemed to think. To conclude, I will review both goals, starting with the second, and then offer some final thoughts about the practical significance of my argument.

Recall Foucault's objection. He claims that while ancient morality emphasized ethics (i.e., the self's relationship with itself) as a self-sufficient moral end, modern morality emphasizes the moral code, or a system of norms to which the subject must remain obedient in order to live in a community with others. The key difference is that while the former involves what Foucault calls a "choice" to live a full and beautiful life, the latter involves the imposition of a moral order, primarily through the instrument of law.[1] From there follows his conclusion: because rights discourse is bound up with the instrument of law and juridical apparatuses, it remains radically distinct from the ethics of the self, and indeed, forms part of a wider modern morality that seeks to exclude and perhaps eliminate ethics altogether.

I have not taken a position as to whether Foucault is right or wrong in general—or I should say, on average—about the role of modern political thought in killing off care of the self as a viable conception of morality. My own sense is that his view is by and large correct: most modern political theories do tend to do so. But that is not to say that his view is exhaustive, and I have attempted to problematize its seeming exhaustiveness by arguing that the value of human rights lies partly in the role they can play in enabling ethical practices of personal transformation and self-care. Or, to state my intervention more directly, I've taken up what Foucault identified as a prime suspect in the demise of the care of the self—rights-based modern political thought, and more specifically still, the juridical subject (*le sujet de droit*) at the heart of this thought—as having the potential to renew care of the self in response to a range of social and political problems.

It helps to revisit the epigraph of my book, which I admit to putting to semi-ironic use. It comes from an interview Foucault gave in 1984, the year of his death: "If I am interested in how the subject constitutes itself in an active fashion through practices of the self, these practices are nevertheless not something invented by the individual himself. They are models that he finds in his culture and are proposed, suggested, imposed upon him by his culture, his society, and his social group."[2] In a nutshell, the authors I treat in this book all do exactly as Foucault says: each is struck by the potential of a discourse and practice widely circulating in his or her own time and place—namely, human rights—to enable subjects to constitute themselves in an active fashion. Perhaps Foucault did not think human rights could bend that way, but these authors do. Now, as we've seen, they do not all do so in the same way. In fact, each author we have looked at highlights a different aspect or dimension of human rights to help care for the self. But over and above these differences, the intuition at the root of this book is that the main authors I discuss each looked at human rights and had the same (and independently arrived at) thought: yes, *this* can be used to care for the self.

Which brings me to the other and main goal of my book: to demonstrate that a concern for the care of the self can be found in the history of human rights. I should say here that I do not believe I have been reading any of the human rights authors featured in this book against the grain. My procedure has not been to ignore what they explicitly say about human rights in order to extract a more shadowy, yet simultaneously more real, set of theses about the care of the self. Not at all. Concern with care of the self is right there in the open at the heart of their work; it *is* the grain of their thinking about human rights. The question, then, is why has it been missed? If, as I claim, care of the self is more or less explicit in key human rights authors and actors, and if, as I also claim, it keeps on being repeated over a 250-year history, why has no one pointed it out before?

For two main reasons. First, although I am not interpreting these particular authors against the grain, I am very much doing so with respect to the overall human rights tradition. As I said at the outset of this book, contemporary thinking about human rights is dominated by two assumptions. One is that the purpose of human rights is to *protect* all human beings from government abuse and neglect. The other stems from the fact that human rights are in the business of advancing global social justice. Especially for people from rich and privileged countries, human rights are seen not as an institution to care for one's *own* self but, much more pressingly, to empower and attend to less fortunate *other* people. And my point is this: even if care of the self has the potential to complement and even enhance mainstream conceptions of human rights, this rich history goes unrecognized due to how far its focus on the self and personal transformation is from prevailing assumptions about what human rights are and do.

The second reason for the neglect of care of the self in human rights can be put down to an issue that I have noted many times already: with the exception of the relationship between Roosevelt and Malik, none of the authors who conceive of human rights in this way refer to one another on this (or really, on any) topic. That is a main reason why the repetition of the care of the self in human rights is hard to detect: there is no acknowledged and reflexive tradition in which one author inherits from another a concern with personal transformation and cultivation of the self. The link between human rights and self-improvement is one each author establishes on his or her own, without reference to (and I would add, without knowledge of) previous attempts in that direction.

Hence the reason I have insisted on the relevance of the concept of the care of the self for the study of human rights. As we know, it is Foucault's concept, and he used it to designate a long tradition in the history of morality that centered on the exhortation for individuals to be concerned with themselves, to attend to themselves, and to work upon themselves. We also know that none of the human rights authors in this book use the term "care of the self" verbatim. Instead, I have brought this concept to the field of human rights in order to name and capture a shared orientation that has so far escaped notice. In other words, Foucault's concept of the care of the self has been my tool to constitute a new object of analysis in human rights. It is an especially handy tool because Foucault left us specific criteria as to what counts as the care of the self. If the reader recalls from chapter 1, care of the self has three main features: it is an ethic that prioritizes personal transformation and self-fashioning; it remains nonprescriptive and allows for individuals to voluntarily adopt a moral code to cultivate the self; and it regards the self and care for oneself as a self-sufficient moral end. Equipped with these criteria, I have identified a series of authors whose thought on human rights satisfies all three. And thus we have the purpose of my book: to show that, even if it is not a "tradition" in the sense of being an idea and practice self-consciously transmitted from generation to generation, care of the self in human rights is, to speak colloquially, a thing. It is a perspective that can be discovered time and again in some of the best thinkers, writing at some of the most critical junctures, in the history of human rights.

To wrap up this summary, permit me a final overall description of care of the self in human rights. As with the criteria of the care of the self, it is threefold, and in many respects redescribes and elaborates those criteria.

Start with the absolute basics. Why should we want to care for ourselves? Here I don't just mean with respect to human rights, but in general—why do it? Well, if we go back to ancient Greek and Roman philosophy (the birthplace of this ethic), and if we agree to suspend the many differences between its leading schools, a clear general answer is offered up: because something in our lives, or more specifically, something about ourselves (and the way we think, feel, and desire), blocks and impedes our potential to flourish and live well. Were we perfect—were we sages, in the lexicon of these schools—there would be no further call to care for the self. Yet as presently constituted, warts and all, work on the self is required if we are to achieve any measure of personal contentment, tranquility, and self-realization. And indeed that is how ancient philosophy presented and promoted itself: as a comprehensive set of discourses and exercises designed to provide the right kind of self-care.

Enter Foucault. Speaking rather loosely, we might say there was one thing he loved and admired about ancient philosophy, and two things he didn't. On the plus side, he very much endorsed its conception of the self as a project, as a material to be worked upon and crafted with the aim of living a rich and beautiful style of life.[3] What he did not like, first and foremost, is its particular conception of the beautiful life, based as it is on domineering virility, dissymmetry, and exclusion of the other.[4] Its second unattractive feature is a lack of historical sense. Now, there are many ways to divide up Foucault's career and important differences to be marked between his early, middle, and late periods. But in one respect he never wavered: Foucault is a historical thinker through and through. The one big question he pursued throughout his life—"Who are we in our actuality?"[5]—could for him only ever be assessed and answered historically: we are who we are thanks to historical and contingent constellations of power, resistance, knowledge, and so forth. That is his diagnostic ethos. But it is not one shared by the ancients he studied in his later work. The kind of problems in light of which they urge care of the self do not have a strong historical index. Ills such as gluttony, quick-temperedness, licentiousness, self-pity, partiality, anxiety about the future, and regret about the past are ahistorical and will forever plague us.

Care of the self in human rights does not primarily address itself to those timeless kinds of problems. Instead, the authors I have surveyed call on human rights to help care for the self in light of a historically generated (or, in Bergson's case, historically exacerbated) harm or danger which they identify as endemic to their own milieu, whether that be chivalry (Wollstonecraft), individualism (Tocqueville), hatred and xenophobia (Bergson), conformity (Roosevelt), or materialism and nihilism (Malik). Human rights are thus not advanced as some all-purpose cure, as if they could be used to transform or improve people in no matter what time or place. To the contrary, each author draws on human rights to provide an appropriate kind of self-care, tailor-made to counteract a particular problem. Earlier (in chapters 2, 6, and 9), I gave this shared orientation a rather cumbersome name: a diagnostic and poetic sensibility. But, in truth, it's not as complicated as it sounds. All I mean is that at its best, care of the self in human rights, first, addresses itself to historically specific forces that threaten the self at a particular moment in time (this is its diagnostic sensibility), and second, works to craft a self that is better able to withstand, resist, or overcome those very forces (this is its poetic—in the sense of poesis and autopoesis—sensibility). And here we have the first of three features of care of the self in human rights that I wish to flag in my concluding overview. Out of homage to Foucault, we could call it an immanent and historicist interpretation of the first criterion of care of the self: care of the self is an ethic that prioritizes personal transformation and self-fashioning—such that the self doing the fashioning with human rights responds to harms and dangers generated from within his or her own social and political world.

The second feature of care of the self in human rights I would like to single out might be termed instrumentalism. In this book I have characteristically written about human rights in a decidedly instrumental register: human rights have been depicted as a tool—as well as a means, medium, instrument, device, and the like—to be used by individuals to cultivate themselves. I have also favored an expression coined by Foucault: human rights have the potential to be a "technique of the self," which he defines as "reflective and voluntary practices by which men [and women] not only set themselves rules of conduct, but seek to transform themselves, to change themselves in their singular being."[6] This instrumentalist vocabulary has been intended to advance a particular interpretation as to how best to conceive of the role of human rights in caring for the self.

Put it this way: the phrase "care of the self in human rights" is open to multiple interpretations. One possibility is that human rights might simply provide the necessary conditions and protections to exercise care of the self. It is perfectly true, after all, that individuals can only meaningfully care for themselves from within a background of relative freedom and security. In this view, then, human rights would be tasked with safeguarding, for example, the requisite negative and positive freedoms for individuals to go on and care for themselves in whatever way they see fit.

I do not object to seeing the relationship between human rights and care of the self in this manner. But it is not at all the sense in which I develop the idea of "care of the self in human rights" in this book. My meaning, built up from the human rights authors featured in the preceding chapters, is that individuals opt to use human rights to *directly* work upon and transform themselves. To mention only two examples we have covered, Wollstonecraft urges women to view themselves from the perspective of the "Rights of Man," and Tocqueville describes how democrats transform themselves by virtue of their day-to-day exercise of universal political rights. My point is that for these thinkers human rights are not about providing the conditions or safeguards for the care of the self, exactly. Human rights are, instead, the direct means or medium with which such care is imagined and practiced. If the reader will forgive a pun, human rights are from this perspective truly human rights *instruments*: tools for individuals to adopt in order to transform and change themselves. We can thus think of this instrumentalism as a gloss on Foucault's second criterion, which is that care of the self is nonprescriptive and allows for individuals to voluntarily adopt a moral code to cultivate the self. Human rights are here envisaged not in terms of obedience to law, but as a technique of the self that people can choose to apply to their own lives in order to, as I cited Foucault a moment ago, "change themselves in their singular being."

Now we revisit the third and final criterion of care of the self. It was always the most fraught with respect to human rights: the object of the care of the self is the self, and in particular, such care is not merely preliminary to the care of others. It is important for me to be clear and firm on this question: care of the self in human rights is undertaken for the sake of one's own self, period. If care of the self does not prioritize the self in this manner, then it is not, well, care of the self but rather something else.

That said, we should absolutely not conclude that such care is thus necessarily egoistic or quietist, or that it shrinks the world down to the size of oneself. As we have seen, care for the self in human rights can and often must take the form of care for others. It all depends on the nature of the problem or danger to be confronted. Recall Tocqueville from chapter 4. He is explicit: care of the self in democracy requires that we take active care and responsibility for a broader social and political world, precisely because democracy inclines us to stultifying self-absorption and private retreat. From his perspective, care for a shared world is good for *me*; such other-oriented care responds to dangers that threatens *my own* psychical well-being. Roosevelt is another fine example. She praises the educative power of human rights to open us up to other people and to listen and attend to what they think and say. But a crucial reason why she praises this power is that only with the kind of openness instilled by human rights can we hope to personally grow and profit from our encounters with others. The same goes for Bergson and Malik, both of whom champion human rights as a means of self-care precisely because it opens people onto broader, and in their cases divine realities. In short, care of the self in human rights is, by definition, undertaken for the self. To cite Foucault's emphatic statement a final time, "[Care of the self] is an activity focused solely on the self and whose outcome, realization, and satisfaction, in the strong sense of the word, is found only in the self. . . . One takes care of the self for oneself, and this care finds its own reward in the care of the self."[7] This holds true with respect to care of the self in human rights. But, at the risk of repeating myself, although care of the self is an end in itself, the form it characteristically assumes in and through human rights is that of care and attention for others and for a wider social, political, and even cosmological world.

A final remark on this topic is in order. In the last several chapters (from chapter 6 onward), I have emphasized the role that human rights can play in fostering an ethic of social and political resistance. The basic idea, taken once again from Foucault, is that effective resistance to dominant social and political powers must involve change in the relationship we have to ourselves. I did not cite it at the time, but a powerful statement on self-care by the poet Audre Lorde is pertinent. She writes, "Caring for myself is not self-indulgence, it is self-preservation, and that is an act of political warfare."[8] Yet here again I need to be explicit about how I have presented the motivation behind such resistance or "warfare" (as Lorde terms it). Care of the self, properly so called, is not undertaken in order to further more effective social and political resistance, as if that were its real and driving goal. Neither, as I said a moment ago, is it preparatory labor to make a self better able to resist, say, for example, by being practiced as a recuperative activity—a kind of breather or time-out[9]—for a restored self to reenter the political fray. The idea, rather, is that care of the self in all the cases we have examined requires active confrontation of and resistance to social and political forces in oneself. Why? The answer is simple: because the forces that threaten the spiritual wellness of the self either have a social and political origin or else underpin hegemonic social and political powers. Whether we are talking about chivalry (with Wollstonecraft), individualism (with Tocqueville), closure and xenophobia (with Bergson), conformity (with Roosevelt), or materialism (with Malik), the main claim made by all the human rights authors I surveyed is that overcoming personal attachment to these dominant (i.e., socially and politically hegemonic) forces is the single most important key to living well. And so the ethic of resistance they envisage is not so much an external "to the barricades" sort—though they by no means dismiss the possibility and need for that kind of protest—but consists instead, to harken back to Foucault's words quoted in chapter 6, of active work on the self to overcome our desire "for the very thing that dominates and exploits us."[10] The result? If successful, and such success is always hard-won and can impose high costs of its own, the result is a self that in its formation and self-understanding is counterpoised to dominant powers of the day. One's own life, to borrow a phrase from Thoreau, has the potential to become "counter-friction to stop the machine": not because self-care is dedicated to overthrowing said machine (that might, in certain circumstances, be a potentially salutary side effect), but because caring for oneself requires it.[11]

That concludes my summary. Care of the self in human rights as I have described it involves, first, a diagnostic and poetic sensibility, second, an instrumental orientation in which human rights are used as tools and techniques of self-care, and third, an ethics-first attitude in which the self is the definitive object of the care of the self. To finish I offer a few suggestions as to the practical significance of all this.

At a more institutional level I won't repeat my earlier claims from chapter 9 that care of the self could serve as another string in the bow of human rights education by providing an alternative outlook and additional resources to inculcate human rights as an ethic and a way of life. I confine myself instead to two observations.

The first concerns what might be called eclecticism: the possibility of personally taking up many of the different techniques to care for the self from the history of human rights. I am reminded of a remark Nietzsche made long ago with respect to all the various schools of ancient philosophy and how a contemporary might go about deciding which one to follow. He simply denied the need to make that kind of choice: "we will not hesitate to adopt a Stoic recipe just because we have profited in the past from Epicurean ones."[12] So too with us. Sadly, as we know all too well, none of the problems raised by the authors I have discussed—even those who wrote two hundred years ago!—have gone away. Individualism, closure and xenophobia, and all the others I listed above, remain in one form or another prominent features of our world. In this book I have not attempted to "update" any of these problems, so to speak, by showing what shape they have taken in the twenty-first century. But such a task could be undertaken, and not just as a scholarly endeavor. A reader of this book might well ask him or herself: "Does what Wollstonecraft (or Bergson, or Roosevelt, and so forth) describes still ring true today? Are her problems still recognizably our own, and if so, can we—can I—follow in her footsteps and use human rights to care for the self in the way she recommends?" Or, to continue with Nietzsche's metaphor, a reader might well wonder: "Can we still cook with these recipes?"

This is where there are advantages to having many at hand. If one no longer feels viable, we can move on to another. Better yet, it may be possible to combine elements of different recipes to more adequately respond to contemporary predicaments. Or, if all else fails and none seem to have remained attractive, then at least by showing so many different attempts I may have succeeded in persuading the reader that, yes, human rights can be used in this way. Only now it's up to us to craft the right recipes for our times.

My parting thought pertains to moralism and the addressee of human rights. Let me frame it this way. Perhaps the most famous piece of writing about human rights in the twentieth century is a chapter from Arendt's *The Origins of Totalitarianism*, "The Decline of the Nation-State and the End of the Rights of Man." Her verdict on human rights can be rendered in the form of a cruel maxim. Human rights: you have them when you don't need them, and you don't have them when you need them. That is to say, given her analysis of how the eighteenth-century doctrine of the Rights of Man became embodied in (and only in) the nation-state, Arendt argues that expulsion from a community of civil and political rights (i.e., the nation-state) is tantamount to expulsion from a community of human rights. Hence the organizing irony of her essay: if any figure in the world should be able to call upon their human rights, it is the refugee; yet, at the very same time, it is precisely the refugee who is prevented from doing so.

In human rights scholarship, all attention is rightly paid to the have-nots of this equation, namely to the refugee who finds him- or herself beyond the pale of both political and human rights. But perhaps it is worth giving some thought to the other side, namely the citizen who has his or her human rights comfortably doubled by civil and political rights. From one perspective, of course, there is nothing to think about. As this person is in the lucky position of being included in the realm of law and rights, we need pay him or her little mind. But what I want to ask is how and why do human rights matter to this person? If he or she is safe and counted in a decent political community, on what level will a traditional human rights discourse concerned exclusively with care and protection of others speak to them?

Well, at its best, such a discourse has the power to awaken or sustain an interest in global justice. It can also energize citizens to take concrete action to try to make that vision a reality. At its worst, however, a discourse framed exclusively in terms of justice for less fortunate and potentially faraway others, runs the risk of moralism, by which I mean concern directed to the improvement of how others live while taking for granted one's own uprightness. Sanctimoniousness is not a new accusation to be leveled at human rights. It was a keynote of the early convergent attacks by Edmund Burke and Karl Marx, and still extends across ideological lines today. But whether or not we accept such criticism, it is difficult to deny that it stems from a reasonable intuition: an institution and discourse as critical and outward looking as human rights cannot but be shadowed by the potential for self-righteousness. It is a standing risk that human rights are seen to apply to everybody except for oneself.

If the care of the self I have discussed has anything to recommend itself, it is this: anyone and everyone becomes the addressee of human rights. Care of the self, as I have presented it, is the opposite of self-satisfaction. At its core it consists of the application of human rights to oneself in order to identify—to diagnose—something wrong and amiss not just in the wider world but, more pointedly, in oneself. From this perspective, human rights are at once sword and salve: a perspective, on the one hand, to reveal and make vivid what is wrong with us—for example, we are enamored with inequality (Wollstonecraft), our love is bound up with hatred (Bergson), we aren't living up to our individuality (Roosevelt), and so on—and a tool, on the other hand, to help us to personally overcome those very faults and deficiencies. As such, human rights don't just speak *to* us in the manner of the familiar other-oriented discourse. They gain the power to speak *of* us, that is, *of* the kind of person we hope and need to become.

Notes

INTRODUCTION

1   Black, ed., *The Eleanor Roosevelt Papers*, vol. 1, 899.
2   Roosevelt, "The Struggle for Human Rights," 903.
3   Roosevelt, "Where Do Human Rights Begin?," 190.
4   Roosevelt, *You Learn by Living*, i.
5   Roosevelt, *You Learn by Living*, i–ii, 11, 25–41.
6   Lefebvre, *Human Rights as a Way of Life*, xv.

CHAPTER 1. The Care of the Self

1   I have the following works in mind: Moyn, *The Last Utopia* and *Christian Human Rights*; Merry, *Human Rights and Gender Violence*; Goodale, *Dilemmas of Modernity* and *Surrendering to Utopia*; Goodale and Merry, eds., *The Practice of Human Rights*; McClennen and Moore, eds., *The Routledge Companion to Literature and Human Rights*; Malkki, *The Need to Help*; Ticktin and Feldman, eds., *In the Name of Humanity*; Reinbold, *Seeing the Myth in Human Rights*; Slaughter, *Human Rights, Inc.*; Hunt, *Inventing Human Rights*; Niezen, *The Origins of Indigenism*; Wahl, *Just Violence*; Hesford, *Spectacular Rhetorics*; Sliwinksi, *Human Rights in Camera*; Zivi, *Making Rights Claims*; Ignatieff, *Human Rights as Politics and Idolatry*; Gregg, *Human Rights as Social Construction*; Donnelly, *Universal Human Rights in Theory and Practice*; Botting, *Wollstonecraft, Mill, and Women's Human Rights*; Lindkvist, *Religious Freedom and the Universal Declaration of Human Rights*; and Joas, *The Sacredness of the Person*.
2   *The Use of Pleasure* and *The Care of the Self* were published simultaneously in 1984. Foucault delivered lectures on ancient philosophy at the Catholic University of Louvain in 1981 (*Wrong-Doing, Truth-Telling*) and Berkeley in 1983 (titled *Fearless Speech* by the publisher), in addition to his annual lectures at the Collège de France, *The Hermeneutics of the Subject* (1981–82), *The Government of Self and Others* (1982–83), and *The Courage of Truth* (1983–84). Among the essays and interviews on the care of the self from this period, the most significant are "On the Genealogy of Ethics" and

"What Is Enlightenment?" For an overview, see Davidson, "Archaeology, Genealogy, Ethics" and "Ethics as Ascetics"; O'Leary, *Foucault and the Art of Ethics*; Elden, *Foucault's Last Decade*; and especially McGuishin, *Foucault's Askesis*.

3   This Introduction was first published independently as "Usage des plaisirs et techniques de soi" in *Le Débat* in 1983. Reprinted in *Dits et écrits II*.

4   Foucault, *The Use of Pleasure*, 25.

5   Foucault, *The Use of Pleasure*, 25.

6   Weighing in at 1,300 pages, Brownlie and Goodwin-Gill, eds., *Basic Documents on Human Rights* shows just how voluminous even the core codes of human rights have become. In the words of one critic, this proliferation of human rights codes is positively "carnivalistic." Baxi, *The Future of Human Rights*, 46.

7   See, for example, Hathaway, "Do Human Rights Treaties Make a Difference?" and Posner, *The Twilight of Human Rights Law*.

8   Foucault, *The Use of Pleasure*, 25, translation modified.

9   Foucault, *The Use of Pleasure*, 26–27.

10 Foucault, "The Ethics of the Concern for Self as a Practice of Freedom," 263. Foucault is not alone in approaching the topic of morality through the lens of the self's relation to itself. Other prominent accounts in English include Taylor, *Sources of the Self*; Larmore, *The Practices of the Self*; and especially Stanley Cavell's later work on moral perfectionism. Within Foucault's own milieu, we could name Paul Veyne, Pierre Hadot, Marcel Detienne, Jean-Pierre Vernant, and Georges Dumézil, all of whom are specialists in classical history and philosophy. What distinguishes Foucault's interpretation of the practices of the self is his framing of the self's relation to itself in terms of care for oneself.

11 As Frédéric Gros (editor of this lecture course) notes, Foucault's memory was faulty on this point. He did not mention the care of the self in the lectures of the previous year.

12 Foucault, *The Hermeneutics of the Subject*, 2, translation modified. Hereafter cited in text as *HOS*, followed by page reference.

13 Another difficulty with the English "care of the self" is that Foucault's phrase in French is *souci de soi*, not *souci du soi*. A more literal translation would be "care of self." Dropping the definite article helps to avoid any connotation of an essential self, which is a notion Foucault criticized over his whole career. Keeping this caveat in mind, I will continue to use "care of the self" as it is the standard translation.

14 Foucault, "The Ethics of the Concern for Self as a Practice of Freedom," 285, translation modified.

15 In his attention to ancient practices of the self, Foucault follows in the footsteps of the French classicist and philosopher Pierre Hadot. It is no exaggeration to say that Hadot's work on spiritual exercises in antiquity is the main influence on Foucault's later period. See Davidson, "Introductory Remarks to Pierre Hadot." I discuss Hadot in chapter 4.

16 Foucault, *The Use of Pleasure*, 95–139; *The Care of the Self*, 99–144.

17 For a book of this kind, that is, an attempt to revive specific classical exercises for us today, see Irvine, *A Guide to the Good Life*. Pierre Hadot makes overtures in this

direction in *What Is Ancient Philosophy?*, 271–81; *The Present Alone Is Our Happiness*, 162–96; and especially *N'oublie pas de vivre*.

18 Foucault, "Le retour de la morale," 1517–18, and "On the Genealogy of Ethics," 256–62. See Veyne, "The Final Foucault and His Ethics."

19 Foucault, "On the Genealogy of Ethics," 256.

20 In "Ethics as Ascetics," Davidson argues that Foucault addresses the practices of ancient sexuality in order to elaborate his conception of ethics. McGuishin is particularly adept at showing why, for Foucault, care of self remains necessary today. See part 2 of *Foucault's Askesis*, "Care of the Self and Parrhesia in the Age of Reason."

21 Foucault, "On the Genealogy of Ethics," 271.

22 Foucault, "On the Genealogy of Ethics," 260.

23 Some critics and interpreters have pointed to this convergence of Foucault's later interest in human rights and care of the self (as a subject-centered philosophy) as indicative of his broader turn to liberalism and humanism. See Paras, *Foucault 2.0*; Wolin, "Foucault the Neohumanist?" and "From the 'Death of Man' to Human Rights"; and Dosse, *Histoire du structuralisme*, vol. 2, 392–94. For convincing critiques that propose that Foucault's tactical and political appeals to human rights serve to critically reclaim key resources of liberalism, see Golder, *Foucault and the Politics of Rights*; and Patton, "Foucault, Critique and Rights," "Foucault and Normative Political Philosophy," and "Historical Normativity and the Basis of Rights."

24 Foucault, "Alternatives to the Prison."

25 Foucault, "Letter to Certain Leaders of the Left."

26 Foucault, "Open Letter to Mehdi Bazargan."

27 Foucault, "The Risks of Security."

28 Foucault, "Sexual Choice, Sexual Act" and "The Social Triumph of the Sexual Will."

29 Foucault, "Confronting Governments."

30 Foucault, "The Social Triumph of the Sexual Will," 157–58.

31 Foucault, *The Courage of Truth*, 2. The word *trip* is in English in the original.

32 Foucault, "The Ethics of the Concern for Self as a Practice of Freedom," 294.

33 Interestingly, the difficulty of translating *sujet de droit* and *personnalité juridique* into English was debated in the drafting of the Universal Declaration of Human Rights in 1948. The term *juridical person* was felt by many, Eleanor Roosevelt included, as too technical and esoteric. The final outcome was Article 6: "Everyone has the right to recognition everywhere as a person before the law" (*Chacun a le droit à la reconnaissance en tous lieux de sa personnalité juridique*). See Roosevelt, "Verbatim Record of the Thirteenth Meeting of the Drafting Committee of the Commission of Human Rights," 568–69.

34 Foucault, *About the Beginning of the Hermeneutics of the Self*, 98–99.

35 See *The Use of Pleasure*, 29–32; "On the Genealogy of Ethics," 266–67; and "An Aesthetics of Existence," 49.

36 I note that much of Foucault's work, especially from his middle period, is critical of a juridical conception of power. He particularly criticizes the belief that social and political life is governed by legal codes and state authority when, in fact, other mechanisms of power are at work (e.g., disciplinary, hermeneutic, and biopolitical).

See Simons, *Foucault and the Political*, 51–59; and Golder, *Foucault and the Politics of Rights*, 13–20.

37 Foucault, "Subjectivity and Truth," 88. For the multiple kinds of "subjects" of government according to Foucault (e.g., souls, households, children, and political subjects), see Burchell, "Liberal Government and the Techniques of the Self."

38 The role of law and juridical institutions in what I've called "political" government is a debated topic in Foucault studies, with some scholars arguing that Foucault expels laws from his analysis of power (see Hunt and Wickham, *Foucault and Law*), and others claiming that his conception of law is illimitable (see Golder and Fitz-patrick, *Foucault's Law*). For Foucault's concepts of government, governance, and governmentality as political techniques, see Lemke, *Foucault, Governmentality, and Critique*, and Lemm and Vatter, eds., *The Government of Life*.

39 Foucault, *The Use of Pleasure*, 29–30, emphasis added, translation modified.

40 For example, Foucault, "On the Genealogy of Ethics," 266.

41 Foucault, "On the Genealogy of Ethics," 266. For an example of Foucault's view that ancient morality is based on personal choice, see his discussion of aphrodisia in *The Use of Pleasure*, 91–93.

42 Robert Hurley's translation of this line is misleading. Foucault writes, "le sujet moral se rapporte à une loi, ou à un ensemble de lois, auxquels il doit se soumettre sous peine de fautes qui l'exposent à un châtiment." Hurley translates this as "the ethical subject refers his conduct to a law, or set of laws, to which he must submit at the risk of committing offenses that may make him liable to punishment." There are two problems here. First, Hurley translates "le sujet moral" as "the ethical sub-ject," even though for Foucault "moral" is the more comprehensive category. Ethics is a part of morality, not the other way around. Second, Foucault does not say that the subject refers his or her "conduct" to a law but, more generally, that the subject refers him or herself to a law.

43 Foucault, "The Aesthetics of Existence," 49.

44 On the congruence between categorical societies and a rule-based conception of morality, see Taylor, *A Secular Age*, 90–145, 270–95; and Schneewind, *The Invention of Autonomy*.

45 Foucault, "Technologies of the Self," 228. See also his lecture remark in *The Herme-neutics of the Subject*, "The theory of political power as an institution usually refers to a juridical conception of the subject of right" (252).

46 Perhaps this is why of all the many strands of modern political thought Foucault names only anarchism (and Max Stirner in particular) as having given a central role to ethics and the aesthetics of the self: it alone is not based on the subject of law (*HOS* 251).

CHAPTER 2. The Juridical Subject as Ethical Subject

1 For a summary, see Golder, *Foucault and the Politics of Rights*, 1–30.

2 Aron and Foucault, *Dialogue*, 22. "Perhaps the role of the philosopher, the role of

the philosopher at present, is not to be a theoretician of totality, but the diagnostician, if you will allow me to use this word, the diagnostician of today."

3 Foucault, *The Hermeneutics of the Subject*, 11.

4 Foucault, *The Use of Pleasure*, 9.

5 Foucault, *The Use of Pleasure*, 8.

6 Foucault, *The Use of Pleasure*, 8.

7 Rabinow also draws attention to Foucault's use of this word. "Introduction," xxxiv–xl. See also Huffer, *Mad for Foucault*: "We might go so far as to call transformation the basic ethical principle in Foucault" (243).

8 I use the term *human rights* even though Wollstonecraft does not. In *Rights of Woman* she refers variously to "natural rights," "inherent rights," and "rights of man." Yet given her argument that such rights should be extended to women (i.e., to all human beings), and in light of my interpretation that such rights are, for her, necessary to help women and men become more fully human, the appropriateness of the term *human rights* outweighs its anachronism.

9 Hodson, *Language and Revolution*, 1.

10 I do not mean to suggest that Paine does not attend to issues of subjectivity and selfhood, or that Wollstonecraft ignores the broader social and political transformation. Politics and ethics are entwined for both authors. My point is that Paine and Wollstonecraft emphasize one topic over the other and, because of this, give different ways to interpret Burke himself. On the Burke–Paine debate, see Lamb, *Thomas Paine and the Idea of Human Rights*.

11 Marx, "On the Jewish Question." In a broadly defined critical tradition, see Douzinas, *Human Rights and Empire*; Anghie, *Imperialism, Sovereignty and the Making of International Law*, 245–72; Baxi, *The Future of Human Rights*; Grear, *Redirecting Human Rights*, 68–95; Hamacher, "The Right Not to Use Rights"; Whyte, "The Fortunes of Natural Man." From a different perspective, the apparent individualism of human rights has been attacked by contemporary Christian critics. For an overview, see Wolterstorff, "Christianity and Human Rights."

12 Bentham, "Anarchical Fallacies"; Waldron, "Nonsense upon Stilts?—A Reply" (chapter 6 of *Nonsense upon Stilts*); and Kundera, "The Gesture of Protest against a Violation of Human Rights" (this chapter is from his novel *Immortality*). See also Hopgood, *The Endtimes of Human Rights*.

13 Badiou, *Ethics*, 4–17; Brown, "The Most We Can Hope For . . ."; Marks, "Four Human Rights Myths"; Baynes, "Towards a Political Conception of Human Rights"; and Slaughter, *Human Rights, Inc.*

14 The most relevant texts by Burke are *Reflections on the Revolution in France* and "A Letter to a Member of the National Assembly." In this latter speech he attacks the French revolutionaries and their doctrine of the rights of man for spreading an "ethics of vanity" (50). In this vein, much Straussian scholarship addresses the corrosive effects of modern natural rights discourse on individual subject formation. See Strauss, *Natural Rights and History*; Stanlis, *Edmund Burke and the Natural Law*; and Canavan, *The Political Reason of Edmund Burke*.

15   Lefebvre, "The Rights of Man and the Care of the Self," 526–34.
16   Wollstonecraft, *A Vindication of the Rights of Woman*, 129. Hereafter cited *VRW* in text, followed by page reference.
17   See Faubert, "Introduction."
18   Tomaselli, "Introduction," xi.
19   Chapter 4 of *Rights of Woman*, "Observations on the State of Degradation to Which Woman Is Reduced by Various Causes," abounds with such characterizations.
20   Tomaselli, "Introduction," xxv.
21   See especially Botting, *Wollstonecraft, Mill, and Women's Human Rights*.
22   Taylor, *Mary Wollstonecraft and the Feminist Imagination*, 214.
23   Taylor, *Mary Wollstonecraft and the Feminist Imagination*, 55–56. Taylor continues: "The heart of Wollstonecraft's feminism was not a campaigning agenda for improvements in women's status, but a complex critique of the impact of power relations on the feminine psyche. . . . It is to this goal, the replacement of artificial Woman with the human creature of God's creation, that the *Rights of Woman* principally devotes itself, rather than to the political rights named in its title" (56–57).
24   Todd, "Introduction," xix, and *Mary Wollstonecraft*, 179; Sapiro, *A Vindication of Political Virtue*, 118; and Bergès, *The Routledge Guidebook to Wollstonecraft's A Vindication of the Rights of Woman*, 22, 26.
25   Taylor and Bergès argue that *Maria, or the Wrongs of Women* (1798) can be seen as Wollstonecraft's promised work on the unjust legal status and treatment of women. See Taylor, *Mary Wollstonecraft and the Feminist Imagination*, 55–56, 228–29, and Bergès, *The Routledge Guidebook to Wollstonecraft's A Vindication of the Rights of Woman*, 89–91. In the Advertisement to *Rights of Woman*, Wollstonecraft signaled her intention to write a second volume on the "laws relative to women, and the consideration of their peculiar duties" (71; see also 235). She did not live to undertake this task, but William Godwin published a series of her notes along with other posthumous works, "Hints [Chiefly Designed to Have Been Incorporated in the Second Part of the *Vindication of the Rights of Woman*]," reproduced in *VRW*, 295–303.
26   O'Neill, *The Burke-Wollstonecraft Debate*, 185–94.
27   Halldenius, "The Primacy of Right," 77. This argument is expanded in *Mary Wollstonecraft and Feminist Republicanism*, 19–50.
28   Bergès, *The Routledge Guidebook to Wollstonecraft's A Vindication of the Rights of Woman*, 22.
29   Slaughter, *Human Rights, Inc.*, 79, 80. See also Donnelly, *Universal Human Rights in Theory and Practice*, 13–17; and Cheah, "Acceptable Uses of People": "[human rights] teach every human being to recognize that he or she is human and, therefore, is entitled to these rights, and to recognize other human beings as having the same rights. They make us human at the level of awareness, cognition, and recognition" (210).
30   Slaughter, *Human Rights, Inc.*, 26.
31   What I call the "Wollstonecraft Paradox" should not be confused with Carole Pateman's similar sounding "Wollstonecraft's Dilemma," which concerns how

women are simultaneously included and excluded from the polity on the basis of the same capacities and attributes. Pateman, "Equality, Difference, Subordination."

32 Locke, *Second Treatise of Government*, §87, §89.

33 Wollstonecraft, *A Vindication of the Rights of Men*, 7.

34 Equal rights as *foreign to their sex* is a phrase of Germaine de Staël's that Wollstonecraft quotes in *Rights of Woman* (185). For Wollstonecraft, Staël typifies the "educated" woman who wishes to exclude women from public affairs.

35 A century later George Eliot will call this kind of education "a girlish instruction comparable to the nibblings and judgments of a discursive mouse." *Middlemarch*, 26.

36 Burke's elegy to chivalry is found in *Reflections on the Revolution in France*, 66.

37 Engster, "Mary Wollstonecraft's Nurturing Liberalism."

38 See especially Wollstonecraft's early works, *On the Education of Daughters*, 43–44, and "The Treatment of Animals," 367–71, both in volume 4 of *The Works of Mary Wollstonecraft*.

39 The sexual division of virtues is the guiding concept of Sapiro's examination of Wollstonecraft's corpus. *A Vindication of Political Virtue*, 128–44.

40 Despite her polemic with Rousseau, Wollstonecraft follows his general argument. "Impulsion by appetite alone," Rousseau states in *The Social Contract*, "is slavery, and obedience to self-imposed law is freedom." *The Essential Rousseau*, 21.

41 Lear, *A Case for Irony*, 3.

42 Ozouf, "Liberty, Equality, Fraternity."

43 Ozouf, "Fraternity," 694.

44 Ozouf, "Liberty, Equality, Fraternity," 86.

45 Though not exclusively. See, for example, her remarks on mother-daughter friendships (*VRW* 122).

46 O'Neill situates Wollstonecraft's criticism of chivalric love in relation to Burke's early writings on beauty, littleness, and contempt. See *The Burke-Wollstonecraft Debate*, 158–73.

47 Wollstonecraft, *Rights of Men*, 9.

48 Foucault, "À propos de la généalogie de l'éthique," 1448. This interview was initially conducted in English and published as "On the Genealogy of Ethics." For the French translation Foucault made modifications and introduced new remarks, including the passage quoted here.

49 Woolf, *The Common Reader*, 163. For a biography that emphasizes Wollstonecraft's life in terms of ongoing brave experimentation, see Gordon's *Vindication*.

50 On this subject of a "style" of existence, I am guided by Veyne's observations on Foucault: "*Style* [for Foucault] does not mean distinction or dandyism. 'Style' takes on the meaning that the word held for the Greeks, for whom an artist was first and foremost an artisan or craftsman." *Foucault*, 106.

51 Substituting the term *genealogy* (or "history of the present") would not fare better. Genealogical analysis is certainly indispensable for the study of human rights, especially given how prone its historiography is to progressivism and teleology. Indeed, one of the great advances made in recent human rights scholarship is that its history has taken a sharp genealogical turn. Moyn's *The Last Utopia*, to name

only the most prominent example, demonstrates how human rights emerged not only recently but also as the result of contingent turns of history rather than rationally inevitable trends. That said, even genealogical analysis requires a measure of filiation (or of relationship, even) between historical authors and events. And it is precisely such filiations that are missing between the authors I have identified as key expositors of the care of the self in human rights.

52 Almost never: the exceptions I have found are a snide ad hominem by Tocqueville about Wollstonecraft (*Democracy in America*, 575), and a handful of dismissive remarks by Malik of Bergson.

53 See Moyn, *The Last Utopia*, 11–43. I discuss this issue in several of the coming chapters.

CHAPTER 3. Critique of Human Rights and Care of the Self

1 See Garber, Hassen, and Walkowitz, eds., *The Turn to Ethics*.

2 Connolly, *The Ethos of Pluralization*, *Why I Am Not a Secularist*, and *Pluralism*. See also Dumm, *Michel Foucault and the Politics of Freedom*. Other applications of Foucault's conception of ethics to political problems (broadly understood) include Faubion, *An Anthropology of Ethics*; Heyes, *Self-Transformations*; and Mahmood, *Politics of Piety*.

3 Critchley, *The Ethics of Deconstruction* and *Infinitely Demanding*; Butler, *Giving an Account of Oneself* and *Precarious Life*; Perpich, *The Ethics of Emmanuel Levinas*; Caygill, *Levinas and the Political*; and Manderson, *Proximity, Levinas, and the Soul of Law*.

4 Nussbaum, *Political Emotions*, *Creating Capabilities*, and *Hiding from Humanity*.

5 See, for example, Button's reinterpretation of social contract theory in terms of the formation of civic character and the cultivation of political self-understanding. "The transformative ethos working throughout the social contract tradition is manifested in widespread concerns about the virtues, habits, and opinions of citizens that are deemed foundational to the long-term sustainability of a just political society." *Contract, Culture, and Citizenship*, 6.

6 See Mouffe, "Which Ethics for Democracy?"; Laclau, "Deconstruction, Pragmatism, Hegemony"; Shulman, "Acknowledgment and Disavowal as an Idiom for Theorizing Politics"; Honig, "The Politics of Ethos."

7 See McNay, "Self as Enterprise"; Foster, "Therapeutic Culture, Authenticity, and Neo-Liberalism"; Furedi, *Therapy Culture*; Illouz, *Saving the Modern Soul*; Brown, *Politics Out of History*; and Dean, "The Politics of Avoidance."

8 Myers, *Worldly Ethics*, 2.

9 Myers, *Worldly Ethics*, 24. See also Myers, "Resisting Foucauldian Ethics."

10 Myers, *Worldly Ethics*, 47. To bolster Myers's case we can also point to the rise of the term *self-care* (that is, #selfcare) on social media, which so often consists of people tending to their own well-being through pampering and consumerism. See Kisner, "The Politics of Conspicuous Displays of Self-Care."

11 Foucault, *The Hermeneutics of the Self*, 107.

12 Plato, *Alcibiades*, in *Complete Works*, 124c–135d.

13 Foucault, "The Ethics of the Concern for Self as a Practice of Freedom," 287.

14 Myers, *Worldly Ethics*, 146, emphasis added.

15 See Ahmed on care of the self in "Selfcare as Warfare" (accessed December 21, 2016), and specifically, this observation: "Neoliberalism sweeps up too much when all forms of self-care become symptoms of neo-liberalism."

16 Moyn, *The Last Utopia*, 11–43; Hoffman, ed., *Human Rights in the Twentieth Century*; Eckel and Moyn, eds., *The Breakthrough*; and Keys, *Reclaiming American Virtue*.

17 Ignatieff, *Human Rights as Politics and Idolatry*, 55, *passim*. I note that a great many of the central concepts and commitments of Ignatieff's lectures—such as his emphasis on moral individualism, minimalism, the protection of the weak from the strong, and hatred of cruelty—derive from the thought of his teacher, Judith Shklar.

18 Brown, "The Most We Can Hope For . . . ," 461.

19 Brown and Forst, *The Power of Tolerance*, 14. Brown's main work on tolerance is *Regulating Aversion*.

20 Brown, "The Most We Can Hope For . . . ," 461.

21 Ignatieff, "Human Rights," 323, quoted by Brown, "The Most We Can Hope For . . . ," 455.

22 Ignatieff, *Human Rights as Politics and Idolatry*, 17–22, 63–77.

23 Brown, "The Most We Can Hope For . . . ," 456.

24 For a sophisticated statement of this view, see Griffin, *On Human Rights*, 9–56.

25 My sense is that it is not fair. The line Brown draws between moral individualism (which Ignatieff certainly favors) and politics is very bright. Yet consider this remark by Ignatieff: "To be a rights-bearer is not to hold some sacred inviolability but to commit oneself to live in a community where rights conflicts are adjudicated through persuasion, rather than violence" (*Human Rights as Politics and Idolatry*, 84). Here, human rights do more than foster an ethos or tend toward a particular sense of self. They *are*, in the strong sense, an ethos: they amount to a disposition or attitude on the part of subjects to lead a deliberative life, that is, to affect others through persuasion rather than through violence. How this sits with the "minimalism" Ignatieff claims for human rights is anyone's guess: tying human rights to an ethos of equality, moral individualism, autonomy, and mutual deliberation seems rather thick and maximalist. But neither does it fit with Brown's picture of human rights as linked to political withdrawal and disengagement. Ignatieff is explicit that the mission of human rights—in fact, the very substance of human rights—is to open up dialogical relationships in order to resolve and direct public affairs.

26 Marks, "Four Human Rights Myths" and "Human Rights and Root Causes."

27 Slaughter, *Human Rights, Inc.*, 90–94. Badiou makes a similar criticism in *Ethics*, 4–17.

28 Hopgood, *The Endtimes of Human Rights*, vii–xvi, 24–46.

29 Moyn, "A Powerless Companion," and Nolan, "Human Rights and Market Fundamentalism in the Long 1970s."

30 See Beetham, "What Future for Economic and Social Rights?"; Baxi, *The Future of Human Rights*; Gill, "Globalisation, Market Civilization and Disciplinary Neoliberalism"; and Grear, *Redirecting Human Rights*.

31 Ignatieff, *Human Rights as Politics and Idolatry*, 90.

32   Brown, "The Most We Can Hope For . . . ," 457.

33   Brown, "The Most We Can Hope For . . . ," 458.

34   See, for example, Douzinas, "The Poverty of (Rights) Jurisprudence" and "The End(s) of Human Rights"; and Baxi, "Reinventing Human Rights in an Era of Hyper-Globalization."

35   Brown, *Undoing the Demos*, 9. In labeling neoliberalism a "normative order of reason" Brown follows Foucault's 1978–79 lectures on neoliberalism as a governing rationality, *The Birth of Biopolitics*.

36   Brown, *Undoing the Demos*, 10.

37   Brown, *Undoing the Demos*, 21–24.

38   Brown, *Undoing the Demos*, 87.

39   Brown, *Undoing the Demos*, 87, emphasis added.

40   Brown, "The Most We Can Hope For . . . ," 456.

41   My term *Homo juridicus* should not be confused with Brown's third persona, *Homo legalis*, which she adapts from Foucault's lectures on biopolitics. Brown, *Undoing the Demos*, 79–99.

42   Brown, *Undoing the Demos*, 110, emphasis added.

43   Brown, *Undoing the Demos*, 39.

44   Brown, *Undoing the Demos*, 43.

45   See what Hopgood calls "Human Rights" (with a capital H and R) in *The Endtimes of Human Rights*. See Indaimo's criticism of the inherent egocentrism of human rights discourse in *The Self, Ethics and Human Rights*. In the popular media, consider the angry backlash against the KONY 2012 film and campaign, which sought to bring attention to the use of child soldiers by Joseph Kony's paramilitary group in Uganda. The backlash came in two waves. The first attacked the perceived moral and factual simplicity of the film. The second criticized its bandwagoners and their light, convenient, self-serving support.

46   https://en.wikipedia.org/wiki/Slacktivism, accessed March 24, 2016.

47   http://www.urbandictionary.com/define.php?term=slacktivism, accessed March 24, 2016.

48   An exception is Foster, "The Therapeutic Spirit of Neoliberalism," 95–96. Drawing on the work of Alasdair MacIntyre and Robert Bellah, his article concludes with an ethical criticism of therapeutic culture.

CHAPTER 4. Human Rights as Spiritual Exercises

1   The most important are *The Inner Citadel*, *What Is Ancient Philosophy?*, *Philosophy as a Way of Life*, and *Exercises spirituels et philosophie antique*.

2   Foucault, *The Use of Pleasure*, 8.

3   On Hadot's cardinal influence on Foucault's later work, see Davidson, "Introductory Remarks to Pierre Hadot," 199–202.

4   For a detailed reconstruction, see Irrera, "Pleasure and Transcendence of the Self." See also Davidson, "Ethics as Ascetics."

5   Hadot, "Reflections on the Idea of the 'Cultivation of the Self,'" 211. Hadot repeats

this criticism in a later essay, "Le sage et le monde," 345–46. The passage critical of Foucault was not included in the English translation of this essay.

6 Foucault, "What Is Enlightenment?," 309–12.

7 Hadot, "Reflections on the Idea of the 'Cultivation of the Self,'" 212.

8 For an engaging account of Tocqueville's and Beaumont's travels, see Damrosch, *Tocqueville's Discovery of America*.

9 Tocqueville, *Democracy in America*, 232. Hereafter cited as DA in text, followed by page reference.

10 See Mansfield, *Tocqueville*, 36, and Mansfield and Winthrop, "Editors' Introduction," xxvii.

11 Tocqueville treats the "French Revolution" from a similar perspective in *The Ancien Régime and the French Revolution*: as a process dating back to Louis XIV and continuing to his day.

12 Moyn, *The Last Utopia*, 13. See Arendt, *The Origins of Totalitarianism*, 267–302, and Tuck, *The Rights of War and Peace* and *Natural Rights Theories*.

13 Moyn, *The Last Utopia*, 13.

14 Of course, such universalism in the United States was far from universal. Equal rights for women and nonwhite Americans were not even on the horizon of conceivability. But generally speaking, by 1820 (that is, eleven years before Tocqueville visited the United States) universal white male suffrage was the norm, and by 1850 almost all requirements to own property or pay taxes in order to vote had been abandoned. Keyssar, *The Rights to Vote*, 29. On property restrictions on the political franchise, which were set state by state, see Ishay, *The History of Human Rights*, 91–99. Tocqueville himself brackets the racial exclusions in the United States as "American without being democratic" and discusses it only in the context of "The Three Races" chapter in *Democracy in America* (DA 302–400). For an excellent account of how Tocqueville may have understood the tragedies of genocide and slavery as internal to democracy, see Lerner, *The Thinking Revolutionary*, 174–91.

15 Or, better put: contemporary human rights treaties—most prominently, the International Covenant on Civil and Political Rights (1976)—serve to guarantee that each state uphold the basic civil and political rights (which, in Tocqueville's day, would have been considered "rights of man") of all individuals within its territory and subject to its jurisdiction.

16 Hadot, *What Is Ancient Philosophy?*, 3.

17 Hadot, *What Is Ancient Philosophy?*, 180. Hadot gives several overviews of spiritual exercises in his work. Three of the most helpful are "Spiritual Exercises," *What Is Ancient Philosophy?*, 1–9, and *The Present Alone Is Our Happiness*, 87–97. Hadot's predecessor on this topic is Rabbow's work on "moral exercises" in *Seelenführung*.

18 Hadot, "Spiritual Exercises," 82, translation modified.

19 See Hadot, *What Is Ancient Philosophy?*, 172–233. Several essays in Davidson and Worms, eds., *Pierre Hadot*, address this topic.

20 Another author who conceives of rights along these lines is J. S. Mill, who, not coincidentally, is influenced by Tocqueville. See Zivi, *Making Rights Claims*, 52–67. "Rights claiming, on [Mill's] account, is a valuable practice for democratic societies

not because it results in specific policy or legal ends but because it provides opportunities for civic engagement and the cultivation of political judgment" (53).

21 Letter to J. S. Mill, November 14, 1839. In Tocqueville, *Alexis de Tocqueville and Gustave de Beaumont in America*, 583.

22 Wolin, *Tocqueville between Two Worlds*, 307.

23 Letter to Louis de Kergolay, December 26, 1836. In the Nolla edition of *Democracy in America*, 32, translation modified.

24 Wolin, *Tocqueville between Two Worlds*, 316; Manent, *Tocqueville and the Nature of Democracy*, xiii; Damrosch, *Tocqueville's Discovery of America*, xvii.

25 Jaume, *Tocqueville*, 141.

26 Foucault, "The Political Technology of Individuals," 145.

27 Wolin, *Tocqueville between Two Worlds*, 7, 531–60.

28 Cited in Schleifer, *The Making of Tocqueville's Democracy in America*, 184.

29 Davidson, "Preface," xii.

30 See Hadot, *What Is Philosophy?*, 3.

31 Tocqueville never witnessed American local government firsthand. His account of the township is indebted to the information supplied by an important American contact (Jared Sparks). See Damrosch, *Tocqueville's Discovery of America*, 100–102.

32 Wolin, *Tocqueville between Two Worlds*, 208.

33 Hadot, "Spiritual Exercises," 103.

34 Tocqueville, *The Ancien Régime and the French Revolution*, 6, translation modified.

35 See Tocqueville, *Democracy in America*, 64, 89, and *The Ancien Régime and the French Revolution*, 6.

36 Hadot, *What Is Ancient Philosophy?*, 29, 59.

37 Wolin, *Tocqueville between Two Worlds*, 211; Pierson, *Tocqueville in America*, 411–12.

38 Hadot, "The Sage and the World."

39 Hadot, *What Is Ancient Philosophy?*, 180.

40 Pascal, *Pensées*, 214 ("Discourse on the Machine").

41 The need for human rights to "remind" the individual that he or she lives in society was also a topic of debate during the drafting of the Universal Declaration in 1948. I return to this issue in my chapters on Roosevelt and Malik.

42 See Nedelsky, "Reconceiving Rights and Constitutionalism"; Ivison, *Rights*, 21–22; Zivi, *Making Rights Claims*, 3–23.

43 Marx, "On the Jewish Question," 52.

44 Hadot, *The Present Alone Is Our Happiness*, 108.

45 Furet and Mélonio, "Introduction," 7.

46 Hadot, *What Is Ancient Philosophy?*, 3.

47 The last two sentences appear as marginal comments in Tocqueville's draft of *Democracy in America*, reproduced in the Nolla edition, 1275.

48 Foucault, *The Hermeneutics of the Subject*, 251.

49 Hellbeck, *Revolution on My Mind*. See also Halfin, *Red Autobiographies*.

50 King, *Where Do We Go from Here?*

51 Freire, *Pedagogy of the Oppressed*, 17–22.

52 Malkki, *The Need to Help*. I address this book at length in chapter 9.

53 Palahniuk, *Fight Club*, 48–50.

54 Foucault, "The Ethics of the Concern for Self as a Practice of Freedom," 291. See Butler's gloss on this idea of Foucault's in "What Is Critique?," 321.

55 Hadot, "Reflections on the Idea of the 'Cultivation of the Self,'" 212.

56 McGushin, *Foucault's Askesis*, 104.

CHAPTER 5. Human Rights as a Way of Life

1 Lefebvre, *Human Rights as a Way of Life*.

2 Soulez and Worms, *Bergson*, 160.

3 Soulez and Worms, *Bergson*, 185.

4 Bergson, *Mélanges*, 1351, 1420–21. In a later work, Bergson deepens the idea that intellectual cooperation can work for international peace: "Anyone who is thoroughly familiar with the language and literature of a people cannot be wholly its enemy. This should be borne in mind when we ask education to pave the way for international understanding." *The Two Sources of Morality and Religion*, 286.

5 Glendon, *The Forum and the Tower*, 3–6.

6 Soulez and Worms, *Bergson*, 263–65. Soulez and Worms caution that these events are perhaps apocryphal. Although reported at the time by friends and commentators, there is no documentary evidence from Bergson himself to serve as confirmation.

7 Moyn's thesis has inspired other works in the history of human rights, including Hoffman, ed., *Human Rights in the Twentieth Century*, and Eckel and Moyn, eds., *The Breakthrough*.

8 Moyn, *The Last Utopia*, 8.

9 Moyn, *The Last Utopia*, 5.

10 Hunt, *Inventing Human Rights*, 27.

11 Hunt, *Inventing Human Rights*, 35–69.

12 Hunt, *Inventing Human Rights*, 146–75. She first develops this argument in the introduction to her documentary history, Hunt, ed., *The French Revolution and Human Rights*.

13 Hunt, *Inventing Human Rights*, 150.

14 Hunt, *Inventing Human Rights*, 147.

15 Hunt, *Inventing Human Rights*, 146. I note that Adams might not have been pleased for Hunt to have given his phrase a positive gloss. The full quote reads: "There will be no End of it. New Claims will arise. Women will demand a Vote. Lads from 12 to 21 will think their Rights not enough attended to, and every Man, who has not a Farthing, will demand an equal Voice with any other in all Acts of State. It tends to confound and destroy all Distinctions, and prostrate all Ranks, to one common Levell." *Papers of John Adams*, 212.

16 Moyn, *The Last Utopia*, 6–8. *Church history* is Moyn's term to describe a type of historiography that treats its cause or guiding idea as "discovered rather than made in history" (6).

17 That said, Hunt's historicism is a model of what Bergson calls the "retrospective illusion." See Bergson, *The Creative Mind*, 73–86.

18 Bergson, *The Two Sources of Morality and Religion*, 101; hereafter cited as *TS* in text, followed by page reference.

19 de Waal, "Morally Evolved," 55. De Waal makes no reference to Bergson.

20 de Waal, "Morally Evolved," 53.

21 de Waal, "The Tower of Morality," 163–64. Another contemporary author close in spirit to Bergson and de Waal is Joshua Greene. In *Moral Tribes* he argues from a combination of utilitarianism and evolutionary theory that morality and love are biological mechanisms enabling cooperation and reproduction, and, more pointedly, that the evolved morality that helps members of a community to cooperate is not conducive to a similar harmony between members of different communities. As he puts it, "Insofar as morality is a biological adaptation, it evolved not only as a device for putting Us ahead of Me, but as a device for putting Us ahead of Them" (24).

22 In Chevalier, *Entretiens avec Bergson*, 215.

23 Jankélévitch, *Henri Bergson*, 158.

24 Jankélévitch, *Henri Bergson*, 153, translation modified. See also Jankélévitch, *The Bad Conscience*, 7–8.

25 Foucault, *The Use of Pleasure*, 10–11.

26 See Kisukidi, *Bergson ou l'humanité créatrice*.

27 Bergson, *Mélanges*, 1566.

28 Jankélévitch, *Henri Bergson*, 155.

29 Lefebvre, *Human Rights as a Way of Life*, 92–100, and Lefebvre, "Jankélévitch on Bergson."

30 Plato, *Symposium*, 210a–212c, in *Complete Works*. See Taubes, *The Political Theology of Paul*, 55.

31 See White, "Habit as a Force of Life in Durkheim and Bergson."

32 Extended discussion of joy can be found in Bergson's very earliest and very last works. Joy features in his very early *Extraits de Lucrèce* (1884), which is not surprising given that it is a commentary on Epicureanism. It is also the first emotion he examines in terms of duration in *Time and Free Will* (1889). His most important discussions of joy are to be found in *Two Sources* and *The Creative Mind* (1934). See Lefebvre, "Bergson, Human Rights, and Joy."

33 Bergson, *Mind-Energy*, 23. Hadot also draws attention to this passage in "Reflections on the Idea of the 'Cultivation of the Self,'" 212.

34 Bergson, *The Creative Mind*, 86. I note that three essays in *Creative Mind* ("The Possible and the Real," "Philosophical Intuition," and "The Life and Work of Ravaisson") conclude with a discussion of joy, and the privileged relation between joy, creation, and philosophy.

35 On the wider tradition, largely Christian but also Romantic, on the connection between joy and self-overcoming, see Potkay, *The Story of Joy*, 30–49.

36 Lefebvre, *Human Rights as a Way of Life*, 3–5, 15–31.

37 Hunt, *Inventing Human Rights*, 147.

38 Lefebvre, *Human Rights as a Way of Life*, 100–109.

39 Lavelle, *The Dilemma of Narcissus*, 99.

CHAPTER 6. On Human Rights Criticism

1 Williams, *Keywords*, 82–83.
2 Hopgood, *Keepers of the Flame*, 73–104, and Neier, *The International Human Rights Movement*, 204–31.
3 Merry, *Human Rights and Gender Violence*, 72–102.
4 Foucault, "The Masked Philosopher," 323.
5 Foucault's 1978 lecture "What Is Critique?" is an important precursor to this essay. See Lorenzini and Davidson, "Introduction," and more generally, their edited volume of Foucault's later writings on criticism, *Qu'est-ce que la critique?*
6 Foucault, "What Is Enlightenment?," 305.
7 Foucault, "What Is Enlightenment?," 312.
8 Foucault, "What Is Enlightenment?," 313.
9 Foucault, "What Is Enlightenment?," 315.
10 Foucault, "What Is Enlightenment?," 319. My interpretation of Foucault is here informed by two excellent guides to his later philosophy: Koopman's *Genealogy as Critique*, 182–216, and especially McGuishin's *Foucault's Askesis*, in which he identifies two methodological anchor points in Foucault's later work: "a diagnostic moment and an *etho-poetic* moment" (22). Closer to the world of human rights and political theory, I note that Goodale, "Human Rights and Moral Agency," and Wall, *Moral Creativity*, also use the term *poetic* in this sense of subject-making.
11 Foucault, "The Political Technology of Individuals," 145.
12 Bergson, *The Creative Mind*, 37.
13 Foucault, "On the Genealogy of Ethics," 271.
14 Foucault, *The Hermeneutics of the Subject*, 251.
15 Foucault, *The Hermeneutics of the Subject*, 251–52.
16 See McGuishin's *Foucault's Askesis* on the risks that Foucault saw in the similarities between ethics and care of the self on the one hand, and contemporary liberal and biopolitical forms of power on the other hand (242–81).
17 Foucault, "Preface," xiii.
18 Slaughter, *Human Rights, Inc.*, 79, 80.
19 Slaughter, *Human Rights, Inc.*, 3.
20 Slaughter, *Human Rights, Inc.*, 4.
21 Slaughter, *Human Rights, Inc.*, 20.
22 Slaughter, *Human Rights, Inc.*, 91–92.
23 See Durkheim, *Moral Education*, 64–127. Surprisingly, given how closely Durkheim matches his theory, Slaughter does not mention him in *Human Rights, Inc.*
24 Wollstonecraft, *Letters Written during a Short Residence in Sweden, Norway, and Denmark*, Letter 6.
25 Freire, *Pedagogy of the Oppressed*, 51–52.
26 Foucault, *The Use of Pleasure*, 8.
27 Slaughter, *Human Rights, Inc.*, 114.
28 Slaughter, *Human Rights, Inc.*, 107.
29 Malik, *Man in the Struggle for Peace*, xxxvi–xxxvii.

30 This formulation comes from a letter from Malik to Bayard Dodge in 1937, cited in Mitoma, "Charles H. Malik and Human Rights," 232.

CHAPTER 7. An Ethic of Resistance I

1 Ignatieff, *Human Rights as Politics and Idolatry*, 53.
2 Morsink, *The Universal Declaration of Human Rights*, xii. See also Flowers, "How to Define Human Rights Education?," 113–14, 121.
3 UN Economic and Social Council, Drafting Committee on an International Bill of Human Rights, 1st Sess., 11th mtg. at 10, UN Doc. E/CN.4/AC.1/SR.11 (June 19, 1947).
4 UN Economic and Social Council, Drafting Committee on an International Bill of Human Rights, 1st Sess., 2nd mtg. at 3, UN Doc. E/CN.4/AC.1/SR.2 (June 11, 1947).
5 Foucault, *The Hermeneutics of the Subject*, 252.
6 Foucault, "Preface," xiii.
7 Another teacher who profoundly influenced Malik at Harvard was the idealist philosopher William Ernest Hocking. I thank Linde Lindkvist for pointing this out to me. "With regard to human rights, Malik and Hocking were clearly on the same page. They both viewed their own philosophical work and the struggle for the internationalization of human rights as analogous projects. The principal aim was to breathe new life into the old notion of the human soul and to affirm the human person's natural responsibility towards himself, his fellow-men and, ultimately, to God. In his talk at the [Commission of the Churches on International Affairs] luncheon in 1949, Malik concluded that this was essentially what the Commission on Human Rights was doing in the struggle to codify human rights: 'We are trying in effect, knowingly or unknowingly, to go back to the Platonic-Christian tradition which affirms man's original, integral dignity and immortality.'" Lindkvist, *Religious Freedom and the Universal Declaration of Human Rights*, 54–55.
8 For Malik's self-characterization as a philosopher, see "The Task Ahead," 25. Edward Said, incidentally, gives a decidedly ambivalent portrait of Malik, his uncle by marriage, in his memoir *Out of Place*. Malik is remembered as an intellectual mentor, but also as prone to self-importance and dogmatism.
9 Malik, "Commission on Human Rights Verbatim Record, Fourteenth Meeting," 507.
10 Roosevelt, "Commission on Human Rights Verbatim Record, Fourteenth Meeting," 508–9.
11 Morsink, *The Universal Declaration of Human Rights*, 37. See chapter 2 of Morsink's book, "World War II as Catalyst," 36–91. For the centrality of Nazism to the drafting process, see also Joas, *The Sacredness of the Person*, 69–96; Glendon, *A World Made New*, 9–10, 176; Ignatieff, *Human Rights as Politics and Idolatry*; and Savelsberg, *Crime and Human Rights*.
12 See Roosevelt, "Statement by Mrs. Franklin D. Roosevelt US Representative to the General Assembly," 972, and Malik, "Speech of Thursday 9 December 1948," 117.
13 As Roosevelt writes in her regular newspaper column "My Day," "The USSR, of course, had wanted to say in this article [Article 27 of the Declaration]—as well as

in every other one—that the law of the individual country must govern rights that were declared or that these rights could only be obtained in measure in which laws of the country permitted them to be obtained." Roosevelt, "My Day, 27 November 1948," 954.

14 Malik, "From Dr. Malik's Diaries," 235.

15 See especially Anderson, *Eyes off the Prize*, 1–7, 97–99, 130–35, 200–201. Anderson argues that despite her reputation as a champion of social equality for African Americans (as depicted, for example, by Black in *Casting Her Own Shadow* and Lash in *Eleanor*), Roosevelt was first and foremost concerned with preserving the reputation of the United States as the moral leader of the free world. In practice, this meant resisting attempts by the Human Rights Commission to include human rights that could be used to attack the United States (foremost, a human right to distributive equality), as well as assuring anxious Southern Democrats that American policy would not come under UN scrutiny.

16 See, for example, Charles Malik (Representative for Lebanon) in UN General Assembly, 3rd Sess., 180th Plenary Meeting at 859–860, UN Doc. A/PV.180 (December 9, 1948). And in a 1950 letter written to George Hakim, Malik writes that "[The Soviets'] keenness and vigor and opposition are necessary [to the Human Rights Commission], even if I do not agree with their point of view." Cited in Mitoma, *Human Rights and the Negotiation of American Power*, 128.

17 A complexity I cannot address in my chapters on Roosevelt and Malik is that a number of communists involved in the drafting process (such as Vladislav Ribnikar and Valentin Tepliakov) are explicit that they do not mean to dismiss the individual. Far from obliterating the self, they argue that selfhood is accessed and enhanced through engagement with collective ideals and practices. See, for example, Tepliakov's remarks in "Commission on Human Rights Verbatim Record, Fourteenth Meeting." As Hellbeck more generally argues in *Revolution on My Mind*, from within such a mindset, "the enlarged life of the collective was seen as the source of true subjecthood. It promised vitality, historical meaning, and moral value, and it was intensely desired" (9). That said, neither Roosevelt nor Malik view communist collectivism in this favorable light. For them it endangers individual autonomy, and they position human rights (and care of the self undertaken with human rights) against it.

18 See Roosevelt, *The Moral Basis of Democracy*, 62.

19 Roosevelt, "The Promise of Human Rights," 162. See also Roosevelt, "Statement on the Purpose of the Declaration of Human Rights," 826–27. René Cassin is another important drafter who thinks of the Declaration in terms of a "moral and educational manifesto." See Prost and Winter, *René Cassin and Human Rights*, 239.

20 See Glendon's chapter on "The Implementation Debate" in *A World Made New*, 79–98.

21 Malik, "The Drafting of the Universal Declaration of Human Rights," 25; Roosevelt, *The Moral Basis of Democracy*, 62–63.

22 Black, "Introduction," xiii. An additional challenge in approaching Roosevelt's (and Malik's) corpus is that there is virtually no scholarship dedicated to her social, political, psychological, and religious thought as distinct from biography, journal-

ism, diplomacy, and activism. The best commentators on Roosevelt, and here I think of Mary Ann Glendon and Allida Black, discuss her life and thought within the context of specific social and political interventions (human rights and diplomacy for Glendon, civil rights and party politics for Black). I do not mean to suggest that Roosevelt's thought can or should be divorced from the particular causes to which she devoted so much of her life. That would not be faithful to her vision of social and political thinking. Still, a synthetic and more theoretical treatment of her corpus has not yet been attempted and, to my mind, would be a rewarding exercise in extracting and organizing themes from her writings on politics, psychology, diplomacy, etiquette, economics, race, gender, religion, and philosophy. The best approximation is Black's extended "Introduction" to *Tomorrow Is Now*.

23 Bergson, *The Creative Mind*, 88–89.

24 Roosevelt, "Address to Americans for Democratic Action," 359.

25 Franklin Delano Roosevelt, "State of the Union Message to Congress (The Four Freedoms)," 99.

26 Franklin Delano Roosevelt, "First Inaugural Address," 29.

27 Roosevelt, *Tomorrow Is Now*, 77.

28 For a sample of Roosevelt's writings on these issues, see *Courage in a Political World*, 34–36, 40–41, 45–57, 120–25, 139, 223–30, 239, 243–44, 265–66, 277–78, 279. See also Black, *Casting Her Own Shadow*, 1–6, 85–150, 199–204.

29 Roosevelt, *Tomorrow Is Now*, 5.

30 Roosevelt, *The Autobiography of Eleanor Roosevelt*, 412.

31 See Roosevelt, *You Learn by Living*, i–ii, 25–41; *The Autobiography of Eleanor Roosevelt*, xix, 410–16; and *Tomorrow Is Now*, 3–5.

32 Roosevelt, *You Learn by Living*, 113–14.

33 Roosevelt, *You Learn by Living*, 111.

34 Wollstonecraft, *Vindication of the Rights of Woman*, 125.

35 Roosevelt, *You Learn by Living*, 11.

36 See Roosevelt, *Tomorrow Is Now*, 5, 77; *The Moral Basis of Democracy*, 72–82; and *The Autobiography of Eleanor Roosevelt*, 409.

37 Roosevelt, *You Learn by Living*, 12–13, 21–22, 133–36, 148, 179.

38 Roosevelt, *You Learn by Living*, 22.

39 Roosevelt, *You Learn by Living*, ii.

40 Roosevelt, *You Learn by Living*, 136.

41 Although Roosevelt does not refer to him in her writings on the spirit of adventure, an author she holds dear has a similar view: Emerson (who took it from Montaigne, who took it from Seneca). See, for example, his essay "Friendship," in which he argues that we access the best part of ourselves through friends. "High thanks I owe you, excellent lovers, who carry out the world for me to new and noble depths, and enlarge the meaning of all my thoughts." *Essays and Lectures*, 343.

42 Roosevelt, *The Autobiography of Eleanor Roosevelt*, 68, emphasis added. She restates this idea later in her autobiography: "I never let an opportunity slip to increase my knowledge of people and conditions. Everything was grist to my mill: not only the things I saw but the people I met" (410).

43   Mill, *On Liberty*, 62.

44   Roosevelt, *You Learn by Living*, 118.

45   Roosevelt, *You Learn by Living*, 114.

46   Roosevelt, *The Autobiography of Eleanor Roosevelt*, 61.

47   Roosevelt, *You Learn by Living*, 118.

48   Roosevelt, *You Learn by Living*, 119.

49   Roosevelt, *You Learn by Living*, 111.

50   See Roosevelt, "Eleanor Roberts Interviews Eleanor Roosevelt."

51   Wittgenstein, *Tractatus Logico-Philosophicus*, 6.43.

52   Roosevelt, "Address to Americans for Democratic Action," 359.

53   See, for example, Roosevelt's criticism of the Daughters of the American Revolution for refusing to rent its auditorium to Marian Anderson because of her race. See Black, *Casting Her Own Shadow*, 42–44.

54   Roosevelt, *Tomorrow Is Now*, 3–5, 13–26, 111.

55   Roosevelt, "Speech on Behalf of Roosevelt College," 549–50. Roosevelt often made the case that racial discrimination in the United States gave the USSR valuable opportunities for criticism. For a series of references on this point, see Black, ed., *The Eleanor Roosevelt Papers*, vol. 2, 362n6.

56   Roosevelt, *Tomorrow Is Now*, 110–19; *You Learn by Living*, 151–68; and *The Moral Basis of Democracy*, 80–82.

57   See Roosevelt, *The Autobiography of Eleanor Roosevelt*, 309–13. See also *You Learn by Living*, 116–17.

58   Roosevelt, "Address to Americans for Democratic Action," 361.

59   Roosevelt, "Speech at the Phi Beta Kappa Association Founders' Day Dinner," 52.

60   Cited in Black, ed., *The Eleanor Roosevelt Papers*, vol. 1, 689.

61   Roosevelt, "My Day, 18 December 1947," 689.

62   Clapham, *Human Rights*, 2. See also Henkin, *The Age of Rights*, 17.

63   The best account is Reinbold, *Seeing the Myth in Human Rights*.

64   Glendon, *A World Made New*, 161. She cites Cassin, *La Pensée et l'action*, 114.

65   http://www.un.org/en/documents/udhr/, emphasis added.

66   I note that this phrase is adapted from the Preamble to the 1789 Declaration of the Rights of Man and Citizen: "The representatives of the French people, constituted as a National Assembly, and considering that ignorance, neglect or contempt of the rights of man are the sole causes of public misfortunes and of the corruption of governments, have resolved to set forth in a solemn Declaration the natural, inalienable, and sacred rights of man: so that by being constantly present to all the members of the social body this Declaration may always remind them of their rights and duties [*afin que cette déclaration, constamment présente à tous les membres du corps social, leur rappelle sans cesse leurs droits et leurs devoirs*]." http://www.textes.justice .gouv.fr/textes-fondamentaux-10086/droits-de-lhomme-et-libertes-fondamentales -10087/Declaration-des-droits-de-lhomme-et-du-citoyen-de-1789-10116.html.

67   I argue this claim at greater length in *Human Rights as a Way of Life*, 76–81.

68   Hadot, *What Is Ancient Philosophy?*, 180.

69   As Roosevelt says in a meeting of the Human Rights Commission, "The Declaration

would have moral, not mandatory, force." Eleanor Roosevelt, Chairman, UN Economic and Social Council, Commission on Human Rights, 3rd Sess., 48th mtg. at 6, UN Doc. E/CN.4/SR.48 (June 4, 1948).

70 Cassin emphasizes this role of the Declaration: "It was quite clear that the Declaration should bear above all an explanatory character," that it should serve as a "guide," and "have the function of keeping the fullest possible list of human rights in everybody's mind." UN Economic and Social Council, Commission on Human Rights, 2nd Sess.

71 Roosevelt, "Where Do Human Rights Begin?," 190.

72 Roosevelt, *The Moral Basis of Democracy*, 53.

73 Roosevelt, "Speech on Behalf of Roosevelt College," 549. See also *Tomorrow Is Now*, 9–13, 110–28.

74 Roosevelt, "Speech before UN General Assembly, 30th Plenary Session," 246–47.

75 Roosevelt, "The Struggle for Human Rights," 903.

76 Roosevelt, "Where Do Human Rights Begin?," 190.

77 Roosevelt, *You Learn by Living*, 112.

78 Roosevelt, *You Learn by Living*, 109–30.

79 Roosevelt, *You Learn by Living*, 119.

80 Roosevelt, *You Learn by Living*, 102.

81 Roosevelt, "The Minorities Question," 394.

82 Roosevelt, "My Day, 18 December 1947," 689.

83 Roosevelt, *You Learn by Living*, 136.

84 See Roosevelt, *You Learn by Living*, 3–41, and *The Autobiography of Eleanor Roosevelt*, xv–xix, 410–20.

85 Rorty, "Human Rights, Rationality, and Sentimentality," 176.

86 Roosevelt, "The Struggle for Human Rights," 903.

CHAPTER 8. An Ethic of Resistance II

1 Morsink, *The Universal Declaration of Human Rights*, 30.

2 See Glendon's chapter on Roosevelt and Malik in *The Forum and the Tower* (199–218).

3 Moyn, *The Last Utopia*, 65.

4 Mitoma, *Human Rights and the Negotiation of American Power*, 104.

5 Malik, "Drafting the Declaration," 242.

6 Cited in Glendon, *A World Made New*, 127.

7 Glendon, *A World Made New*, 128.

8 John Humphrey, the UN Secretariat's human rights director, spoke especially highly of him (despite initial misgivings). See *Human Rights and the United Nations*, 23, and *On the Edge of Greatness*, 144–46.

9 See Rawls, *The Law of Peoples*, 15; Ignatieff, *Human Rights as Politics and Idolatry*, 54; Nussbaum, *Women and Human Development*, 83, and *Creating Capabilities*, 182; Habermas, *Between Facts and Norms*, 98; Lefort, *Democracy and Political Theory*, 40; and Rorty, "Human Rights, Rationality, and Sentimentality."

10 Rorty, "Human Rights, Rationality, and Sentimentality," 169–70. See also his interview on post-metaphysical culture in *Take Care of Freedom and Truth Will Take Care
of Itself*, 46–55.

11 I note that the contemporary philosophy of human rights is not unanimous in
adopting a post-metaphysical approach. A recent campaign by such thinkers as
Chris Brown, John Tasioulas, and Jeremy Waldon insists that you cannot sidestep
human nature as a ground for human rights. Moreover, the wide interest recently
in theorizing human dignity points to the fact that an important current in the
philosophy of human rights is moving in a post-post-metaphysical direction. That
said, to my knowledge none of this literature draws on Malik. See Brown, "Human
Rights and Human Nature" and "'Human Nature,' Science and International
Political Theory"; Waldron, *Dignity, Rank, and Rights*; and Tasioulas, "Towards a
Philosophy of Human Rights." For my own part, I have built on Bergson's attempt to
propose a theory of human rights connected to key facts about human nature. See
Lefebvre, *Human Rights as a Way of Life*, 27–31, 51–57, 68–70.

12 Malik, "An International Bill of Rights," 58. See also Malik's remarks on Article 1 of
the Declaration in the Third Session of the Human Rights Commission. "The first
article of the Declaration should state those characteristics of human beings which
distinguished them from animals, that is, reason and conscience. Without reason
the very work [we] are engaged in would be impossible; what, then, more 'reasonable' than the explicit mention of the fact which constitutes the basis of [our]
work, in the very first article?" Charles Malik, Rapporteur, UN Economic and Social
Council, Commission on Human Rights, 3rd Sess., 50th mtg., UN Doc. E/CN.4/
SR.50 (June 4, 1948), 12.

13 Malik, "The Challenge of Human Rights," 157.

14 The most extended (and most curious) philosophical debate concerning the "nature
of man" during the drafting process took place in the United Nations' Third Committee, November 24, 1948. On this occasion delegates considered whether the
eponymous hero of Daniel Defoe's *Robinson Crusoe* served as an adequate stand-in
for humankind. See Whyte, "The Fortunes of Natural Man," for a detailed summary
and analysis. Slaughter treats this episode in *Human Rights, Inc.*, 45–63.

15 On several occasions, and always in response to Malik, delegates on the Human
Rights Commission tried to steer the conversation away from deep discussion of
human nature. See, for example, Hansa Mehta's (of India) plea that "we should
not enter this maze of ideology" at the Fourteenth Meeting of the Human Rights
Commission (February 4, 1947). Reproduced in Malik, "Four Basic Principles," 31.
See also Roland Lebeau's (of Belgium) response to Malik in the Third Session of the
Human Rights Commission "that a Declaration on Human Rights need not begin
with a definition of what constitutes the human being," a suggestion seconded by
the British and Indian delegates. Charles Malik, Rapporteur, UN Economic and
Social Council, Commission on Human Rights, 3rd Sess., 50th mtg., UN Doc. E/
CN.4/SR.50 (May 27, 1948), 12–13.

16 See Mitoma, *Human Rights and the Negotiation of American Power*, 116.

17 Maritain, *Man and the State*, 77. In *Human Rights as Politics and Idolatry*, Ignatieff

borrows this phrase from Maritain (though without attribution) as a building block for his own theory of human rights as "politics." "The Universal Declaration," says Ignatieff channeling Maritain, "enunciates rights; it does not explain why people have them" (77). Another relevant anecdote, this time involving Malik, points to a similar reluctance to discuss foundational issues. It is Roosevelt's recounting of the first meeting between Malik, Chang, Humphrey, and herself at her Washington Square apartment: "[A]s we settled down over the teacups one of them made a remark with philosophical implications, and a heated discussion ensued. Dr. Chang was a pluralist and held forth in a charming fashion on the proposition that there is more than one kind of ultimate reality. . . . [Malik promptly retorted] as he expounded at some length the philosophy of Thomas Aquinas. Dr. Humphrey joined enthusiastically in the discussion, and I remember that at one point Dr. Chang suggested that the Secretariat might well spend a few months studying the fundamentals of Confucianism! But by that time I could not follow them, so lofty had the conversation become, so I simply filled the teacups again and sat back to be entertained by the talk of these learned gentlemen." Roosevelt, *The Autobiography of Eleanor Roosevelt*, 317. Glendon recounts this episode in *The Forum and the Tower* as evidence of great clashes of opinion that potentially threatened to derail the Human Rights Commission (207). To my mind it is better read as a foretaste of the resistance that such "lofty talk" would meet in committee. Roosevelt herself is the most interesting (and sympathetic) character in this vignette, and seems less dazzled by the conversation than resigned to it. In sitting back to be "entertained by the talk of these learned gentlemen," do we not see the good-humored patience (combined with a bit of eye-rolling) of someone who, quite reasonably, wants to get down to work?

18   Malik, "An International Bill of Rights," 59.

19   Many categories, some anachronistic, could be used to connect Malik with Schmitt: "right-wing," "Christian," perhaps even "fascist" (here I allude to Malik's role in the creation of the Lebanese Front for Freedom and Man, later the Lebanese Forces, in the late 1970s, which I do not discuss). But it is a shared "political" sensibility that draws them closest. "The high points of politics," Schmitt famously argued in *The Concept of the Political*, "are simultaneously the moments in which the enemy is, in concrete clarity, recognized as the enemy" (67). It is well known that Schmitt was no fan of international humanitarian and human rights law, which he regarded either as an obfuscation of the political (see, for example, *The Nomos of the Earth*, 214–80) or else as a disguised intensification of the political that enables belligerents to wage war in the name of humanity (see, for example, *Theory of the Partisan*, 64–68). But what Schmitt did not consider is how human rights could be used to designate a real, concrete enemy. They do not "de-humanize" others by casting them beyond the purview of humankind. Instead, they help to draw out and oppose different conceptions of the human. One way to read Malik's life and work is as an endeavor—just as determined as the Cromwells and Lenins of political history whom Schmitt so admires in *The Concept of the Political*—to name and identify the real enemy. In his case, the enemy is the materialist streak of modernity and its

contemporary communist incarnation. Malik is innovative in that he uses human rights to do so in a way that is not incompatible with Schmitt's own descriptive and normative account of the political.

20 Malik, "The Challenge of Human Rights,"160.

21 Malik, "The Tide Must Turn," unnumbered page.

22 See, for example, UN Economic and Social Council, Commission on Human Rights, 3rd Sess., 64th mtg., UN Doc. E/CN.4/SR.64 (June 8, 1948), 17, where Malik "[calls] attention to the need for establishing the kind of social and economic conditions . . . in which the individual could develop and in which his rights could be guaranteed."

23 See Morsink, The Universal Declaration of Human Rights, 281–90. See also Malik, "The Challenge of Human Rights": "Up to the very last stage in the formation of this document the word 'endowed' was followed by the two words 'by nature.' Owing, however, to a certain confusion in the French and Spanish translations of the phrase 'by nature,' it was finally decided to drop it. And I was more sorry than any other member was when it was dropped" (162).

24 Chapelle, La Déclaration universelle des droits de l'homme et le catholicisme, 86.

25 Malik, "The Challenge of Human Rights." "We discern, in the doctrine of the Declaration, a partial and implicit return to the law of nature. A careful examination of the Preamble and of Article 1 will reveal that the doctrine of natural law is woven at least into the intent of the Declaration" (161).

26 Charles Malik, Rapporteur, UN Economic and Social Council, Drafting Committee on an International Bill of Human Rights, 1st Sess., 13th mtg., UN Doc. E/CN.4/AC.1/SR.13 (June 20, 1947), 19–20.

27 UN Economic and Social Council, Drafting Committee on an International Bill of Human Rights, 2nd Sess., 38th mtg., UN Doc. E/CN.4/AC.1/SR.38 (May 18, 1948), 8–15.

28 Morsink, The Universal Declaration of Human Rights; Glendon, A World Made New, 123–42; and Mitoma, "Charles H. Malik and Human Rights" and Human Rights and the Negotiation of American Power, 103–33.

29 Malik, "Spiritual Implications of Universal Declaration" and "A Christian Reflection on Martin Heidegger." For Malik's debt to Heidegger, see Woessner, "Provincializing Human Rights?," 70–79.

30 Malik, "The Individual in Modern Society," Will the Future Redeem the Past?, and The Wonder of Being.

31 Malik, Will the Future Redeem the Past?, 8.

32 Malik, "The Tide Must Turn," unnumbered page.

33 Slaughter, Human Rights, Inc., 107. The quote inside the quote—"the modernizing of the world," which I argued is cited out of context by Slaughter—is from Malik, Man in the Struggle for Peace, xxxvi.

34 Mitoma, Human Rights and the Negotiation of American Power, 105.

35 Moyn, Christian Human Rights, 8.

36 Malik is tricky to place theologically. Born into an Orthodox Greek family he remained committed to this faith his whole life. But he was also strongly influenced

by other strains of Christianity, and Catholicism in particular. In *The Wonder of Being* he remarks that the Great Schism of 1054, which divided the Eastern and Western Churches, is arguably "the greatest tragedy in history" (13). His repeated tributes to Saint Thomas, along with his philosophical, theological, and diplomatic writings, show strong markings of personalism (itself heavily influenced by Thomism thanks to Maritain and Karol Wojtyla). A good place to begin tracing these sources is the semiautobiographical remarks on faith that Malik makes in the opening pages of *The Wonder of Being*, 11–21, and "The Two Tasks."

37   Moyn, *Christian Human Rights*, 70.

38   Cited in Moyn, *Christian Human Rights*, 2. As Moyn makes clear, Pius XII is not the first pope to have appealed to the discourse of human rights. His predecessor, Pius XI, broke this ground for him. In his 1937 encyclical letter "Mit brennender Sorge," Pius XI writes, "Man, as a person, possesses rights that he holds from God and which must remain, with regard to the collectivity, beyond the reach of anything that would tend to deny them, to abolish them, or to neglect them." Cited in *Christian Human Rights*, 75.

39   Malik, "The Challenge of Human Rights," 158–59.

40   On learning to recognize what we already know, see Malik's *Survival in an Age of Revolution*: "He is likely to survive who is not ashamed of the deepest he knows, and nothing is more disgusting or shameful than the spectacle of people shamed or apologetic about the deepest they know" (25).

41   See Glendon's chapter on "The Implementation Debate" in *A World Made New*, 79–98.

42   For example, "An International Bill of Human Rights," 60; "Spiritual Implications of the Declaration," 137; "The Metaphysics of Freedom"; and *The Wonder of Being*, 96–97.

43   These remarks come from the fourteenth meeting of the Human Rights Commission. Reproduced in Malik, "Four Basic Principles," 38.

44   As Malik says in "The Tide Must Turn," "[Modern man] has lost his distinctive personality. He is not looked upon, nor does he look upon himself, as an end: he is treated, and he treats himself, as a mere means. He thinks as his group thinks; he acts as his group acts; he cannot assert any genuine personal freedom" (unnumbered page).

45   Malik, "From Dr. Malik's Diaries," 235, emphasis added.

46   Malik, "Spiritual Implications of the Universal Declaration," 135.

47   Malik, "Human Rights in the United Nations," 210.

48   Malik, "Human Rights in the United Nations," 210.

49   Charles Malik, Rapporteur, UN Economic and Social Council, Commission on Human Rights, 3rd Sess., 50th mtg., UN Doc. E/CN.4/SR.50 (May 27, 1948), 5–6.

50   Malik, "Human Rights in the United Nations," 210.

51   Malik, "Excerpts from the 'International Bill,'" 105.

52   UN General Assembly, 3rd Sess., 180th Plenary Meeting, UN Doc. A/PV.180 (December 9, 1948), 864–67. Ishay uses this image of the portico and four pillars as an organizing metaphor for *The History of Human Rights*, 3–4, 222–23.

53   UN General Assembly, 3rd Sess., 180th Plenary Meeting, UN Doc. A/PV.180 (December 9, 1948), 866.

54   Malik, "The Tide Must Turn," unnumbered page.

55   Malik, *Christ and Crisis*, x. For other examples, see part 2 ("The World: The Evil of Sufficiency") of *The Wonder of Being*, 75–104, and the introduction to *Man in the Struggle for Peace*, ix–xliv.

56   Malik, *The Wonder of Being*, 114.

57   Roosevelt, "My Day, 10 December 1948," 970. For Roosevelt's more general reflections on the Christian underpinnings of democracy, see *The Moral Basis of Democracy*, 42–82.

58   Roosevelt, "My Day, 10 December 1948," 970.

59   Taylor, *A Secular Age*, 19–21, 26–28, 242–69.

60   Malik, *Man in His Struggle for Peace*, xvi.

61   Malik, "Excerpts from the International Bill," 106.

62   Malik, "Human Rights in the United Nations," 211.

63   Malik, "The Challenge of Human Rights," 161.

64   Malik, *The Wonder of Being*, 108.

65   Moyn, *Christian Human Rights*, 176.

CHAPTER 9. Human Rights Education

1   Baxi, *The Future of Human Rights*, 6.

2   See Katz and Spero, eds., *Bringing Human Rights Education to US Classrooms*; Baxi and Mann, eds., *Human Rights Learning*; Tibbitts, "Women's Human Rights Education Trainers in Turkey"; Bajaj, *Schooling for Social Change*.

3   See Gerber, *Understanding Human Rights*, 1–23; Bajaj, *Schooling for Social Change*, 13–27, and *Human Rights Education*; Tibbitts, "Building a Human Rights Education Movement in the United States" and "Evolution of Human Rights Education Models."

4   Several essays in the first academic volume dedicated to HRE make this argument. Andreopoulos and Claude, eds., *Human Rights Education for the Twenty-First Century*.

5   UN General Assembly, Resolution 66/137, "United Nations Declaration on Human Rights Education and Training" (December 19, 2011), emphasis added.

6   I note that this section of the Resolution was adapted from Amnesty International's *Guidelines for Human Rights Friendly Schools*.

7   UN Educational, Scientific and Cultural Organization, General Conference, 18th Sess., *Recommendation Concerning Education for International Understanding, Co-Operation and Peace and Education Related to Human Rights and Fundamental Freedoms*, UN Doc. ST/HR/1/Rev.5(Vol.I/Part2), (November 19, 1974).

8   UN General Assembly, Resolution 49/184, "United Nations Decade for Human Rights Education" (December 23, 1994).

9   UN Office of the High Commissioner for Human Rights, "The Right to Human Rights Education: A Compilation of Provisions of International and Regional Instruments Dealing with Human Rights Education" (September 2014).

10 "HRE20/20: Global Coalition for Human Rights Education," http://www.hre2020 .org/newsticker, accessed June 10, 2016.

11 UN General Assembly, Resolution 49/184, "United Nations Decade for Human Rights Education" (December 23, 1994).

12 UN General Assembly, Resolution 62/171, "International Year of Human Rights Learning" (December 18, 2007).

13 UN Development Programme and Office of the High Commissioner for Human Rights, *Toolkit for Collaboration with National Human Rights Institutions*, xiv.

14 UN Educational, Scientific and Cultural Organization, 61st Annual DPI/NGO Conference, "Reaffirming Human Rights for All" (September 3–5, 2008).

15 http://unchronicle.un.org/article/human-rights-way-life/, accessed June 12, 2016. Koenig is the author of this article.

16 http://www.pdhre.org/about.html, accessed June 10, 2016.

17 Reardon, "Human Rights Learning," 47.

18 Flowers, "How to Define Human Rights Education?," 122.

19 Koenig, "In Our Hands" and "The Nature of Human Rights Learning."

20 Mayor, "Opening Address," 28.

21 Bajaj, *Schooling for Social Change*, 55.

22 Bajaj, *Schooling for Social Change*, 11–13, 53–75.

23 Bajaj, *Schooling for Social Change*, 53–75.

24 Bajaj, "Teaching to Transform, Transforming to Teach," 208, and *Schooling for Social Change*, 116–30.

25 See Celermajer's critique of the UN Office of the High Commissioner for Human Rights' *Pocket Book for Human Rights for the Police*: "[This] training material and training practices are dominated by the transmission of information about rules and laws. . . . More pointedly, it would appear that often training is in fact an exercise in transmitting information about rules, with the possible effect of increasing trainees' knowledge about the content of human rights (and this result would only be achieved if this transmission is achieved effectively)." Celermajer, "International Review," 13. See also Bajaj, "Human Rights Education"; and Flowers, "What Is Human Rights Education?"

26 Koenig, "In Our Hands," 5.

27 This remark attributed to Voltaire is the epigraph for the volume *Human Rights Learning*, prepared by the People's Movement for Human Rights Learning and edited by Baxi and Mann.

28 Koenig, "Human Rights as a Way of Life," "Imposed Ignorance Is a Human Rights Violation," and "Learning and Integrating Human Rights as a Way of Life."

29 Koenig, "Human Rights as a Way of Life." This story is repeated in "The Nature of Human Rights Learning," "In Our Hands," and "Imposed Ignorance Is a Human Rights Violation."

30 See Frésard's comprehensive study of combatant attitudes and behaviors toward international humanitarian law, undertaken on behalf of the International Committee of the Red Cross, *The Roots of Behaviour in War*.

31 See Celermajer and Grewal's critique of HRE in the security sector as proceeding

in almost total absence of research and evidence as to what underpins problematic attitudes and abusive behaviors, which factors can be effectively influenced by working with personnel, and which models of learning can best bring reform. "Preventing Human Rights Violations 'From the Inside.'"

32 Koenig relates several stories similar to this one. Here is another example—a highly infantilizing and orientalizing one, I might add—from the same article: "In a Dalit village, after sharing with women that food, education, health, housing and work at liveable wages are inalienable human rights, they clapped their hands, danced and repeated these five human rights imperatives as a mantra." "Human Rights as a Way of Life."

33 UN Secretary-General, General Assembly, 51st Sess., *Report of the United Nations High Commissioner for Human Rights on the implementation of the Plan of Action for the United Nations Decade for Human Rights Education*, UN Doc. A/51/506/Add.1 (December 12, 1996), 6.

34 Malkki, *The Need to Help*, 2.

35 Malkki, *The Need to Help*, 3.

36 Malkki, *The Need to Help*, 25–26.

37 Malkki, *The Need to Help*, 25. For a complementary analysis of the plurality of motivations behind humanitarian work (including caring for oneself), see Dawes, *That the World May Know*.

38 Malkki, *The Need to Help*, 8.

39 Malkki, *The Need to Help*, 117.

40 Malkki, *The Need to Help*, 137.

41 Malkki, *The Need to Help*, 162.

42 Malkki, *The Need to Help*, 4.

43 I note that depending on where HRE is applied, attempts are often made to provide contextually specific motivations as to why people should learn from it. This is especially true of vocational contexts. Judges, for example, are instructed that respecting human rights would assist them in making decisions that would not be overturned. Police, too, are told that human violations have a negative effect on public confidence, that it impedes the possibility of building good relations with community, and that it may even lead to prosecution and punishment. See Celermajer, "International Review," 10. But these motivations remain instrumental reasons as to why human rights should modify professional attitudes and conduct. At the existential level I address, my objection stands: HRE does not address why individuals would want to adopt human rights—in the robust "way of life" sense—as a personal day-to-day ethic.

44 UN General Assembly, Resolution 66/137, "United Nations Declaration on Human Rights Education and Training" (December 19, 2011), Article 3.

45 See what Bajaj calls "HRE for coexistence" in "Human Rights Education."

46 See what Tibbitts calls the "accountability model" in "Understanding What We Do" and "Evolution of Human Rights."

47 Note that I am using the terms *critical* and *criticism* in a different sense than in chapter 6. There my goal was to show how care of the self involves a positive (what

I called "poetic") kind of criticism. Here I propose that care of the self is critical in the sense of self-limiting. These two senses are, however, complementary and work together in the following way: care of the self limits itself to particular kinds of problems ("critical" in the sense of this chapter) so that it has the appropriate conditions to practice positive and poetic criticism ("critical" in the sense of chapter 6).

48 Bajaj, "Human Rights Education," 507–8.

49 Tibbitts, "Women's Human Rights Education Trainers in Turkey," 52. Bajaj reports similar findings in her work with HRE teachers in India (i.e., personal transformation and empowerment as a result of HRE). See *Schooling for Social Change*, 122–30.

50 Tibbitts, "Women's Human Rights Education Trainers in Turkey," 53.

51 See, for example, Meintjes, "Human Rights Education as Empowerment."

52 Tibbitts, "Women's Human Rights Education Trainers in Turkey," 46.

53 Tibbitts, "Evolution of Human Rights Models."

54 Print et al., "Moral and Human Rights Education," 122.

55 Baxi, "Introduction," 15.

56 Baxi, "Introduction," 16.

CONCLUSION

1 Foucault, "On the Genealogy of Ethics," 271.

2 Foucault, "The Ethics of the Concern for Self as a Practice of Freedom," 291.

3 See Veyne, "The Final Foucault and His Ethics."

4 Foucault, "On the Genealogy of Ethics," 256–62.

5 Foucault, "The Political Technology of Individuals," 145.

6 Foucault, *The Use of Pleasure*, 10–11.

7 Foucault, *The Hermeneutics of the Subject*, 177.

8 Lorde, *A Burst of Light*, 131. I am uncertain whether my interpretation of Lorde's sentence is faithful to her meaning. The issue is further complicated by the fact that it has itself become a catchphrase in the recent rise of the term *self-care* (#selfcare) on social media. See Harris's instructive piece, "A History of Self-Care," in which she traces a genealogy of self-care starting from 1960s medical practice in the United States, extending to the civil rights movement, and then to contemporary black and feminist activism.

9 Consider the following fact: in the weeks following the election of Donald Trump to the U.S. presidency, Google Trends reports that searches for the term *self-care* spiked. Journalists and bloggers on the left suggest it is because disheartened liberals sensed that if they hope to bring a strong self to future political struggles they need, for the time being, to withdraw and recharge. In this sense, the self-care they envisage is self-preservative and self-restorative rather than self-transformative. See Spechler, "The Rise of Donald Trump Demands We Embrace a Harder Kind of Self-Care"; and Meltzer, "Soak, Steam, Spritz."

10 Foucault, "Preface," xiii.

11 Thoreau, "Civil Disobedience," 133. I admit to taking liberties in citing Thoreau's

phrase in this context. In "Civil Disobedience" his ambition is quite plainly to inspire fellow Americans to follow his example and to stop the machine. That said, if this same phrase were used to frame a reading of *Walden* I wager we would find an ethic highly compatible with care of the self.

12 Nietzsche, *Posthumous Fragments* (fall 1881), cited in Hadot, *What Is Ancient Philosophy?*, 322.

Bibliography

Adams, John. *The Papers of John Adams*. Cambridge, MA: Harvard University Press, 2003.

Ahmed, Sara. "Selfcare as Warfare." *feministkilljoys*, 2014. https://feministkilljoys.com/2014/08/25/selfcare-as-warfare/.

Amnesty International. *Guidelines for Human Rights Friendly Schools*. London: Amnesty International, 2009.

Anderson, Carol. *Eyes off the Prize: The United Nations and the African American Struggle for Human Rights, 1944–1955*. Cambridge, MA: Cambridge University Press, 2003.

Andreopoulos, George J., and Richard Pierre Claude, eds. *Human Rights Education for the Twenty-First Century*. Philadelphia: University of Pennsylvania Press, 1997.

Anghie, Anthony. *Imperialism, Sovereignty and the Making of International Law*. Cambridge: Cambridge University Press, 2007.

Arendt, Hannah. *The Origins of Totalitarianism*. New York: Harcourt, Brace, 1968.

Aron, Raymond, and Michel Foucault. *Dialogue*. Paris: Nouvelles Éditions Lignes, 2007.

Badiou, Alain. *Ethics: An Essay on the Understanding of Evil*. Translated by Peter Hallward. London: Verso, 2002.

Bajaj, Monisha. "Human Rights Education: Ideology, Location, and Approaches." *Human Rights Quarterly* 33 (2011): 481–508.

———, ed. *Human Rights Education: Theory, Research, Praxis*. Philadelphia: University of Pennsylvania Press, 2017.

———. *Schooling for Social Change: The Rise and Impact of Human Rights Education in India*. New York: Continuum International, 2012.

———. "Teaching to Transform, Transforming to Teach: Exploring the Role of Teachers of Human Rights Education in India." *Educational Research* 53, no. 2 (2011): 207–21.

Baxi, Upendra. *The Future of Human Rights*, 3rd ed. New Delhi: Oxford University Press, 2012.

———. "Introduction." In *Human Rights Learning: A People's Report*, ed. Upendra Baxi and Kenny Mann, 1–16. New York: People's Movement for Human Rights Learning, 2006.

————. "Reinventing Human Rights in an Era of Hyper-Globalization: A Few Wayside Remarks." In *Cambridge Companion to Human Rights Law*, ed. Conor Gearty and Costas Douzinas, 150–70. Cambridge: Cambridge University Press, 2012.

Baxi, Upendra, and Kenny Mann, eds. *Human Rights Learning: A People's Report.* New York: People's Movement for Human Rights Learning, 2006.

Baynes, Kenneth. "Towards a Political Conception of Human Rights." *Philosophy and Social Criticism* 35, no. 4 (2009): 371–90.

Beetham, David. "What Future for Economic and Social Rights?" *Political Studies* 43 (1995): 41–60.

Bentham, Jeremy. "Anarchical Fallacies." In *Nonsense Upon Stilts: Bentham, Burke, and Marx on the Rights of Man*, ed. Jeremy Waldron, 46–76. London: Routledge, 2014.

Bergès, Sandrine. *The Routledge Guidebook to Wollstonecraft's A Vindication of the Rights of Woman.* London: Routledge, 2013.

Bergson, Henri. *The Creative Mind.* Translated by Mabelle L. Andison. Mineola, NY: Dover, 2007.

————. *Extraits de Lucrèce avec un commentaire des notes.* Paris: Librairie Ch. Delagrave, 1972.

————. *Mélanges.* Paris: PUF, 1972.

————. *Mind-Energy.* Translated by H. Wildon Carr. London: Palgrave Macmillan, 2007.

————. *Time and Free Will: An Essay on the Immediate Data of Consciousness.* Translated by F. L. Pogson. Mineola, NY: Dover, 2001.

————. *The Two Sources of Morality and Religion.* Translated by R. Ashley Audra and Cloudesley Brereton. Notre Dame, IN: University of Notre Dame, 1977.

Black, Allida. *Casting Her Own Shadow.* New York: Columbia University Press, 1997.

————, ed. *The Eleanor Roosevelt Papers*, vol. 1: *The Human Rights Years, 1945–1948.* Farmington Hills, MI: Thomson Gale, 2007.

————. "Introduction." In Eleanor Roosevelt, *Tomorrow Is Now.* New York: Penguin, 2012.

Bolla, Peter de. *The Architecture of Concepts: The Historical Formation of Human Rights.* New York: Fordham University Press, 2013.

Botting, Eileen Hunt. *Wollstonecraft, Mill, and Women's Human Rights.* New Haven, CT: Yale University Press, 2016.

Brown, Chris. "'Human Nature,' Science and International Political Theory." *Journal of International Relations and Development* 16, no. 4 (2013): 435–54.

————. "Human Rights and Human Nature." In *Human Rights: The Hard Questions*, ed. Cindy Holder and David Reidy, 23–38. Cambridge: Cambridge University Press, 2013.

Brown, Wendy. "'The Most We Can Hope For . . .': Human Rights and the Politics of Fatalism." *South Atlantic Quarterly* 103, nos. 2–3 (2004): 451–63.

————. *Politics Out of History.* Princeton, NJ: Princeton University Press, 2001.

————. *Regulating Aversion: Tolerance in the Age of Identity and Empire.* Princeton, NJ: Princeton University Press, 2008.

————. *Undoing the Demos: Neoliberalism's Stealth Revolution.* New York: Zone, 2015.

Brown, Wendy, and Rainer Forst. *The Power of Tolerance: A Debate.* New York: Columbia University Press, 2014.

Brownlie, Ian, and Guy S. Goodwin-Gill, eds. *Basic Documents on Human Rights*. Oxford: Oxford University Press, 2010.

Burchell, Graham. "Liberal Government and the Techniques of the Self." *Economy and Society* 22, no. 3 (2006): 267–82.

Burke, Edmund. "A Letter to a Member of the National Assembly." In *Further Reflections on the French Revolution*, ed. Daniel E. Ritchie, 27–72. Indianapolis: Liberty Fund, 1997.

———. *Reflections on the Revolution in France*. Indianapolis: Hackett, 1987.

Butler, Judith. *Giving an Account of Oneself*. New York: Fordham, 2005.

———. *Precarious Life: The Power of Mourning and Violence*. London: Verso, 2004.

———. "What Is Critique? An Essay on Foucault's Virtue." European Institution for Progressive Cultural Policies, 2001. http://eipcp.net/transversal/0806/butler/en.

Button, Mark. *Contract, Culture, and Citizenship: Transformative Liberalism from Hobbes to Rawls*. University Park: Pennsylvania State University Press, 2008.

Canavan, Francis. *The Political Reason of Edmund Burke*. Durham, NC: Duke University Press, 1960.

Cassin, René. *La pensée et l'action*. Boulogne-sur-Seine: F. Lalou, 1972.

Caygill, Howard. *Levinas and the Political*. London: Routledge, 2005.

Celermajer, Danielle. "International Review: Current Approaches to Human Rights Teaching in the Law Enforcement and Security Sectors." (2015): 1-40. http://sydney.edu.au/arts/research/ehrp/downloads/EHRP_International_Training_Review.pdf.

Celermajer, Danielle, and Kirwan Grewal. "Preventing Human Rights Violations 'From the Inside.'" *Journal of Human Rights Practice* 5, no. 2 (2013): 243–66.

Chapelle, Philippe. *La Déclaration universelle des droits de l'homme et le catholicisme*. Montreal: Pensée, 2011.

Cheah, Pheng. "Acceptable Uses of People." In *Human Rights at the Crossroads*, ed. Mark Goodale, 210–26. New York: Oxford University Press, 2013.

Chevalier, Jacques. *Entretiens avec Bergson*. Paris: Plon, 1959.

Clapham, Andrew. *Human Rights: A Very Short Introduction*. Oxford: Oxford University Press, 2007.

Connolly, William. *The Ethos of Pluralization*. Minneapolis: University of Minnesota Press, 1995.

———. *Pluralism*. Durham, NC: Duke University Press, 2005.

———. *Why I Am Not a Secularist*. Minneapolis: University of Minnesota Press, 2000.

Critchley, Simon. *The Ethics of Deconstruction: Derrida and Levinas*. Oxford: Blackwell, 1992.

———. *Infinitely Demanding: Ethics of Commitment, Politics of Resistance*. London: Verso, 2013.

Damrosch, Leo. *Tocqueville's Discovery of America*. New York: Farrar, Straus and Giroux, 2011.

Davidson, Arnold I. "Archaeology, Genealogy, Ethics." In *Foucault: A Critical Reader*, ed. David Couzens Hoy, 221–33. Oxford: Blackwell, 1986.

———. "Ethics as Ascetics: Foucault, the History of Ethics, and Ancient Thought." In *Cambridge Companion to Foucault*, ed. Gary Gutting, 123–48. Cambridge: Cambridge University Press, 2005.

———. "Introductory Remarks to Pierre Hadot." In *Foucault and His Interlocutors*, ed. Arnold I. Davidson. Chicago: University of Chicago Press, 1996.

———. "Spiritual Exercises, Improvisation, and Moral Perfectionism: With Special Reference to Sonny Rollins." In *The Oxford Handbook of Critical Improvisation Studies*, vol. 1, ed. George E. Lewis and Benjamin Piekut, 523–38. Oxford: Oxford University Press, 2016.

Davidson, Arnold I., and Frédéric Worms, eds. *Pierre Hadot, L'enseignement des antiques, l'enseignement des modernes*. Paris: Editions rue d'Ulm, 2013.

Dawes, James. *That the World May Know: Bearing Witness to Atrocity*. Cambridge, MA: Harvard University Press, 2007.

Dean, Jodi. "The Politics of Avoidance." *Hedgehog Review* 7, no. 2 (2005): 55–65.

de Waal, Frans. "Morally Evolved: Primate Social Instincts, Human Morality, and the Rise and Fall of 'Veneer Theory.'" In *Primates and Philosophers: How Morality Evolved*, ed. Stephen Macedo and Josiah Ober, 1–58. Princeton, NJ: Princeton University Press, 2006.

———. "The Tower of Morality." In *Primates and Philosophers: How Morality Evolved*, ed. Stephen Macedo and Josiah Ober, 161–82. Princeton, NJ: Princeton University Press, 2006.

Donnelly, Jack. *Universal Human Rights in Theory and Practice*. Ithaca, NY: Cornell University Press, 2013.

Dosse, François. *Histoire du structuralisme: Le chant du signe, 1967 à nos jours*, vol. 2. Paris: Editions de la Découverte, 1992.

Douzinas, Costas. "The End(s) of Human Rights." *Melbourne University Law Review* 26 (2002): 445–65.

———. *Human Rights and Empire: The Political Philosophy of Cosmopolitanism*. London: Routledge, 2007.

———. "The Poverty of (Rights) Jurisprudence." In *The Cambridge Companion to Human Rights Law*, ed. Conor Gearty and Costas Douzinas, 56–78. Cambridge: Cambridge University Press, 2012.

Dumm, Thomas. *Michel Foucault and the Politics of Freedom*. Lanham, MD: Rowman and Littlefield, 2002.

Durkheim, Émile. *Moral Education: A Study in the Theory and Application of the Sociology of Education*. Translated by Everett Wilson and Herman Schnurer. New York: Free Press, 1961.

Eckel, Jan, and Samuel Moyn, eds. *The Breakthrough: Human Rights in the 1970s*. Philadelphia: University of Pennsylvania Press, 2013.

Elden, Stuart. *Foucault's Last Decade*. Cambridge: Polity, 2016.

Eliot, George. *Middlemarch*. New York: Penguin, 2003.

Emerson, Ralph Waldo. *Essays and Lectures*. New York: Library of America, 1983.

Engster, Daniel. "Mary Wollstonecraft's Nurturing Liberalism: Between an Ethic of Justice and Care." *American Political Science Review* 95, no. 3 (2001): 577–88.

Faubert, Michelle. "Introduction." In Mary Wollstonecraft, *Mary, a Fiction and the Wrongs of Woman, or Maria*, 11–50. Peterborough, ON: Broadview, 2012.

Faubion, James. *An Anthropology of Ethics*. Cambridge: Cambridge University Press, 2011.

Flowers, Nancy. "How to Define Human Rights Education? A Complex Answer to a Simple Question." In *International Perspectives in Human Rights Education*, ed. Viola Georgi and Michael Seberich, 105–27. Gütersloh, Germany: Bertelsmann Foundation, 2004.

———. "What Is Human Rights Education?" In *A Survey of Human Rights Education*. Hamburg: Bertelsmann Verlag, 2003.

Foster, Roger. "Therapeutic Culture, Authenticity, and Neo-Liberalism." *History of the Human Sciences* 29, no. 1 (2016): 99–116.

———. "The Therapeutic Spirit of Neoliberalism." *Political Theory: An International Journal of Political Philosophy* 44, no. 1 (2016): 82–105.

Foucault, Michel. "À propos de la généalogie de l'éthique." In *Dits et écrits II: 1976–1988*, 1428–50. Paris: Gallimard, 2001.

———. *About the Beginning of the Hermeneutics of the Self: Lectures at Dartmouth College 1980*. Translated by Graham Burchell. Chicago: University of Chicago Press, 2015.

———. "An Aesthetics of Existence." In *Politics, Philosophy, Culture: Interviews and Other Writings, 1977–1984*, ed. Lawrence Kritzman. London: Routledge, 1990.

———. "Alternatives to the Prison: Dissemination or Decline of Social Control?" *Theory, Culture, and Society* 26, no. 6 (2009): 12–24.

———. *The Birth of Biopolitics*. Translated by Graham Burchell. London: Palgrave Macmillan, 2010.

———. "Confronting Governments: Human Rights." In *Power: Essential Works of Michel Foucault, 1954–1984*, ed. James Faubion, 474–76. New York: New Press, 2000.

———. *The Courage of Truth: Lectures at the Collège de France, 1983–1984*. Translated by Graham Burchell. New York: Palgrave Macmillan, 2011.

———. "The Ethics of the Concern for Self as a Practice of Freedom." In *Ethics: Subjectivity and Truth*, ed. Paul Rabinow, 281–302. New York: New Press, 1997.

———. *The Government of Self and Others: Lectures at the Collège de France, 1982–1983*. Translated by Graham Burchell. New York: Palgrave MacMillan, 2010.

———. *The Hermeneutics of the Subject: Lectures at the Collège de France, 1981–82*. Translated by Graham Burchell. New York: Palgrave MacMillan, 2005.

———. *The History of Sexuality*, vol. 2: *The Use of Pleasure*. Translated by Robert Hurley. New York: Pantheon, 1985.

———. *The History of Sexuality*, vol. 3: *The Care of the Self*. Translated by Robert Hurley. New York: Vintage, 1986.

———. "Letter to Certain Leaders of the Left." In *Power: Essential Works of Foucault, 1954–1984*, ed. James Faubion, 439–42. New York: New Press, 2000.

———. "The Masked Philosopher." In *Ethics: Subjectivity and Truth*, ed. Paul Rabinow, 321–28. New York: New Press, 1997.

———. "On the Genealogy of Ethics." In *Ethics: Subjectivity and Truth*, ed. Paul Rabinow, 253–80. New York: New Press, 1997.

———. "Open Letter to Mehdi Bazargan." In *Power: Essential Works of Michel Foucault, 1954–1984*, ed. James Faubion, 439–42. New York: New Press, 2000.

———. "The Political Technology of Individuals." In *Technologies of the Self: A Seminar with Michel Foucault*, ed. Luther H. Martin, Huck Gutman, and Patrick H. Hutton, 145–62. Amherst: University of Massachusetts Press, 1988.

———. "Preface." In Félix Guattari and Gilles Deleuze, *Anti-Oedipus: Capitalism and Schizophrenia*, xi–xiv. Minneapolis: University of Minnesota Press, 1983.

———. *Qu'est-ce que la critique? Suivie de La culture de soi*. Paris: Vrin, 2015.

———. "Le retour de la morale." In *Dits et écrits II: 1976–1988*, 1515–25. Paris: Gallimard, 2001.

———. "The Risks of Security." In *Power: Essential Works of Michel Foucault, 1954–1984*, ed. James Faubion, 365–81. New York: New Press, 2000.

———. "Sexual Choice, Sexual Act." In *Ethics: Subjectivity and Truth*, ed. Paul Rabinow, 141–56. New York: New Press, 1997.

———. "The Social Triumph of the Sexual Will." In *Ethics: Subjectivity and Truth*, ed. Paul Rabinow. New York: New Press, 1997.

———. "Subjectivity and Truth." In *Ethics: Subjectivity and Truth*, ed. Paul Rabinow, 87–92. New York: New Press, 1997.

———. "Technologies of the Self." In *Ethics: Subjectivity and Truth*, ed. Paul Rabinow, 223–52. New York: New Press, 1997.

———. "Usage des plaisirs et techniques de soi." In *Dits et écrits II: 1976–1988*, 1358–80. Paris: Gallimard, 2001.

———. "What Is Critique?" In *The Politics of Truth*, ed. Sylvère Lotringer. Los Angeles: Semiotext(e), 2007.

———. "What Is Enlightenment?" In *Ethics: Subjectivity and Truth*, ed. Paul Rabinow, 303–20. New York: New Press, 1997.

———. *Wrong-Doing, Truth-Telling: The Function of Avowal in Justice*. Translated by Stephen W. Sawyer. Chicago: University of Chicago Press, 2014.

Freire, Paulo. *Pedagogy of the Oppressed*. London: Bloomsbury, 2000.

Frésard, Jean-Jacques. *The Roots of Behaviour in War: A Survey of the Literature*. Geneva: International Committee of the Red Cross, 2004.

Furedi, Frank. *Therapy Culture: Cultivating Vulnerability in an Uncertain Age*. London: Routledge, 2003.

Furet, François, and Françoise Mélonio. "Introduction." In Alexis de Tocqueville, *The Old Regime and the Revolution*, 1–82. Chicago: University of Chicago Press, 1998.

Garber, Marjorie, Beatrice Hanssen, and Rebecca Walkowitz, eds. *The Turn to Ethics*. London: Routledge, 2000.

Gerber, Paula. *Understanding Human Rights: Educational Challenges for the Future*. Cheltenham, UK: Edward Elgar, 2013.

Gill, Stephen. "Globalisation, Market Civilization and Disciplinary Neoliberalism." *Millennium Journal of International Studies* 24, no. 3 (1995): 399–423.

Glendon, Mary Ann. *The Forum and the Tower: How Scholars and Politicians Have Imagined the World, from Plato to Eleanor Roosevelt*. Oxford: Oxford University Press, 2011.

———. *A World Made New: Eleanor Roosevelt and the Universal Declaration of Human Rights*. New York: Random House, 2001.

Golder, Ben. *Foucault and the Politics of Rights*. Stanford, CA: Stanford University Press, 2015.

Golder, Ben, and Peter Fitzpatrick. *Foucault's Law*. London: Routledge, 2009.

Goodale, Mark. *Dilemmas of Modernity: Bolivian Encounters with Law and Liberalism.* Stanford, CA: Stanford University Press, 2008.

———. "Human Rights and Moral Agency." In *Human Rights: The Hard Questions*, ed. Cindy Holder and David Reidy, 418–35. Cambridge: Cambridge University Press, 2012.

———. *Surrendering to Utopia: An Anthropology of Human Rights.* Stanford, CA: Stanford University Press, 2009.

Goodale, Mark, and Sally Engle Merry, eds. *The Practice of Human Rights: Tracking Law between the Global and the Local.* Cambridge: Cambridge University Press, 2007.

Gordon, Lyndall. *Vindication: A Life of Mary Wollstonecraft.* New York: HarperCollins, 2005.

Grear, Anna. *Redirecting Human Rights: Facing the Challenge of Corporate Legal Humanity.* London: Palgrave MacMillan, 2010.

Greene, Joshua. *Moral Tribes: Emotion, Reason, and the Gap between Us and Them.* New York: Penguin, 2014.

Gregg, Benjamin. *Human Rights as Social Construction.* Cambridge: Cambridge University Press, 2013.

Griffin, James. *On Human Rights.* Oxford: Oxford University Press, 2008.

Habermas, Jürgen. *Between Facts and Norms: Contributions to a Discourse Theory of Law and Democracy.* Translated by William Rehg. Cambridge, MA: MIT Press, 1996.

Hadot, Pierre. *Exercices spirituels et philosophie antique.* Paris: Institut d'Études augustiennes, 1993.

———. *The Inner Citadel: The Meditations of Marcus Aurelius.* Translated by Michael Chase. Cambridge, MA: Harvard University Press, 1998.

———. *N'oublie pas de vivre: Goethe et la tradition des exercices spirituels.* Paris: Albin Michel, 2008.

———. "Philosophy as a Way of Life." In *Philosophy as a Way of Life*, 264–76. Oxford: Blackwell, 1995.

———. *The Present Alone Is Our Happiness: Conversations with Jeannie Carlier and Arnold I. Davidson.* Translated by Marc Djaballah. Stanford, CA: Stanford University Press, 2009.

———. "Reflections on the Idea of the 'Cultivation of the Self.'" In *Philosophy as a Way of Life,* 206–13. Oxford: Blackwell.

———. "The Sage and the World." In *Philosophy as a Way of Life*, 251–63. Oxford: Blackwell, 1995.

———. "Le sage et le monde." In *Exercices spirituels et philosophie antique*, 343–60. Paris: Albin Michel, 2002.

———. "Spiritual Exercises." In *Philosophy as a Way of Life*, 81–125. Oxford: Blackwell, 1995.

———. *What Is Ancient Philosophy?* Translated by Michael Chase. Cambridge, MA: Harvard University Press, 2002.

Halfin, Igal. *Red Autobiographies: Initiating the Bolshevik Self.* Seattle: University of Washington Press, 2011.

Halldenius, Lena. "The Primacy of Right: On the Triad of Liberty, Equality and Virtue in Wollstonecraft's Political Thought." *British Journal for the Philosophy of History* 15, no. 1 (2007): 75–99.

————. *Mary Wollstonecraft and Feminist Republicanism*. London: Routledge, 2016.

Hamacher, Werner. "The Right Not to Use Rights: Human Rights and the Structure of Judgments." In *Political Theologies: Public Religions in a Post-Secular World*, ed. Hent de Vries and Lawrence E. Sullivan, 671–90. New York: Fordham University Press, 2006.

Harris, Aisha. "A History of Self-Care: From Its Radical Roots to Its Yuppie-Driven Middle Age to Its Election-Inspired Resurgence." *Slate*, April 5, 2017. http://www.slate.com/articles/arts/culturebox/2017/04/the_history_of_self_care.html.

Hathaway, Oona. "Do Human Rights Treaties Make a Difference?" *Yale Law Journal* 111, no. 8 (2002): 1935–2042.

Hellbeck, Jochen. *Revolution on My Mind: Writing a Diary under Stalin*. Cambridge, MA: Harvard University Press, 2006.

Henkin, Louis. *The Age of Rights*. New York: Columbia University Press, 1990.

Hesford, Wendy. *Spectacular Rhetorics: Human Rights Visions, Recognitions, Feminisms*. Durham, NC: Duke University Press, 2011.

Heyes, Cressida. *Self-Transformations: Foucault, Ethics, and Normalized Bodies*. Oxford: Oxford University Press, 2007.

Hodson, Jane. *Language and Revolution in Burke, Wollstonecraft, Paine, and Godwin*. London: Hampshire UK, 2007.

Hoffman, Stefan-Ludwig. "Introduction: Genealogies of Human Rights." In *Human Rights in the Twentieth Century*, ed. Stefan-Ludwig Hoffman, 1–28. Cambridge: Cambridge University Press, 2010.

Honig, Bonnie. "The Politics of Ethos." *European Journal of Political Theory* 10, 3 (2011): 422–29.

Hopgood, Stephen. *The Endtimes of Human Rights*. Ithaca, NY: Cornell University Press, 2013.

————. *Keepers of the Flame: Understanding Amnesty International*. Ithaca, NY: Cornell University Press, 2006.

Huffer, Lynne. *Mad for Foucault: Rethinking the Foundations of Queer Theory*. New York: Columbia University Press, 2009.

Humphrey, John. *Human Rights and the United Nations: A Great Adventure*. Dobbs Ferry, NY: Transnational, 1984.

————. *On the Edge of Greatness: The Diaries of John Humphrey*. vol. 1. Kingston, ON: McGill-Queens University Press, 1995.

Hunt, Alan, and Gary Wickham. *Foucault and Law: Towards a Sociology of Law as Governance*. London: Pluto, 1994.

Hunt, Lynn. *The French Revolution and Human Rights: A Brief Documentary History*. New York: St. Martin's, 1996.

————. *Inventing Human Rights: A History*. New York: W. W. Norton, 2008.

Ignatieff, Michael. "Human Rights." In *Human Rights in Political Transitions: Gettysburg to Bosnia*, ed. Carla Hesse and Robert Post, 313–24. New York: Zone Books, 1999.

———. *Human Rights as Politics and Idolatry*. Princeton, NJ: Princeton University Press, 2003.

Illouz, Eva. *Saving the Modern Soul: Therapy, Emotions, and the Culture of Self-Help*. Berkeley: University of California Press, 2008.

Indaimo, Joseph. *The Self, Ethics and Human Rights: Lacan, Levinas and Alterity*. Abingdon, UK: Routledge, 2015.

Irrera, Orazio. "Pleasure and Transcendence of the Self: Notes on 'A Dialogue Too Soon Interrupted' between Michel Foucault and Pierre Hadot." *Philosophy and Social Criticism* 36, no. 9 (2010): 995–1017.

Irvine, William B. *A Guide to the Good Life: The Ancient Art of Stoic Joy*. Oxford: Oxford University Press, 2008.

Ishay, Micheline R. *The History of Human Rights: From Ancient Times to the Globalization Era*. Berkeley: University of California Press, 2008.

Ivison, Duncan. *Rights*. Stocksfield, UK: Acumen, 2008.

Jankélévitch, Vladimir. *The Bad Conscience*. Translated by Andrew Kelley. Chicago: University of Chicago Press, 2015.

———. *Henri Bergson*. Translated by Nils F. Schott. Durham, NC: Duke University Press, 2015.

Jaume, Lucien. *Tocqueville: The Aristocratic Sources of Liberty*. Translated by Arthur Goldhammer. Princeton, NJ: Princeton University Press, 2013.

Joas, Hans. *The Sacredness of the Person: A New Genealogy of Human Rights*. Washington, DC: Georgetown University Press, 2013.

Katz, Susan Roberta, and Andrea McEvoy Spero, eds. *Bringing Human Rights Education to US Classrooms: Exemplary Models from Elementary Grades to University*. London: Palgrave, 2015.

Keys, Barbara J. *Reclaiming American Virtue: The Human Rights Revolution of the 1970s*. Cambridge, MA: Harvard University Press, 2014.

Keyssar, Alexander. *The Right to Vote: The Contested History of Democracy in the United States*. New York: Basic Books, 2009.

King, Martin Luther, Jr. *Where Do We Go from Here: Chaos or Community?* Boston: Beacon, 2010.

Kisner, Jordan. "The Politics of Conspicuous Displays of Self-Care." *New Yorker*, March 14, 2017.

Kisukidi, Nadia Yala. *Bergson ou l'humanité créatrice*. Paris: CRNS, 2013.

Koenig, Shulamith. "Human Rights as a Way of Life." *United Nations Chronicle* 49, no. 3 (2012). https://unchronicle.un.org/article/human-rights-way-life.

———. "Imposed Ignorance Is a Human Rights Violation." Centre for Development and Human Rights, 2015. http://www.cdhr.org.in/human-rights-education/on-the-value-of -human-rights-education/.

———. "In Our Hands: Human Rights as a Way of Life." In *Our Freedoms: A Decade's Reflection on the Advancement of Human Rights*. London: International Bar Association, 2007.

———. "The Nature of Human Rights Learning: For All to Know Human Rights as a

Way of Life." People's Movement for Human Rights Learning, 2008. http://pdhre.org
/shula-vienna.pdf.

Koopman, Colin. *Genealogy as Critique: Foucault and the Problems of Modernity.* Blooming-
ton: Indiana University Press, 2013.

Kundera, Milan. *Immortality.* Translated by Peter Kussi. New York: HarperCollins,
1999.

Laclau, Ernesto. "Deconstruction, Pragmatism, Hegemony." In *Deconstruction and Pragmatism,* ed. Simon Critchley and Chantal Mouffe, 47–68. London: Routledge, 1996.

Lamb, Robert. *Thomas Paine and the Idea of Human Rights.* Cambridge: Cambridge University Press, 2015.

Larmore, Charles. *The Practices of the Self.* Chicago: University of Chicago Press, 2010.

Lash, Joseph P. *Eleanor: The Years Alone.* New York: W. W. Norton, 2014.

Lavelle, Louis. *The Dilemma of Narcissus.* Translated by William Gairdner. London:
George Allen and Unwin, 1973.

Lear, Jonathan. *The Case for Irony.* Cambridge, MA: Harvard University Press, 2014.

Lefebvre, Alexandre. "Bergson, Human Rights, and Joy." *Continental Philosophy Review* 50,
no. 1 (2016): 1–23.

———. *Human Rights as a Way of Life: On Bergson's Political Philosophy.* Stanford, CA:
Stanford University Press, 2013.

———. "Jankélévitch on Bergson: Living in Time." In Vladimir Jankélévitch, *Henri Bergson,* xi–xxvii. Durham, NC: Duke University Press, 2015.

———. "The Rights of Man and the Care of the Self." *Political Theory: An International
Journal of Political Philosophy* 44, no. 4 (2016): 518–40.

Lefort, Claude. *Democracy and Political Theory.* Translated by David Macey. Cambridge:
Polity, 1990.

Lemke, Thomas. *Foucault, Governmentality, and Critique.* London: Routledge, 2012.

Lemm, Vanessa, and Miguel Vatter, eds. *The Government of Life: Foucault, Biopolitics, and
Neoliberalism.* New York: Fordham University Press, 2014.

Lerner, Ralph. *The Thinking Revolutionary: Principle and Practice in the New Republic.*
Ithaca, NY: Cornell University Press, 1988.

Lindkvist, Linde. *Religious Freedom and the Universal Declaration of Human Rights.* Cambridge: Cambridge University Press, 2017.

Locke, John. *Second Treatise of Government.* Indianapolis: Hackett, 1980.

Lorde, Audre. *A Burst of Light: Essays.* New York: Firebrand, 1988.

Lorenzini, Daniele, and Arnold I. Davidson. "Introduction." In Michel Foucault, *Qu'est-ce
que la critique? Suivie de La culture de soi,* 11–32. Paris: Vrin, 2015.

Mahmood, Saba. *Politics of Piety: The Islamic Revival and the Feminist Subject.* Princeton,
NJ: Princeton University Press, 2011.

Major, Federico. "Opening Address." *Human Rights Teaching* 8 (1993): 26–33.

Malik, Charles. "The Challenge of Human Rights." In *The Challenge of Human Rights:
Charles Malik and the Universal Declaration,* ed. Habib C. Malik, 153–66. Oxford:
Charles Malik Foundation, 2000.

———. *Christ and Crisis.* Grand Rapids, MI: Wm. B. Eerdmans, 1962.

———. "A Christian Reflection on Martin Heidegger." *The Thomist* 41, no. 1 (1977): 1–61.

———. "Commission on Human Rights Verbatim Record, Fourteenth Meeting." In *The Eleanor Roosevelt Papers: The Human Rights Years, 1945–1948*, ed. Allida Black, 506–14. Farmington Hills, MI: Thomson Gale, 2007.

———. "Drafting the Declaration." In *The Challenge of Human Rights: Charles Malik and the Universal Declaration*, ed. Habib C. Malik, 242–54. Oxford: Charles Malik Foundation, 2000.

———. "The Drafting of the Universal Declaration of Human Rights." *Bulletin of Human Rights* 86, no. 1 (1986): 18–26.

———. "Excerpts from the 'International Bill.'" In *The Challenge of Human Rights: Charles Malik and the Universal Declaration*, ed. Habib C. Malik, 101–6. Oxford: Charles Malik Foundation, 2000.

———. "Four Basic Principles." In *The Challenge of Human Rights: Charles Malik and the Universal Declaration*, ed. Habib C. Malik, 27–50. Oxford: Charles Malik Foundation, 2000.

———. "From Dr. Malik's Diaries." In *The Challenge of Human Rights: Charles Malik and the Universal Declaration*, ed. Habib C. Malik, 234–35. Oxford: Charles Malik Foundation, 2000.

———. "Human Rights in the United Nations." In *The Challenge of Human Rights: Charles Malik and the Universal Declaration*, ed. Habib C. Malik, 205–13. Oxford: Charles Malik Foundation, 2000.

———. "The Individual in Modern Society." In *The One and the Many: The Individual in the Modern World*, ed. John Brooks. New York: Harper and Row, 1962.

———. "An International Bill of Rights." In *The Challenge of Human Rights: Charles Malik and the Universal Declaration*, ed. Habib C. Malik, 53–60. Oxford: Charles Malik Foundation, 2000.

———. *Man in the Struggle for Peace*. New York: Harper and Row, 1963.

———. "The Metaphysics of Freedom." *New Scholasticism* 40, no. 3 (1966): 312–30.

———. "Speech of Thursday 9 December 1948." In *The Challenge of Human Rights: Charles Malik and the Universal Declaration*, ed. Habib C. Malik, 117–25. Oxford: Charles Malik Foundation, 2000.

———. "Spiritual Implications of Universal Declaration." In *The Challenge of Human Rights: Charles Malik and the Universal Declaration*, ed. Habib C. Malik, 134–40. Oxford: Charles Malik Foundation, 2000.

———. *Survival in an Age of Revolution*. New York: Coca-Cola Company, 1972.

———. "The Tide Must Turn." In *To Meet the Communist Challenge: Addresses delivered by Dr. Edward Teller and Dr. Charles Malik*. St. Louis: St. Louis University Press, 1961.

———. "The Two Tasks." In *The Two Tasks of the Christian Scholar: Redeeming the Soul, Redeeming the Mind*, ed. William Lane Craig and Paul M. Gould, 55–66. Wheaton, IL: Crossway Books, 2007.

———. *War and Peace*. New York: Overlook, 1950.

———. *Will the Future Redeem the Past?* Williamsburg, VA: Colonial Williamsburg, 1960.

———. *The Wonder of Being*. Waco TX: Word Press, 1974.

Malkki, Liisa H. *The Need to Help: The Domestic Arts of International Humanitarianism*. Durham, NC: Duke University Press, 2015.

Manderson, Desmond. *Proximity, Levinas, and the Soul of Law*. Kingston, ON: McGill-Queens University Press, 2007.

Manent, Pierre. *Tocqueville and the Nature of Democracy*. Translated by John Waggoner. Lanham, MD: Rowman and Littlefield, 1996.

Mansfield, Harvey. *Tocqueville: A Very Short Introduction*. Oxford: Oxford University Press, 2010.

Mansfield, Harvey, and Delba Winthrop. "Editors' Introduction." In Alexis de Tocqueville, *Democracy in America*. Chicago: Chicago University Press, 2000.

Maritain, Jacques. *Man and the State*. Washington, DC: Catholic University of America Press, 1998.

Marks, Susan. "Four Human Rights Myths." In *Human Rights: Old Problems, New Possibilities*, ed. David Kinley, Wojciech Sadurski, and Kevin Walton, 217–35. London: Routledge, 2013.

———. "Human Rights and Root Causes." *Modern Law Review* 74, no. 1 (2011): 57–78.

Marx, Karl. "On the Jewish Question." In *Nonsense upon Stilts: Bentham, Burke, and Marx on the Rights of Man*, ed. Jeremy Waldron, 137–50. London: Routledge, 2014.

McClennen, Sophia A., and Alexandra Schultheis Moore, eds. *The Routledge Companion to Literature and Human Rights*. London: Routledge, 2015.

McGushin, Edward F. *Foucault's Askesis: An Introduction to the Philosophical Life*. Chicago: Northwestern University Press, 2007.

McNay, Lois. "Self as Enterprise: Dilemmas of Control and Resistance in Foucault's 'The Birth of Biopolitics.'" *Theory, Culture, and Society* 26, no. 6 (2009): 55–77.

Meintjes, Garth. "Human Rights Education as Empowerment." In *Human Rights Education for the Twenty-First Century*, ed. George J. Andreopoulos and Richard Pierre Claude, 64–79. Philadelphia: University of Pennsylvania Press, 1997.

Meltzer, Marisa. "Soak, Steam, Spritz: It's All Self-Care." *New York Times*, December 10, 2016.

Merry, Sally Engle. *Human Rights and Gender Violence: Translating International Law into Local Justice*. Chicago: Chicago University Press, 2006.

Mill, John Stuart. *On Liberty and Other Writings*. Cambridge: Cambridge University Press, 1989.

Mitoma, Glenn. "Charles H. Malik and Human Rights: Notes on a Biography." *Biography* 33, no. 1 (2010): 222–41.

———. *Human Rights and the Negotiation of American Power*. Philadelphia: University of Pennsylvania Press, 2013.

Morsink, Johannes. *The Universal Declaration of Human Rights: Origins, Drafting, and Intent*. Philadelphia: University of Pennsylvania Press, 1999.

Mouffe, Chantal. "Which Ethics for Democracy?" In *The Turn to Ethics*, ed. Marjorie Garber, Beatrice Hanssen, and Rebecca Walkowitz. London: Routledge, 2000.

Moyn, Samuel. *Christian Human Rights*. Philadelphia: University of Pennsylvania Press, 2015.

———. *The Last Utopia: Human Rights in History*. Cambridge, MA: Harvard University Press, 2010.

———. "A Powerless Companion: Human Rights in the Age of Neoliberalism." *Law and Contemporary Problems* 77, no. 4 (2014): 147–69.

Myers, Ella. "Resisting Foucauldian Ethics: Associative Politics and the Limits of the Care of the Self." *Contemporary Political Theory* 7, no. 2 (2008): 125–46.

———. *Worldly Ethics: Democratic Politics and Care for the World.* Durham, NC: Duke University Press, 2013.

Nedelsky, Jennifer. "Reconceiving Rights and Constitutionalism." *Journal of Human Rights* 7 (2008): 139–73.

Neier, Aryeh. *The International Human Rights Movement: A History.* Princeton, NJ: Princeton University Press, 2012.

Niezen, Ronald. *The Origins of Indigenism: Human Rights and the Politics of Identity.* Berkeley: University of California Press, 2003.

Nolan, Mary. "Human Rights and Market Fundamentalism." European University Institute, Max Weber Programme for Postdoctoral Studies, 2014. http://cadmus.eui.eu /bitstream/handle/1814/31206/MWP_LS_Nolan_2014_02.pdf.

Nussbaum, Martha. *Creating Capabilities: The Human Development Approach.* Cambridge: Cambridge University Press, 2011.

———. *Hiding from Humanity: Disgust, Shame, and the Law.* Princeton, NJ: Princeton University Press, 2006.

———. *Political Emotions: Why Love Matters for Justice.* Cambridge, MA: Belknap Press, 2015.

———. *Women and Human Development: The Capabilities Approach.* Cambridge: Cambridge University Press, 2000.

O'Leary, Timothy. *Foucault and the Art of Ethics.* London: Continuum, 2006.

O'Neill, Daniel I. *The Burke-Wollstonecraft Debate: Savagery, Civilization, and Democracy.* University Park: Pennsylvania State University Press, 2007.

Ozouf, Mona. "Fraternity." In *A Critical Dictionary of the French Revolution*, ed. François Furet and Mona Ozouf, 694–703. Cambridge, MA: Harvard University Press, 1989.

———. "Liberty, Equality, Fraternity." In *Realms of Memory*, ed. Pierre Nora, 77–114. New York: Columbia University Press, 1998.

Palahniuk, Chuck. *Fight Club: A Novel.* New York: W. W. Norton, 2005.

Paras, Eric. *Foucault 2.0: Beyond Power and Knowledge.* New York: Other Press, 2006.

Pascal, Blaise. *Pensées.* Translated by Roger Ariew. Indianapolis: Hackett, 2005.

Pateman, Carole. "Equality, Difference, Subordination: The Politics of Motherhood and Women's Citizenship." In *Carole Pateman: Democracy, Feminism, Welfare*, ed. Terrell Carver and Samuel Chambers, 114–27. New York: Routledge, 2011.

Patton, Paul. "Foucault and Normative Political Philosophy." In *Foucault and Philosophy*, ed. Timothy O'Leary and Christopher Falzon. London: Wiley-Blackwell, 2010.

———. "Foucault, Critique and Rights." *Critical Horizons* 6 (2005): 267–87.

———. "Historical Normativity and the Basis of Rights." In *Re-Reading Foucault: On Law, Power and Rights*, ed. Ben Golder. Abingdon: Routledge, 2012.

———. "History, Normativity, and Rights." In *The Meaning of Rights: The Philosophy and Social Theory of Human Rights*, ed. Costas Douzinas and Conor Gearty, 233–50. Cambridge: Cambridge University Press, 2014.

Perpich, Diane. *The Ethics of Emmanuel Levinas.* Stanford, CA: Stanford University Press, 2008.

Pierson, George Wilson. *Tocqueville in America*. Baltimore: Johns Hopkins University Press, 1996.

Plato. *Complete Works*, ed. John M. Cooper and D. S. Hutchinson. Indianapolis: Hackett, 1997.

Posner, Eric. *The Twilight of Human Rights Law*. Oxford: Oxford University Press, 2014.

Potkay, Adam. *The Story of Joy: From the Bible to Late Romanticism*. Cambridge: Cambridge University Press, 2007.

Print, Murray, Caroline Ugarte, Concepción Naval, and Anja Mihr. "Moral and Human Rights Education: The Contribution of the United Nations." *Journal of Moral Education* 37, no. 1 (2008): 115–32.

Rabbow, Paul. *Seelenführung: Methodik der Exerzitien in der Antike*. Munich: Kösel-Verlag, 1954.

Rabinow, Paul. "Introduction." In *Ethics: Subjectivity and Truth*, ed. Paul Rabinow, xi–xlii. New York: New Press, 1997.

Rawls, John. *The Law of Peoples*. Cambridge, MA: Harvard University Press, 2001.

Reardon, Betty. *Human Rights Learning: Pedagogies and Politics of Peace*. San Juan: University of Puerto Rico, 2010.

Reinbold, Jenna. *Seeing the Myth in Human Rights*. Philadelphia: University of Pennsylvania Press, 2016.

Roosevelt, Eleanor. "Address to Americans for Democratic Action." In *The Eleanor Roosevelt Papers: The Human Rights Years, 1949–1952*, ed. Allida Black, 359–63. Charlottesville: University of Virginia Press, 2012.

———. *The Autobiography of Eleanor Roosevelt*. Boston: Da Capo Press, 1992.

———. "Commission on Human Rights Verbatim Record, Fourteenth Meeting." In *The Eleanor Roosevelt Papers: The Human Rights Years, 1945–1948*, ed. Allida Black, 506–14. Farmington Hills, MI: Thomson Gale, 2007.

———. *Courage in a Dangerous World*. New York: Columbia University Press, 2000.

———. "Eleanor Roberts Interviews Eleanor Roosevelt." In *The Eleanor Roosevelt Papers: The Human Rights Years, 1945–1948*, ed. Allida Black, 658–62. Farmington Hills, MI: Thomson Gale, 2007.

———. "The Minorities Question." In *The Eleanor Roosevelt Papers: The Human Rights Years, 1945–1948*, ed. Allida Black, 392–95. Farmington Hills, MI: Thomson Gale, 2007.

———. *The Moral Basis of Democracy*. New York: Howell, Soskin, 1940.

———. "My Day, 18 December 1947." In *The Eleanor Roosevelt Papers: The Human Rights Years, 1945–1948*, ed. Allida Black, 689–90. Farmington Hills, MI: Thomson Gale, 2007.

———. "My Day, 27 November 1948." In *The Eleanor Roosevelt Papers: The Human Rights Years, 1945–1948*, ed. Allida Black, 955–56. Farmington Hills, MI: Thomson Gale, 2007.

———. "My Day, 10 December 1948." In *The Eleanor Roosevelt Papers: The Human Rights Years, 1945–1948*, ed. Allida Black, 969–70. Farmington Hills, MI: Thomson Gale, 2007.

———. "The Promise of Human Rights." In *Courage in a Dangerous World: The Political*

Writings of Eleanor Roosevelt, ed. Allida Black, 156–61. New York: Columbia University Press, 2000.

———. "Speech before UN General Assembly, 30th Plenary Session." In *The Eleanor Roosevelt Papers: The Human Rights Years, 1945–1948*, ed. Allida Black, 246–48. Farmington Hills, MI: Thomson Gale, 2007.

———. "Speech on Behalf of Roosevelt College." In *The Eleanor Roosevelt Papers: The Human Rights Years, 1945–1948*, ed. Allida Black, 548–51. Farmington Hills, MI: Thomson Gale, 2007.

———. "Speech at the Phi Beta Kappa Association Founders' Day Dinner." In *The Eleanor Roosevelt Papers: The Human Rights Years, 1949–1952*, ed. Allida Black, 49–62. Charlottesville: University of Virginia Press, 2012.

———. "Statement by Mrs. Franklin D. Roosevelt US Representative to the General Assembly." In *The Eleanor Roosevelt Papers: The Human Rights Years, 1945–1948*, ed. Allida Black, 972–73. Farmington Hills, MI: Thomson Gale, 2007.

———. "The Struggle for Human Rights: Speech at the Sorbonne, Paris." In *The Eleanor Roosevelt Papers: The Human Rights Years, 1945–1948*, ed. Allida Black, 900–910. Farmington Hills, MI: Thomson Gale, 2007.

———. *Tomorrow Is Now.* New York: Penguin, 2012.

———. "Verbatim Record of the Thirteenth Meeting of the Drafting Committee of the Commission of Human Rights." In *The Eleanor Roosevelt Papers: The Human Rights Years, 1945–1948*, ed. Allida Black, 567–74. Farmington Hills, MI: Thomson Gale, 2007.

———. "Where Do Human Rights Begin?" In *Courage in a Dangerous World: The Political Writings of Eleanor Roosevelt*, ed. Allida Black, 190–91. New York: Columbia University Press, 2000.

———. *You Learn by Living: Eleven Keys for a More Fulfilling Life.* New York: Harper and Brothers, 1960.

Roosevelt, Franklin Delano. "The First Inaugural Address." In *Great Speeches*, ed. John Grafton, 28–33. Mineola, NY: Dover, 1999.

———. "State of the Union Message to Congress ('The Four Freedoms')." In *Great Speeches*, ed. John Grafton, 92–100. Mineola, NY: Dover, 1999.

Rorty, Richard. "Human Rights, Rationality, and Sentimentality." In *Truth and Progress: Philosophical Papers*, vol. 3, 167–85. Cambridge: Cambridge University Press, 1998.

———. *Take Care of Freedom and Truth Will Take Care of Itself: Interviews with Richard Rorty.* Stanford, CA: Stanford University Press, 2006.

Rousseau, Jean-Jacques. *The Essential Rousseau.* Translated by Lowell Bair. New York: Signet, 1974.

Said, Edward. *Out of Place: A Memoir.* New York: Vintage, 2000.

Sapiro, Virginia. *A Vindication of Political Virtue: The Political Theory of Mary Wollstonecraft.* Chicago: University of Chicago Press, 1992.

Savelsberg, Joachim J. *Crime and Human Rights: Criminology of Genocide and Atrocities.* London: Sage, 2010.

Schleifer, James T. *The Making of Tocqueville's Democracy in America*, 2nd ed. Indianapolis: Liberty Fund, 2000.

Schmitt, Carl. *The Concept of the Political*. Translated by George Schwab. Chicago: Chicago University Press, 2007.

———. *The Nomos of the Earth*. Translated by G. L. Ulmen. New York: Telos, 2006.

———. *Theory of the Partisan: Intermediate Commentary on the Concept of the Partisan*. Translated by G. L. Ulmen. New York: Telos, 2007.

Schneewind, Jerome. *The Invention of Autonomy: A History of Modern Moral Philosophy*. Cambridge: Cambridge University Press, 1997.

Shulman, George. "Acknowledgment and Disavowal as an Idiom for Theorizing Politics." *Theory and Event* 14, no. 1 (2011).

Simons, John. *Foucault and the Political*. London: Routledge, 2013.

Slaughter, Joseph R. *Human Rights, Inc.: The World Novel, Narrative Form, and International Law*. New York: Fordham University Press, 2007.

Sliwinski, Sharon. *Human Rights in Camera*. Chicago: University of Chicago Press, 2011.

Soulez, Philippe, and Frédéric Worms. *Bergson*. Paris: PUF, 2002.

Spechler, Diana. "The Rise of Donald Trump Demands We Embrace a Harder Kind of Self-Care." *Quartz*, November 11, 2016. https://qz.com/834607/the-rise-of-donald -trump-demands-a-new-kind-of-self-care/.

Stanlis, Peter J. *Edmund Burke and the Natural Law*. New Brunswick, NJ: Transaction, 2003.

Strauss, Leo. *Natural Right and History*. Chicago: University of Chicago Press, 1999.

Tasioulas, John. "John Tasioulas Recommends the Best Books on Human Rights." 2016. http://fivebooks.com/interview/human-rights/.

———. "Towards a Philosophy of Human Rights." *Current Legal Problems* 65 (2012): 1–30.

Taubes, Jacob. *The Political Theology of Paul*. Translated by Dana Hollander. Stanford, CA: Stanford University Press, 2004.

Taylor, Barbara. *Mary Wollstonecraft and the Feminist Imagination*. Cambridge: Cambridge University Press, 2003.

Taylor, Charles. *A Secular Age*. Cambridge, MA: Harvard University Press, 2007.

———. *Sources of the Self: The Making of Modern Identity*. Cambridge: Cambridge University Press, 1992.

Taylor, Natalie. *The Rights of Woman as Chimera: The Political Philosophy of Mary Wollstonecraft*. London: Routledge, 2006.

Tepliakov, Vladimir. "Commission on Human Rights Verbatim Record, Fourteenth Meeting." In *The Eleanor Roosevelt Papers: The Human Rights Years, 1945–1948*, ed. Allida Black, 506–14. Farmington Hills, MI: Thomson Gale, 2007.

Thoreau, Henry David. "Civil Disobedience." In *The Essays of Henry David Thoreau*, ed. Lewis Hyde, 125–45. New York: North Point, 2002.

Tibbitts, Felisa. "Building a Human Rights Education Movement in the United States." In *Bringing Human Rights Education to US Classrooms: Exemplary Models from Elementary Grades to University*, ed. Susan Roberta Katz and Andrea McEvoy Spero, 3–14. London: Palgrave, 2015.

———. "Evolution of Human Rights Models." In *Human Rights Education: Theory,*

Research, Praxis, ed. Monisha Bajaj. Philadelphia: University of Pennsylvania Press, 2016. https://www.academia.edu/19607660/Evolution_of_Human_Rights_Education_Models.

———. "Transformative Learning and Human Rights Education: Taking a Closer Look." *Intercultural Education* 16, no. 2 (2005): 107–13.

———. "Understanding What We Do: Emerging Models of Human Rights Education." *International Review of Education* 48 nos. 3–4 (2002): 159–71.

———. "Women's Human Rights Education Trainers in Turkey: Situated Empowerment for Social Change." *Journal of Peace Education* 13, no. 1 (2016): 41–59.

Ticktin, Miriam, and Ilana Feldman, eds. *In the Name of Humanity: The Government of Threat and Care*. Durham, NC: Duke University Press, 2010.

Tocqueville, Alexis de. *Alexis de Tocqueville and Gustave de Beaumont in America: Their Friendship and Their Travels*. Translated by Arthur Goldhammer. Charlottesville: University of Virginia Press, 2011.

———. *The Ancien Regime and the French Revolution*. Translated by Arthur Goldhammer. Cambridge: Cambridge University Press, 2011.

———. *Democracy in America*. Translated by Harvey C. Mansfield and Delba Winthrop. Chicago: University of Chicago Press, 2000.

———. *Democracy in America*, ed. Eduardo Nolla. Translated by James T. Schleifer. Indianapolis: Liberty Fund, 2010.

Todd, Janet. "Introduction." In Mary Wollstonecraft, *A Vindication of the Rights of Men*, vii–xxxiv. Oxford: Oxford University Press, 1994.

———. *Mary Wollstonecraft: A Revolutionary Life*. London: Weidenfeld and Nicolson, 2000.

Tomaselli, Sylvana. "Introduction." In Mary Wollstonecraft, *A Vindication of the Rights of Men and A Vindication of the Rights of Woman*, ix–xxix. Cambridge: Cambridge University Press, 1995.

Tuck, Richard. *Natural Rights Theories: Their Origin and Development*. Cambridge: Cambridge University Press, 1982.

———. *The Rights of War and Peace: Political Thought and the International Order from Grotius to Kant*. Cambridge: Cambridge University Press, 2001.

UN Development Programme and Office of the High Commissioner for Human Rights. *Toolkit for Collaboration with National Human Rights Institutions*. 2010. http://www.ohchr.org/Documents/Countries/NHRI/1950-UNDP-UHCHR-Toolkit-LR.pdf.

UN Economic and Social Council. Commission on Human Rights, 3rd Sess., 48th mtg., UN Doc. E/CN.4/SR.48 (June 4, 1948).

———. Commission on Human Rights, 3rd Sess., 50th mtg., UN Doc. E/CN.4/SR.50 (May 27, 1948).

———. Commission on Human Rights, 3rd Sess., 64th mtg., UN Doc. E/CN.4/SR.64 (June 8, 1948).

———. Drafting Committee on an International Bill of Human Rights, 1st Sess., 11th mtg., UN Doc. E/CN.4/AC.1/SR.11 (June 19, 1947).

———. Drafting Committee on an International Bill of Human Rights, 1st Sess., 2nd mtg., UN Doc. E/CN.4/AC.1/SR.2 (June 11, 1947).

————. Drafting Committee on an International Bill of Human Rights, 1st Sess., 13th
   mtg., UN Doc. E/CN.4/AC.1/SR.13 (June 20, 1947).
————. Drafting Committee on an International Bill of Human Rights, 2nd Sess., 38th
   mtg., UN Doc. E/CN.4/AC.1/SR.38 (May 18, 1948).
UN Educational, Scientific and Cultural Organization. 61st Annual DPI/NGO Conference, "Reaffirming Human Rights for All" (September 3–5, 2008). http://www.un.org
   /webcast/dpingo/archive.asp.
————. General Conference, 18th Sess., *Recommendation Concerning Education for International Understanding, Co-Operation and Peace and Education Related to Human Rights
   and Fundamental Freedoms*, UN Doc. ST/HR/1/Rev.5(Vol.I/Part2), (November 19,
   1974).
UN General Assembly. Resolution 49/184, "United Nations Decade for Human Rights
   Education" (December 23, 1994).
————. Resolution 62/171, "International Year of Human Rights Learning" (December
   18, 2007).
————. Resolution 66/137, "United Nations Declaration on Human Rights Education
   and Training" (December 19, 2011).
————. 3rd Sess., 180th Plenary Meeting, UN Doc. A/PV.180 (December 9, 1948).
————. 3rd Sess., 3rd Committee, 142nd mtg., UN Doc. A/C.3/SR.154 (November 24,
   1948).
UN Office of the High Commissioner for Human Rights. "The Right to Human Rights
   Education: A Compilation of Provisions of International and Regional Instruments
   Dealing with Human Rights Education" (September 2014). http://www.ohchr.org/EN
   /Issues/Education/Training/Compilation/Pages/Listofcontents.aspx.
UN Secretary-General. General Assembly, 51st Sess., *Report of the United Nations High
   Commissioner for Human Rights on the Implementation of the Plan of Action for the United
   Nations Decade for Human Rights Education*, UN Doc. A/51/506/Add.1 (December 12,
   1996).
Veyne, Paul. "The Final Foucault and His Ethics." In *Foucault and His Interlocutors*, ed.
   Arnold I. Davidson, 225–33. Chicago: University of Chicago Press, 1997.
————. *Foucault: His Thought, His Character*. Translated by Janet Lloyd. Cambridge:
   Polity, 2010.
Wahl, Rachel. *Just Violence: Torture and Human Rights in the Eyes of the Police*. Stanford,
   CA: Stanford University Press, 2016.
Waldron, Jeremy, ed. *Dignity, Rank, and Rights*. New York: Oxford University Press, 2012.
————. *Nonsense upon Stilts: Bentham, Burke, and Marx on the Rights of Man*. London:
   Routledge, 2014.
Wall, John. *Moral Creativity: Paul Ricoeur and the Poetics of Possibility*. Oxford: Oxford
   University Press, 2005.
White, Melanie. "Habit as a Force of Life in Durkheim and Bergson." *Body and Society* 19,
   nos. 2–3 (2013): 240–62.
Whyte, Jessica. "The Fortunes of Natural Man: Robinson Crusoe, Political Economy,
   and the Universal Declaration of Human Rights." *Humanity: An International Journal of
   Human Rights, Humanitarianism, and Development* 5, no. 3 (2014): 301–21.

Williams, Raymond. *Keywords: A Vocabulary of Culture and Society.* New York: Oxford University Press, 1985.

Wittgenstein, Ludwig. *Tractatus Logico-Philosophicus.* Translated by D. F. Pears and B. F. McGuinness. London: Routledge, 2001.

Woessner, Martin. "Provincializing Human Rights? The Heideggerian Legacy from Charles Malik to Dipesh Chakrabarty." In *Human Rights from a Third World Perspective: Critique, History, and International Law,* ed. José-Manuel Barreto, 65–101. Cambridge: Cambridge Scholars, 2013.

Wolin, Richard. "Foucault the Neohumanist?" *Chronicle of Higher Education,* September 2006. http://chronicle.edu/article/Foucault-the-Neohumanist-/23118.

———. "From the 'Death of Man' to Human Rights: The Paradigm Change in French Intellectual Life." In *Histories of Postmodernism,* ed. M. Bevir, J. Hargis, and S. Rushing. Abingdon, UK: Routledge, 2007.

Wolin, Sheldon S. *Tocqueville between Two Worlds.* Princeton, NJ: Princeton University Press, 2001.

Wollstonecraft, Mary. "Hints [Chiefly Designed to Have Been Incorporated in the Second Part of the Vindication of the Rights of Woman]." In *A Vindication of the Rights of Men and a Vindication of the Rights of Woman,* ed. Sylvana Tomaselli, 295–303. Cambridge: Cambridge University Press, 1995.

———. *Letters Written during a Short Residence in Sweden, Norway, and Denmark.* Oxford: Oxford University Press, 2009.

———. *A Vindication of the Rights of Men and a Vindication of the Rights of Woman.* Cambridge: Cambridge University Press, 1995.

———. *The Works of Mary Wollstonecraft,* ed. Janet Todd and Marilyn Butler, vol. 4. London: William Pickering, 1989.

Wolterstorff, Nicholas P. "Christianity and Human Rights." In *Human Rights and Religion,* ed. John Witte and M. Christian Green, 42–55. Oxford: Oxford University Press, 2011.

Woolf, Virginia. *The Common Reader.* Back Bay, MA: Mariner, 2003.

Zivi, Karen. *Making Rights Claims: A Practice of Democratic Citizenship.* Oxford: Oxford University Press, 2012.

Index

American Psycho (movie), 82
American Revolution, 65–67, 81
ancient philosophy: care of self and, 11, 13–16,
  51, 62, 108, 179, 185, 188; Hadot on, 61–62,
  67–68, 72–75, 78–79, 82–83
Arendt, Hannah, 193

Bajaj, Monisha, 172
Baxi, Upendra, 165
Bergson, Henri, 2, 5, 83, 109, 191; on benefits
  of open love, 99–100; biography of, 86–87;
  on closed morality during war, 90–91; death
  of, 87; on great thinkers, 125; human rights
  and naturalist account of morality of, 91–92;
  human rights as open love and care of self
  and, 5, 85–86, 95–96, 101–5; human rights
  as technique of the self, 96; human rights
  based on closed morality critique, 92–94;
  on joy, 100–101; on limited emotional life
  guided by closed morality, 94–96, 99–100;
  as president of Commission for Intellectual
  Cooperation (League of Nations), 87; on
  problems and solutions, 109; rejection of
  "honorary Aryan" title by, 87; role of entry
  of U.S. into WWI and, 86–87. See also *Two
  Sources of Morality and Religion* (Bergson)
Brown, Wendy, 53–59
Burke, Edmund, 27–28, 194

care of self, 2–4, 81–92, 192–93; ancient philosophy and, 11, 13–16, 51, 62, 108, 179, 185,
188; in contemporary humanitarianism,
  175–78; criteria for, 15–17, 101–3, 155–56,
  166–67, 187, 189–90; critique of, 47–52, 60,
  82–83, 105–6; as *epimeleia heautou* (ancient
  Greek), 13, 179; human rights education and,
  10, 167–68, 174–78; human rights as personal transformation and, 132, 181–83, 189;
  in human rights history and authors, 4–7,
  45–46, 52–53, 186–88; as life-long process,
  178–79; and relation to care for other people,
  3–4, 47, 82–84, 186, 190–91, 193–94; as resistance to political power, 110–12, 119–21,
  191–94; as style of existence, 44–45; as therapeutic response to local contexts, 175–78;
  as undertaken for the self, 82–84, 190–91,
  194. *See also* human rights and human rights
  critiques; human rights authors and author
  studies
Cassin, René, 159
Chang, P. C., 119
chauvinism, 81–82
chivalry, Wollstonecraft's attack on, 10, 12, 26,
  35–45, 71, 108, 115
Christianity, 96–98, 102; human rights and
  Catholicism in late 1930s and, 153–54; of
  Malik, 152–54, 161–62
Clapham, Andrew, 132
collectivism, 118, 120, 125, 132, 142, 148–49,
  151–52, 154–55, 157, 161
communism, 145–54
conformity, 10; Roosevelt on freedom from,
  120, 125–32

equality as care of self and, 39–41; juridical and political theory of human rights of, 30–32; liberty as care of self and, 41–42; resistance to and awareness of oppression of, 115–16; scholarship on theory of rights and education of, 31–33; views of women of, 29–30, 128; *Vindication of the Rights of Men* by, 34. See also *Vindication of the Rights of Women*

World War I, Bergson's role in U.S. entry into, 86–87

xenophobia, 10, 86, 96, 192

You Live by Learning: Eleven Keys for a More Fulfilling Life (Roosevelt), 2, 127, 129, 138–39